DANCING
with the
DEVIL

A MEMOIR

GRETCHEN ROSE
IN COLLABORATION WITH MEGHAN ROSE

Indigo River Publishing

Indigo River Publishing
3 West Garden Street Ste. 352 M
Pensacola, FL 32502
www.indigoriverpublishing.com

Ordering Information:
Quantity sales: Special discounts are available on quantity purchases by corporations, associations, and others. For details, contact the publisher at the address above.

Orders by U.S. trade bookstores and wholesalers: Please contact the publisher at the address above.

Printed in the United States of America

Editors: Regina Cornell and Faith Green
Cover Designer: John Lucas
Interior Design: mycustombookcover.com

Library of Congress Control Number: 2018938887
ISBN: Paperback: 978-1-948080-22-4
Ebook: 978-1-948080-70-5

First Edition

With Indigo River Publishing, you can always expect great books, strong voices, and meaningful messages. Most importantly, you'll always find ... words worth reading.

"THERE WAS A STAR DANCED,
AND UNDER THAT WAS I BORN."

— William Shakespeare, *Much Ado about Nothing*

Gretchen and Meghan Rose in 2005, the year Meghan began dancing

PREFACE

Meghan and I dedicate this book to the memories of David Root, Read Lowe, Gus Wallen, and Olivia Garrison, all of whom died alcohol- or drug-related deaths. We offer our sincere thanks to their families for providing us with painful details surrounding the tragic deaths of their loved ones. It is our wish that this book will serve as a cautionary tale to anyone who travels down the road to addiction.

As the writer, I would particularly like to commend my daughter for her candor, for allowing me to portray her as she was in those very dark, drug-addled days. In her words, "If the telling of my story prevents just one person from following the path that I did, if it gives just one family hope that a cure for addiction is possible, then the degradation and abuse I suffered as a result of my own addiction will have been worth it."

This book is based on a true story, and I want to add the following disclaimer: I have tried to be as accurate as possible, but some episodes Meghan recounted to me occurred when she was heavily under the influence. If I've gotten anything wrong, I apologize.

I wish to thank Darlene Forage for the information she provided regarding her late husband, Dr. Paul Forage, as well as to thank Dr. Raymond Dean, Chef Farnsworth, and Jerry Burr for their contributions.

But most of all, I want to thank Miss Frances Watson. It was she and her siblings, "God's own angels on Earth," who directed the Restoration House Ministries and returned my daughter to me.

Unfortunately, the doors to Restoration House are currently shuttered. Poor health and a lack of funding make it impossible for Ms. Frances and her siblings to continue their ministry. But that doesn't mean Frances is giving up; that's not her nature. She holds to the belief that God is sending someone to help her reopen the doors of RH in order that the work she and her sisters started might continue.

Due to the nature of this chronicle, the names of many people and places have been changed to protect both the innocent and the guilty. You know who you are, and I hope you agree that I have portrayed you accurately.

The Velvet Pony has also closed its doors. Meghan and I pray no one reopens them.

November 30, 2013

I COULDN'T FEEL MY LEGS, WAS BARELY CAPABLE OF PUTTING ONE FOOT BEFORE THE OTHER. But I was intensely aware of the two burning lead weights that were my arms. Would I ever be able to lift them? As though from a great distance, I heard voices from the crowd; they were chanting my name, yelling for me to finish. In a moment of déjà vu, I saw myself cradling a lacrosse ball in my wicket, racing toward the goal, and from deep within some well of reserve, I summoned the will to go on.

I staggered mulishly across the uneven deck and, with the last vestiges of strength I possessed, demanded that my right arm rise to this final task. When I rang the bell, the crowd erupted.

In the next instant, I was surrounded. Fellow contestants, Coast Guardsmen, Navy SEALs, and reporters applauded me, clapped my back, and offered congratulations. But I was near collapse, dead on my feet. Then my mother's arms were around me.

"You did it," she whispered in my ear. "You really did it, baby girl."

My breath hitched in my throat, and I reconnected with the universe. Realization dawned. Despite all odds, *I had done it*!

Someone thrust an open water bottle toward me. Greedily, I sucked the contents down, and the ringing in my ears gradually subsided. I began to process the conversations swirling around me. I was the cause célèbre. It was crazy and wonderful. And I needed to sit before my legs gave out entirely.

A journalist stopped snapping photos and shoved a tape recorder in my face. "How much do you weigh?" he asked.

"One twenty." I bent at the waist, palms on knees.

"Your height?"

"Five four."

"A mere slip of a girl," he muttered.

"Huh?"

"What inspired you to attempt the Navy SEAL Challenge?" He was rapidly firing questions at me, and I had all I could do to process them. But when he asked, "What was your motivation?" my muddled brain cleared quickly. What *had* possessed me to attempt this most grueling of contests, to push myself beyond my own strength and endurance? The Navy SEAL Challenge would be an achievement for any normal girl, but for me, it held special meaning. It was a way for me to prove to the world I had overcome my demons, a mile marker of how far I'd traveled from that dopey, lost girl I'd once been. Then and there, I gave thanks to the Creator of all Creation for bringing me through fire to this defining point in my formerly miserable existence.

CHAPTER ONE

October 2008

I WAS DIRTY, HAD NO IDEA HOW LONG IT HAD BEEN SINCE I'D BATHED. MY HAIR WAS A TANGLE; MY COMPLEXION, ASHEN. But I was far beyond caring about appearances, a fact confirmed by my outfit: a grease-stained XL tee that I swam in and a pair of threadbare shorts. Under normal circumstances, I wouldn't have been caught dead in such a get-up. But normal had been a long time ago.

More remarkable was my footwear: cheap rubber flip-flops in a cheesy camouflage pattern, purchased at a truck stop in the middle of nowhere. I had enough difficulty navigating in my impaired state. The crummy flip-flops didn't help matters any.

On that particular visit to the ER, my toenail polish was . . . Reckless Ruby? Reprehensible Red? Whatever the shade, it was badly chipped. Usually, that would drive me crazy, but I hadn't given a thought to my grooming or personal hygiene in weeks. Quite a contrast to the Bridge Challenge girl, wouldn't you say? There was another difference between that strong, capable girl and this filthy, dopey, wretched one: unlike that spunky competitor, I was thoroughly and utterly terrified.

I could barely string two words together but was somehow cognizant of the activity going on around me, which is precisely what scared the living daylights out of me. A kind of duality existed, as though I were two people. Despite the fact that I was plummeting down off my methadone high, I possessed an awareness of the external phenomena, the comings and goings of doctors and nurses and the conversations drifting about me, as well as of my own sorry state. What is so horrifying about that? You wonder. The truth of the matter is that I was not only outside of my body—outside, hovering, looking down at myself—I was also peering behind me, as if I had eyes in the back of my head. My feet looked as though they were on backward, sticking out the other side of me.

I was *twisted*.

I was dancing with the Devil. He'd grabbed hold of me, and though I tried to shake him off, he held me fast!

Now that's some scary mojo! I was quaking, and the tremors weren't merely a result of crashing from my whopping overdose. In the weeks leading up to this sorry state of affairs, I'd come to believe I was insane. I could hear that old Satan, and he wasn't singing me a lullaby. He was cackling inside my head while distorting the world around me. Rooms alternately contracted and expanded. Walls and people pressed in only to whoosh away and change in dimension. It was like standing in front of the world's worst funhouse mirror.

But I knew it was the Devil. He'd latched on to my foot, which explains why I kept losing shoes. Shoe, I should say, for it was always just one shoe that went missing. He would clasp my foot, draw me to him, and twirl me round and around in a crazed, macabre dance.

CHAPTER TWO

Mexican Hat Dance

I WAS JUST A TODDLER WHEN I FIRST EXHIBITED MY OBSESSION WITH
SHOES, A TRAIT THAT HAS CONTINUED ON TO THE PRESENT. I was beautiful then, before the gawky, awkward days of my adolescence. In old
photographs, I appear as an elfin creature with large hazel eyes and
a mass of golden hair.

As the story goes, one Sunday afternoon in May, my parents
dragged me along with them to a pool party hosted by a fellow Ki-
wanian. (My dad was big into Kiwanis. At least he was before he got
big into alcohol.) Anyway, it was Florida and it was hot. Most of the
women, in their sundresses and heels, declined to take a dip, opting
instead for the shade and a cool beverage so as not to risk running
makeup and deflating coifs. But the men had no such qualms; they
seized the opportunity to dunk their male compatriots, under the
guise of fair play, in a boozy game of water polo.

The pool deck was littered with shoes, and while the women gos-
siped and the men played on in their testosterone-fueled contest, I was
having the time of my life. I'd slip my itty foot into one large shoe and
clop, clop, clop around. Then I'd find another more interesting shoe
and repeat the exercise. Bright sunlight shone down on me in little
bits and pieces, sieved through the loosely woven straw hat someone
had laughingly placed on my small head, as I tried on shoe after shoe.
The gentleman who hosted the party was the first to notice me.

"Un Zapato," he said, winking conspiratorially. It was he who prophetically dubbed me Un Zapato. One Shoe—some kind of portent, I'd say.

Mine was a very happy and rather uneventful childhood. At the age of seven, I began training with the Indian River County Soccer Association. From the get-go, I was a tiger. Like my older brother, Michael, I welcomed any excuse to run. I continued to play on the local league until the age of fourteen. My dad coached for a few seasons, and that was really fun because the girls on the team all looked up to me. Dad was Coach. Cool! It was a very happy, innocent time. Still, I believe the tiny, innocuous seed of corruption was planted when I began competing with other like-minded girls.

In middle school, I was diagnosed with Attention Deficit Hyperactivity Disorder. An average student, I occasionally distinguished myself in the annual poetry contest. But if my scholarly achievements were less than stellar, I made up for it in athletics. All those years tagging along after Michael and his best friend, Gus, had toughened me up and given me a cocky sense of invulnerability that served me well in team sports. I was fearless, and I could run like the wind. So it came as no surprise when, as a lowly freshman, I was selected to play as a starter in both the varsity soccer and lacrosse teams.

Michael and I attended St. Edward's, an exclusive private school on Vero's barrier island. My years in both lower and middle school were a delight. I adored all of my teachers, and I forged friendships with classmates that endure to this day. It wasn't until upper school that I began veering off course. That bastion of academic excellence was lost on me. I couldn't seem to concentrate in class and had a hard time completing assignments. But the worst of it was, I got all caught up in the one-upmanship game.

Scads of super-wealthy kids attended St. Ed's, and once they became teenagers, designer labels suddenly became really important to the girls. And it goes without saying that haute couture fashion simply doesn't cut it unless one is possessed of the super-svelte frame to hang it on. I was naturally curvy and had muscular legs. I wasn't happy with my body. I wanted to be whip thin, and dieting wasn't getting me there. Add to that the fact that my addictive personality was just beginning to manifest, that everything I undertook I did to the extreme, and you can understand how my life was fast becoming one big competition.

It was about that time, when the braces came off and the baby fat dissolved, I realized—as did everyone else, unfortunately—I'd been transformed from a tomboy into a pretty young woman with curves. Guys would crane their necks and none too subtly give me the eye as I passed by in the hallway. I had the same effect on older men, like my friends' dads. Heady stuff for a formerly awkward, pimply chubbette! It wasn't long before I became accustomed to this new reality. I learned to pretend I didn't feel the heat of lustful eyes following me wherever I went.

In my clique, eating disorders—anorexia and bulimia—were the norm, and I was the poster child. It wasn't enough that I ran my legs off on the playing field and worked out daily in the gym. Eventually, I began abusing laxatives and over-the-counter diet pills. All the popular girls did. It got so our tender ears could detect the sound of a girl retching behind a restroom door. We'd just raise our eyebrows and exchange knowing looks. No biggie.

Despite the peer pressure, most of my fellow students thrived in that rarified atmosphere. As they matured, they were able to distinguish what was really important from the inconsequential and apply themselves to their studies. It just didn't prove a good fit for Little Miss Un Zapato. This round peg refused to fit into that square hole, and I got sidetracked by the superficial. Worse yet, I was laying the groundwork for my future addiction.

It wasn't long before I transitioned from supplements and carbbusters to recreational drugs. Again, it seemed like everyone—except the biggest nerds, of course—was doing a line or two of coke at a party, mixing it up with oxys and alcohol. There was always weed, but that seemed plebeian, so public school. I never liked smoking grass because it made me ravenous and turned the whites of my eyes red. My crowd, the elite, did whatever was available. We weren't particular. It was fooling-around kind of stuff. Or so we all thought back then—before my father; my best friend, Olivia; my first crush, David; before Read and Gus, who were like brothers to me—before they all died senseless drug- or alcohol-related deaths.

CHAPTER THREE

The Beguine

MY PARENTS BELIEVED A KID SHOULD EARN HIS OWN SPENDING MONEY AND LEARN THE VALUE OF A DOLLAR. By the time he was fourteen, my brother was employed at John's Island, the luxury oceanfront development managed by my father. Wanting to avoid any claim of nepotism, Dad sent him to work under the direction of Chef Farnsworth, who presided over his own large staff. John's Island's beachfront and golf course restaurants were far removed from Dad's jurisdiction.

From the lowly task of burning bones for stock, to prep, to working the line, Farnsworth took Michael under his wing and generously shared his skills. When there was no more Chef Farnsworth could teach my brother, he sent him to study at the Culinary Institute of America in Hyde Park, to absorb under the tutelage of some of the Big Apple's finest. Today my brother is an accomplished chef in his own right. He made a success of it.

My early work experiences, on the other hand, were disasterous. My very first job was babysitting, which I adored. Caring for other people's children was fun and easy, but not very profitable. I was acquiring expensive tastes, craved Gucci sunglasses and Louis Vuitton handbags, and five bucks an hour wasn't going to get them for me. I segued into waitressing, hustling for tips. The world is kind to pretty people, and I had no qualms about working that angle. I never had difficulty getting a job. It was keeping one that was the problem.

On weekdays, Dad enjoyed having breakfast with a few of his cronies at the Beachside Café. The Beachside was a homey joint where local professionals could gossip over their eggs and freshly ground before devoting themselves to the daily grind. Over the years, my dad had forged a relationship with Judy, the proprietress. When I turned sixteen and he decided it was high time I became gainfully employed, he wasn't above asking for favors. I was hired, and it went well for a while. (It always did.) I looked cute in the uniform, a tiny skirt and fitted blouse, and I liked the fast pace of waiting tables.

About that time, I'd started dating Keith. I was gaga, convinced he was the love of my life. Needless to say, I don't have great taste in men, a common aspect of PGS, pretty girl syndrome. I always figured men were attracted to me because of my looks. Deep down, I felt I was unworthy of their attention. Of all the guys I could have been seeing—and believe me, I could have had my pick—I chose the surly, brooding Keith, a ne'er-do-well who literally hailed from the other side of the tracks. He was my Heathcliff with none of the charm.

The first time drugs landed me unconscious in the ER, I'd been with Keith. He'd taken me to a party in the groves west of town, and somehow my drink had been laced with GHB, the date-rape drug. I'm not sure, but I suspect Keith was to blame. It was the first time I had sex, and I don't remember a thing. One moment, I was laughing at a kegger with a group of people I thought were my friends, and the next thing I recalled was waking up to a violently throbbing head and a tube being shoved down my throat.

Sometimes my smart mouth gets me in trouble. Add to that the fact that I'm a natural athlete, strong and plucky, and it's a recipe for disaster. Never mind the fact that I'm a lightweight, I always figure I can go toe-to-toe with any guy. And once engaged in a confrontation, I'm too stubborn to ever back down. My mother says I was born without the caution gene. Most people, when they detect danger lurking, seek a way around it, she explained. Their brains issue warnings, "Careful, careful," as the adrenaline releases, heightening their senses. Not me; I thrill to the adrenaline rush. Feeling invincible, I charge recklessly forward. It's a knee-jerk reaction that's gotten me into a whole lot of hot water.

Bad as it was, my temper didn't compare to Keith's; his was mercurial. The slightest thing could, and often did, send him into a rage. He was built for bullying: stocky, with biceps like footballs and hands the size of Perdue roasting hens. There was nothing Keith liked better than a good fight.

They say love is blind, and I certainly had been. But suddenly, I was beginning to see Keith more clearly. There was no ring on my finger, and I wanted out. At the same time, I was becoming intensely aware of a senior, Rob Madden. Gorgeous with his chiseled jaw, Rob was from the right side of the tracks. I was a lowly freshman, but when I realized Rob was shooting me the looks, I had the nerve to ask him to the Sadie Hawkins dance, and he said yes! What a gentleman he was, as different from Keith as Dior is from Maybelline.

When he came to pick me up in his shiny red convertible, Rob presented me with a bouquet of fresh flowers. He knew how to treat a lady, and he made me feel like one. We had a great time at the dance. When Rob finally delivered me to my doorstep, he crushed me in his arms, and I thought I'd died and gone to heaven. He was a beautiful guy with lovely manners. All night long, I'd breathed in the clean, sweet scent of him: lemons and leather. I was so over Keith, so ready to end that toxic relationship.

The very next evening, I was working a shift at the Beachside Café, and who do you think strutted in all hot under the collar? You guessed it. It was none other than the former love of my life. I was in the kitchen loading up a tray when I heard him holler for me.

"Meghan," Keith growled. "Get out here!"

I knew then and there that this was going to end badly, that there'd probably be no more Beachside Café for me, and that really burned me. I liked this job! The wise thing would have been for me to have tucked tail and run. But as I've explained, that wasn't my style.

Judy, who'd been out on the floor schmoozing customers, came barreling through the Dutch doors into the kitchen.

"Don't go out there, Meghan," she warned.

"Meghan Rose," Keith bellowed. "You little bitch! You'd better get yourself out here, or I'll come in after you and drag you out by that ditsy blonde head of yours."

And people accused me of being a drama queen! My blood was beginning to boil at the injustice of it all. This big lummox's temper was about to get me canned, and I hadn't done a thing wrong. I was going to kill that creep if it was the last thing I did! I released my tray, sending it crashing onto the stainless-steel countertop. Before the clattering subsided, I'd palmed the heaviest sauté pan within reach. Thank heavens I didn't grab a knife, or things might have turned out differently. In the next instant, I charged out the swinging doors, eyes wild.

"You big-mouthed idiot," I screeched, wielding the pan over my head. "Get out of here. Get out of my life!"

All of this transpired in a matter of seconds, and in that brief period, the diners were temporarily paralyzed with disbelief. This was unbelievable, so far removed from normal parameters, I'm sure some thought they'd been secretly signed on as extras in a B movie.

On this particular evening, Dad's newly hired Chief of Security, Jerry Burr, had chosen to dine at the Beachside. As the former Grand Blanc, Michigan, Chief of Police, Jerry had over twenty years of experience dealing with misfits and criminals. Who could blame him for seeking out a cushy job in paradise? The former chief exuded an inner core of strength that came from a lifetime spent protecting the innocent and putting away bad guys. Keith was a bad guy. It was no wonder Jerry was the first to rise from his chair. In the next instant, Jerry's two companions, also former badges, pushed away from the table and followed suit.

In the meantime, Keith had effortlessly deflected the sauté pan and gripped my wrist in a tourniquet-like vise. He twisted my arm behind me and wrenched it upward in an effort to inflict pain.

"You little slut," he sneered, holding me to him with his free hand.

And then it was over. Jerry and one of his pals tackled Keith, bringing him down. The third fellow wrapped me in a bear hug and pulled me out of harm's way.

Keith went to jail, and I was fired. Judy said she knew it hadn't been my fault, but she had to let me go anyway. It was just too much drama, she explained. Good-bye, Beachside Café.

It didn't last with Rob either. He was simply too normal for me. Sometimes I wish I'd stuck with him. I'd be Mrs. Madden now, living in a big house with a luxury SUV in our three-car garage. Not a bad life: one day a week at the spa, Junior League functions, and five kids. He was so devoted and sweet, but there was no challenge in it for me. I'd developed a taste for bad boys, a sense of danger, and I craved more.

Blithely, I skipped from job to job, from the arms of one creep to those of another. With my devil-may-care attitude, I sailed through my high school years, constantly pushing the envelope. When I was a junior, alcohol poisoning landed me in the ER for the second time, and as he would do so many times in the ensuing years, my brother came to my rescue. Whenever I threatened to implode, Michael would be there, ready to pick up all of my messy pieces.

My second soiree in the ER occurred after my date dumped me at my brother's place. I was falling-down drunk, and Michael and his wife, Mary, muscled me into their bathroom. Between bouts of consciousness, I retched until I thought my guts might come up. At some point, fearing that I might be dying, Michael and Mary bundled me into their car and drove me to the hospital. Again, a tube was shoved down my throat so that my stomach could be pumped. Once I was in the ER, my parents were contacted, and I was busted big time. When I came to my senses, I felt like the victim; bad things just seemed to happen to me. I was very good at deflecting blame. It never occurred to me that I might have a problem.

Let's take a tally: My grandfather had been an alcoholic, as were two of my aunts. My great-grandfather drank himself into a stupor before blowing his brains out. Years later, my dad managed to kill himself with drink.

I guess it's fair to say I come by addiction honestly. But in my teens, I simply considered myself a wild child. I enjoyed living on the edge, and there wasn't a rule I wasn't meant to break. When I was sixteen, two major events occurred that affected me far more than I realized. First, my mom divorced my dad. His drinking had become an all-day affair, and she'd had enough of it. Talk about a reversal of fortune! Dad not only lost his job and his esteemed position in the community, he lost his family. It bothered me, but I didn't allow myself to dwell on it, especially given the fact that my parents remained on amicable terms and I saw Dad from time to time. Then, much to my mother's chagrin, I managed to get myself kicked out of St. Ed's. She'd already purchased a lovely white dress for me to wear at my graduation. But there'd be no walking in the white dress for me! I preferred to tell people I'd stacked up too many demerits for defying the dress code, and I *had* accumulated a good number for hiking up my skirts above the knee and wearing makeup. But it was the joyride off campus for a forbidden lunch with a senior that tipped the scales against me.

St. Edward's was finally cleaning house, and when I transferred to John Carroll Catholic High School, I was in good company. I finished my senior year without getting into too much trouble, graduated, and pushed away the regret. I didn't allow myself to think about the mistakes I'd made. There'd be plenty of time for that.

College . . . Let's just say it passed in a blur. I was there and then I wasn't, and not much of anything worthwhile transpired in between. St. Leo University is an obscure Catholic institution of higher learning with a reputation for turning out baseball greats who turn pro. Baseball not being my sport, what was I doing there? The answer was simple: my mother was bound and determined I'd go to college, but given my dismal academic record, St. Leo was the only university to which I was accepted.

During my freshman year, I didn't study at all. My sole achievement was obtaining my lifeguard certification. I studiously avoided my academic classes with the same intensity with which I shied away from my musty little hovel of a dorm room.

It was then, during that crazy first year at university, I started spinning out of control. Without my family to ground me, to tame the wild Un Zapato child in me, I was always looking for the next high—guys, booze, drugs, whatever. I exercised my power through my sexuality, and I was having the time of my life. But this lifestyle was killing me, deadening me in little bits and pieces, one brain cell at a time, and my behavior was becoming ever more erratic.

I was a heck of a lifeguard, though, and looked killer in my black speedo, but it wasn't enough. Eventually, inevitably, I flunked out. I ended up back with Mom, aimlessly searching for some meaning to my life. In the fall, Mom persuaded me to enroll at Indian River State College where I slogged through basic required courses and a few interior design classes, but my heart wasn't in it. The overwhelming emptiness inside me refused to be ignored, and I began trying to fill that hole with whatever I thought might satisfy the desperate, gnawing need.

CHAPTER FOUR

Skipping the Light Fantastic

I WAS NINETEEN WHEN I GOT MY FIRST DUI. AS WAS MY CUSTOM, I DID IT WITH FLARE. No late under-cover-of-night altercations with the law for me! It was at the mall, the center of the universe, where I was cited for driving the wrong way—exiting on the entrance road—while intoxicated. Two of my closest girlfriends and I had been celebrating a birthday. We'd started at noon. The bartender thought we were cute and failed to ask for our IDs. He didn't do us any favors, kept the rum and Cokes coming for the better part of three hours, and we belted them down with abandon. We were totally blasted when I slid behind the wheel of the car my dad had recently purchased for me. Our plan was to hit the beach, check out the action, and try to score more free booze. We didn't get over the causeway. In fact, we didn't make it out of the mall proper. Instead, I got myself plastered across the front page of the next morning's *Press Journal*.

When I navigated onto the entrance ramp, the girls started screaming like banshees. Two lanes of oncoming cars were surging toward us. I reacted by doing the first thing that came to mind: I rammed the car into reverse and backed up over the dividing median. The underbelly of the car scraped against concrete, making a sickening crunch as the car skewed and shimmied over the cement retainer. The back wheels bounced down onto the asphalt pavement, and the next thing you know, I found myself careening straight into the path of a middle-aged woman behind the wheel of some nondescript automobile. She didn't see me coming until I was on top of her. I slammed right into her, ass-backward. The rear end of my car crumpled in on itself like metal origami while destroying the grill and headlights of the terrified woman's car. She was forced into the next lane of traffic, and in the next instant, there was one percussive boom after another. Unable to brake in time, an elderly guy rammed her from behind. That fellow's vehicle was struck by the car behind him. It was quite a pileup: four vehicles totaled, and all before five o'clock in the afternoon! Although I wasn't going more than twenty miles an hour at the time of impact, the results were calamitous. Fortunately, the airbags in all four cars deployed, thus preventing any life-threatening injuries. The woman I hit was the worst off, having suffered whiplash and a slipped disc. It was just minor cuts, scrapes, and bruises for the rest of us, and not a broken bone to show for all the spectacle! Still, a total of seven individuals were whisked to the hospital via ambulance.

After I'd sobered up, I didn't spend a minute worrying about any of it. With the exception of the $500 deductible that my dad forked out, our insurance paid for everything. The adjusters from both insurance companies wrangled about a settlement for the injured woman. My court date was set for three weeks hence, and I went on about my charmed life. What were they going to do to a pretty, privileged girl like me? Throw me in the slammer? Not a chance! I figured, with my luck, I'd be sentenced to community service and be done with the whole sorry episode.

That's not how it went down.

The day of my hearing, I had the good sense to dress demurely. I went for a preppy look, donning a crepe skirt and a lightweight cotton sweater. With my long blonde tresses clipped up on top of my head, I thought I appeared very innocent looking. But my appearance had no effect; Judge Joe Wilde was not to be swayed, pretty girl or no. Instead, he threw the book at me, sentencing me to sixty days in the county jail, after which I was required to complete fifty hours of community service and mandatory alcohol and drug counseling. I was stunned, couldn't believe what I was hearing. I felt as though I were in a bad dream. One minute, Wilde was pronouncing his verdict, and the next, the uniformed guard herded me off to the side of the bench to take my fingerprints. I gazed at my mom imploringly while this humiliating procedure was performed. But there was no help for me. I was escorted out the door and down the hallway to a holding room where I would remain until the day's hearings were completed.

That afternoon in the holding cell, time took on a new dimension. It was my first experience simply waiting, like a caged animal, for the penal system to do with me as it would. I soon learned that waiting with absolutely nothing to do is excruciating. There was to be a lot more of that in the sixty days that loomed ahead. I remember thinking, as the minutes and hours ticked slowly by, that my life was over. But life, it seemed, had much more in store for this chastened girl.

In retrospect, my first stint in jail wasn't too bad. I learned the ropes and kept away from the really criminal types, the big women with crude tattoos and foul mouths. Instead, I quickly made friends with other girls like me, those whose only crime had been getting mixed up with drugs or alcohol. There were a good number of us. The worst aspect of jail time was the mind-numbing boredom. Not being able to go outside to see the light of day was torture. We were supposed to be allowed to exercise outdoors, yet seldom were. To help relieve the tedium, we read whatever we could lay our hands on, recounted our life stories to one another—the mistakes we'd made and misfortunes we'd endured—and wrote letters home. We also attended Bible study and AA meetings whenever the opportunity to do so arose, more to pass the time than from any commitment to either endeavor.

Upon my release, I realized that my formerly carefree lifestyle had come to an end. I no longer had a car, and even if I did, I couldn't have driven. I wouldn't qualify for a valid driver's license for at least two years, after which time I'd be eligible for a hardship license, one that would permit me to drive to work, school, and church, provided I had an interlock device installed. Mom chauffeured me around town for several months, dropping me off at DUI school, driving me to and from Monte's where I worked as a waitress—always nagging me about what I was going to do with my life and whether or not I was ever going to finish school. Blah, blah, blah. Eventually, I couldn't take it any longer; her carping was driving me up a wall. I took the easy way out. I moved in with my newest boyfriend, Nick—another loser.

Nick loved me in a strange, obsessive way, and I truly believed I loved him back. I continued to think so for years, even long after we'd broken up. For one, he was good looking in that slick Italian way, with his creamy olive skin, great hair, and long, lean-muscled body that turned me on. Two, he was a great lay. How I loved that man in my bed! Three, he came from a very nice family. His father was a local architect and well thought of. Nick, however, was the black sheep of the family. He had never finished college and wasn't qualified for any employment other than as a day laborer or a waiter. He'd chosen the latter and was working at Monte's, which is how I met him. This relationship made sense to me, if only for the convenience of the arrangement: he could drive us both to and from work!

We rented a rundown apartment in town where we partied after hours, drinking and doing lines of coke whenever we could score the stuff. Nick loved coke, but I joined him only to be sociable. My ADHD kept things going at a fast enough clip.

Occasionally, I would see my mom. She'd take me to lunch or dinner, harp on me about completing my community service hours, what I was going to do about my future. I know now that she meant well, but I was always glad to escape into Nick's arms. In his eyes, I was perfect, and that validated me. All this time, I was receiving court-ordered counseling, but it had no effect. I thought it was useless. I know now that I was stuck somehow, not moving forward in any constructive way, but rather just drifting and waiting for the next shoe to fall.

In 2004, Vero Beach was visited by not one, but two hurricanes.

First, that harpy Hurricane Frances paid her respects. It appeared as though she couldn't wait to get at us, for she hurtled toward the Treasure Coast like a runaway freight train. Yet once having arrived at her destination, Frances revealed her cantankerous and changeable nature and dallied. Like most travelers, she seemed to enjoy her sojourn on the Treasure Coast and was reluctant to depart. More's the pity. Frances kept battering us till we thought she'd never leave. Two weeks later, storm-weary residents were just beginning to pick up the pieces of their disrupted lives and restore order, and who blew into town but Frances's ugly sibling, Hurricane Jeanne!

Nick and I were living in that tumbledown apartment in downtown Vero when the warning for the first hurricane was issued. I would have gone to Mom's place, but it was on the barrier island where there was a mandatory evacuation. Everyone was frantically boarding up windows and scurrying to purchase bottled water and canned goods, laying in for a long siege. Our flat was a second-story unit, so we figured we'd be safe. Why, I'm not sure, but we did. Nick and I, and the couple who rented below us, treated the whole thing like a madcap caper. When the wind picked up that evening, we sat around the linoleum-laminate table drinking beer and doing lines while some inane sitcom aired on the television. Around ten, the wind really started howling. The lights began to flicker, and we lost reception. Undeterred, we inserted a DVD and settled in. We knew it was only a matter of time before the power would go altogether. Sure enough, about a half hour later, we lost electricity, and the air conditioner ceased to cool. We were plunged into darkness with only the sound of the wind roaring in our ears. As the storm raged on and rain pelted against the windowpanes, the four of us sought higher ground. We huddled together on the bed to wait it out. It was a wild night, but eventually we crashed and slept. The next morning, we awoke to chaos.

Although the apartment had withstood the storm, it was the worse for wear. Leaves, raffia, and small twigs were plastered against the windowpanes, and puddles of water pooled beneath the sills. Outside, a huge Washingtonia palm had toppled and laid recumbent across the driveway like a dinosaur corpse. Nick's car had narrowly escaped being flattened, and we had a heck of a time clearing away the monster tree so we could get to the car. The electricity was still out, and it was wicked hot and sauna humid. We desired nothing more than to get somewhere cool. Since there would be no shifts at Monte's anytime soon, Nick and I decided to head to Orlando where we could find a cheap hotel with A/C, maybe catch a theme park, and make the most of this window of opportunity.

Driving out of Indian River County was an eye-opener; there was devastation everywhere: buildings with roofs peeled away like lids from sardine cans, cars and boats tossed about, downed trees and utility poles. I had no long-term plans. Perhaps, I thought fleetingly, I'd come back when the lights were on again.

When we did return, Nick got arrested for pulling a knife on a guy at a local bistro. He was sentenced to six months, which meant he'd be getting out about the time I'd be coming off probation. I decided I didn't have it in me to keep the home fires burning and quickly found a replacement in the form of one Derrick Kelly. Like Nick, Derrick was olive-skinned, ropey-muscled, and swarthy. I'm always drawn to that type, and Derrick seemed sweet enough. But he wasn't Italian, he was Irish, and his drug of choice was booze. That was okay with me because I really wasn't into cocaine, but I could drink with the best of them.

Derrick and I moved to Daytona where, it was reputed, one could make an easy buck during Bike Week when the place was teeming with bikers partying from dawn till dusk. If one is unemployed in Daytona during Bike Week, he is either supremely lazy or too high to perform a simple task. It didn't take me long to realize that Derrick fit nicely into both categories. The man had little ambition other than to drink himself silly. We were crashing in a fleabag of a motel until what little money we had ran out, and finally having had enough of his sloth, I ran out on him. With no resources and nowhere to go, I found myself walking a back alley in a sleazy section of downtown Daytona, all of my worldly possessions stuffed into an oversized sports duffel. Next thing I knew, a door flew open, spilling light and trouble onto the pavement and sealing my destiny. A giant of a man—shaved head, muscles bulging beneath his straining tee—exploded from the building, dragging a partially clad and exceedingly ornery brunette behind him.

"Out," he cried, thrusting the thrashing creature into the alleyway. He turned, grabbed a large tote overflowing with personal belongings—clothes, hairdryer, and the like—and hurled it into the street after her. Items flew from the bag, and the girl scrambled to collect them.

The bouncer shook his head in disgust. "And don't come back! I got enough trouble without your drama."

"You son of a bitch, Lonnie." The girl darted about collecting her things and stuffing them into her bag. "I'll get you for this!" Face mottled, she rose from the pavement and strutted off in a vain attempt to regain some small shred of dignity. "I don't need your shit, you pig," she added as she trotted around the corner.

Suddenly, Lonnie saw me trembling there in horror. Pointing a fleshy finger in my direction, he bellowed, "You! Get your ass over here."

Despite my lack of the caution gene, I was immediately overawed by this fellow, and my bones seemed to melt on the spot. Still, I managed to shuffle toward him.

"What the hell you doing sneaking around back here?" he asked.

Like a fish dying in air, my mouth closed and opened, but no words came out. It's safe to say I was scared speechless.

The monster gave me the once-over and then slowly nodded his head approvingly. "Sweetheart, you need a job?" he asked, turning on the charm. In an instant, his expression softened, and he didn't look nearly so threatening.

But I wasn't really processing much of anything. Then my brain kicked in. Well yeah, I did, I thought. "Sure," I said, when I was capable of speech. "Whattaya got?"

"Come on inside, girly. I'll show you around," he said, flashing an insincere smile my way.

And that's how I started dancing.

Two months later, I waltzed into the Mercedes dealership and purchased a brand- spanking-new champagne-colored E 320 Sport sedan.

Paid cash.

As strip clubs go, the Velvet Pony was one of the more upscale establishments, so it wasn't difficult fooling myself into believing that fate had led me there. When Lonnie showed me the lay of the land, I asked if I could just tend bar. I enjoyed bartending; the work was fast-paced and didn't allow me time to think, which is just the way I liked it.

"Sure you can, sweetheart," Lonnie said. "But you'll end up dancing. They always do. The money's just too good to pass up. And with your looks, you're gonna make a killing."

He was right. In no time, I was riding the pole, shaking my fanny and baring my breasts. And as Lonnie had predicted, the money was flowing in hand over G-string. In case you didn't know, the really big money in dancing isn't in dancing at all. Big surprise there, huh? No. It's in the VIP, the miserable little chambers where, for a fee, a guy can have a bit of a one-on-one with the babe of his choice. Rules are: no touching, but rules are made to be broken. Truth of the matter is, the girl calls the shots; she can do as little or as much as she pleases. And with Lonnie or one of his minions within earshot, the guys generally go along with the plan.

In those back rooms, I was much in demand—a high-energy new girl with the face of an angel and a body built for sin. It wasn't long before I was popping a Xanax before my sets to make the sleaziness of my occupation seem less so.

There were always tension and drama at the Pony. Although we dancers sedated ourselves, tempers often flared. The pecking order was as follows: I, the blonde bombshell, was the top girl, followed by the dark and sultry Storm. The two of us were completely opposite in coloring and therefore dubbed Salt and Pepper. Tina, a redhead, was cute and perky and third in line. Don't get me wrong; all the girls in the Pony stable were pretty, but some of them had bad teeth or sallow complexions, and a few of them looked hardened because they were. Gigi and Giselle, siblings from Romania, were counted among the latter. Both were small breasted and rather emaciated looking. The fact that they were identical twins is what made them unique. G. and G. were highly sought after for twosomes, which is kind of funny because, like a lot of sisters, that pair could get on each other's nerves. Sometimes they'd come storming through the back door, raving like lunatics, and Lonnie or another bouncer would have to separate them for fear there'd be blood.

On just such an occasion, the two Gs were going at it in the dressing room, Giselle hurling insults at her twin in their native tongue. None of the rest of us understood a word, but we got the gist. While this transpired, all of us dancers, the two Gs included, were either applying makeup or styling wigs. Apparently, Giselle was the injured party. She sat before her mirror lining her eyes with kohl. Every so often, she would cut away to spit out venomous accusations in her sister's direction. It was quite a performance. Storm and I raised our eyebrows, struggling to contain our giggles.

Gigi made a show of ignoring her sibling, affecting nonchalance as she scrutinized her own reflection in the mirror. Primping, she turned her head from side to side as waves of vitriol washed over her. But then Giselle must have said something so vile it could not be ignored, or maybe Gigi had simply taken all the abuse she could tolerate. In any case, the smile disappeared from her face only to be replaced by a murderous expression. In the next moment, Gigi leapt out of her chair and pounced on Giselle, throttling her sister's neck with both hands. The rest of us froze, unable to comprehend what was transpiring before our eyes. There was little Giselle could do to repel this offense, although she struggled mightily, throwing ineffective punches at Gigi's midsection.

It's not easy to strangle a person. Months later, I'd find myself employing a rope to that end, and even that wouldn't work. This particular attempt didn't seem to be meeting with much success either. Gigi was putting a lot of effort into the exercise, but her twin wasn't about to surrender. At one point, Giselle's fingers scrabbled across her dressing table and locked around a pair of tweezers. The grooming tool became a weapon in her hands, and Giselle began stabbing Gigi repeatedly about the neck.

That was enough to rouse us bystanders from our drug-induced languor, and we shrieked at the sight of blood. Storm and I jumped up and rushed the twins, attempting to wrest the tweezers from Giselle's grasp. But she turned on us, wielding her double-pronged dagger, and we retreated.

A footnote regarding the condition of our lockers: they were pitiful, much worse than the ones I'd used in high school, for they'd never been properly affixed to the walls. We were always complaining to Vinnie or Freddy, whoever would listen, that the lockers were not merely unstable but downright dangerous. Stowing our personal items was touch and go, for we were afraid the darn things would come crashing down on us at any moment. Wily Giselle used this failing to her advantage. She lunged at the locker nearest her sister and gave it a mighty shove. Sure enough, the contraption came toppling down on Gigi, who in turn crumpled like a paper doll. By this time, we all were yowling, trying to restrain Giselle while at the same time attempting to extricate Gigi. Finally Lonnie arrived, and that put an end to the hullabaloo.

Gigi was rescued and, except for a few shallow puncture wounds to her neck and an egg on the back of her head, was none the worse for wear. Lonnie read the twins the riot act and hustled them out the back door, warning them not to return until they were prepared to behave like human beings.

And the freak show went on as usual.

CHAPTER FIVE

Lyle's Hustle

OVER THE COURSE OF THE SIX MONTHS I'D BEEN DANCING AT THE
PONY, I BECAME AWARE OF THE FACT THAT THE OWNERS, THE ROMANO
BROTHERS, WERE *CONNECTED*. That is to say, they were also involved in il-
legal gambling and who knows what other illicit dealings. Like the other
dancers, I made it a practice to stay clear of Vinnie, Freddy, and Ricco.
Pills helped us turn a blind eye to their shenanigans.

During that time, I had lots of "dates," and some of those guys
became my regulars. If I was having a slow night and it didn't look as
though I'd clear my personal preset minimum of a thousand bucks, I'd
call up one or more of the regulars and invite them to a special party. I
hadn't hooked up with anyone exclusively, and I was sharing an apartment with Storm. But this all changed when Lyle sauntered in and his
eyes latched on mine. I knew immediately that he'd be requesting time in
the VIP with the newest filly in the Pony stable. What I didn't know was
that this was to mark the beginning of another ignoble chapter of my life.

After my set, I slid off the bar and toddled over to him. His eyes
were glued on me as I crossed the distance, my six-inch Lucite heels
making a click-clicking sound on the terrazzo floor. "Hi," I said. "Buy
a girl a drink?"

"Sure." He patted the empty stool beside him. "What's your pleasure?"

"I'll have a Cosmo."

"A Cosmo for the little lady," he called to the bartender. "And another Michelob with lemon for me."

"So, I haven't seen you here before," I said.

"Which is why I haven't seen you," he countered. "I'm a pretty busy guy. It's been a while since I've been back here."

"Oh. What do you do?"

"I'm a CPA, have my own office on Yong Street. And what do you do?" he asked slyly.

I laughed. "You mean when I'm not taking my clothes off?"

"Yeah, in your spare time."

My Cosmo arrived, and I ran my tongue around the sugared rim, fully aware of the effect I was having on this guy. "Um . . . Well, I like to work out. And I run. And I really love playing soccer and lacrosse."

"No kidding?" he exclaimed, eyeing me speculatively. I'm sure he'd figured me for a bimbo, but it was obvious he was making a reassessment. "You're not like the other girls."

"No?"

"You're a class act, aren't you?"

"I've always thought so. What's your name?" I asked.

"Lyle Bennett," he said. "And you are?"

"Meghan Rose," I said, extending a hand.

"Pleased to meet you, ma'am," Lyle said, and we shook on it.

When we finished our drinks, I did some more shaking with him in the VIP. Afterward, I could see he was a bit overcome. He opened his wallet, said, "Here, take it. There's three hundred dollars."

I made as if to refuse, but not with any enthusiasm.

"No, I mean it," he said. "You're worth every penny."

Lyle became my number-one regular, and it wasn't long before he offered to put me up in one of his rental properties. I considered it for a few weeks, finally coming to the conclusion that I needed someone to take care of me. Left to my own devices, I didn't seem to be doing a very good job of it. Add to that the fact that I'd had my fill of stripping. I was tired of pretending that what I did in that sordid VIP was okay—pretending that I could deal with it, that I didn't feel anything. I was tired of assuaging my misgivings by repeating the mantra, "A girl has to make a living," when all I really wanted was a way out. Lyle was the ticket. At least, that's what I thought.

Lyle was married, but that didn't bother me. Most of my regulars were married. He set me up in a spiffy little duplex. One unit was occupied by a solitary old geezer who seldom ventured outside, and the other was to be mine all mine. I thought this the perfect arrangement; I was able to maintain my independence while Lyle saw to my apartment's upkeep.

I'd imagined that once Lyle had his very own love nest, he'd bankroll me so that I could stop dancing. But I'd been mistaken. He wanted me to continue working, said he got a kick out of knowing that, at the end of the day, the lust object of every man at the Pony would be coming home to him. It was weird, but I felt indebted to him so I let it slide.

At that same time, I started ratcheting up my pill consumption—oxys, roxies, whatever I could get my hands on. Just two pills to take the edge off and I could sail through the long nights at the Velvet Pony. Given my hyperactive brain, I especially liked the feeling of things slooo . . . wiiiing . . . dooo . . . wn. Narcotics made me feel normal, as though I could actually catch hold of life instead of letting it slide through my fingers.

I was self-medicating, and it would come back to bite me.

CHAPTER SIX

The Bump and Grind

DAYTONA IS A BITCHIN' SIN CITY, AND AN AMBITIOUS GIRL CAN DO WELL THERE. Trouble is, it's easy to get sucked up into the sordidness of it all. At first, I thought the bikers, with their screaming Hogs, were fun. God knows they spent money like water. But in the end, I came to despise the sound of their vroom-vroom-screeching wheels nearly as much as I did the thunderous, deafening roar of the racetrack. It was like living in a carnival night and day, ticky-tacky and phony. But I made the most of it. I was *the* girl at the Velvet Pony. And I was bringing home more money than I'd ever dreamed possible.

Like Madonna, I was a material girl and could now afford all the designer clothing, handbags, and sunglasses my little heart desired, and I indulged my passion for fashion. On the downside, my self-medication had turned into an addiction. It started out innocently enough: just a few pills before my shift to soften the harsh edges. And it wasn't like I was the only one. All the girls doped. Pills helped keep us from obsessing over what we were doing in the VIP, which we jokingly referred to as "very intense pussy." We laughed it off. It was just a brief phase in our young lives. Not one of us planned on doing that sort of thing for very long, but it was hard to walk away from that seemingly endless flow of cash.

I spent half a year riding bareback at the Pony before I decided to pursue more legitimate work. I figured I might be able to break away from dancing and segue into a modeling career. I had professional head and body shots taken in Orlando, and I sent them out to modeling agencies everywhere. I did get some work. But for the most part, I was asked to take my clothes off, and that's not what I was after. I modeled at a few trade shows in Orlando, which is how I came to meet Michael Serious. (Seriously, that's his name.) Mike represented a guy who created designs for application on surfboards, boogie boards, skateboards, posters, all kinds of things. He had me sit for the guy, and sure enough, my image now graces all of the above. Did I get paid? No. Was I gullible? Yes.

And then there was the time I was asked to accompany one of the race car drivers to his vehicle on the track.

"Are you for real?" I asked, thinking the guy was pulling my leg.

"Oh yeah," he said. "You get to wait up top in the air-conditioned VIP area. It's a trip."

"VIP?" My smile hardened as my suspicious mind conjured unpleasant scenarios. "And just what is it I'm supposed to do?"

"Nothing! You get dolled up real nice, take the race car driver by the arm, and lead him to his car. That's it."

"And for that I get—?"

"Five hundred bucks and all the food and booze you can put away before and after you do your bit. Plus, you get to watch the races for free in cool, quiet comfort with all the high rollers."

"You're on," I said.

On race day, I was so nervous I took one pill too many. Combine that with an unending supply of Cosmos, and it's a miracle I was able to walk the poor sucker to his car. I can't even remember his name.

And I never did get the five hundred bucks.

Karl Jankovic, the fellow who was renting the other half of Lyle's duplex, was a cool old dude, but it took a while for me to notice. Most days I didn't crawl out of bed till mid-afternoon. I was up so late working nights that by the time I got home Karl was all tucked in. It's little wonder we seldom saw one another. Monday, my day off, was the most likely time our paths might cross.

Karl enjoyed sitting on his little front porch, having a smoke and watching the world go by. On those rare occasions when I happened to catch sight of him, he'd invite me over to join him, and I usually obliged. Like most elderly people, he tended to ramble, could fill the hours reminiscing about his past. I didn't mind; I enjoyed listening to Karl jabber away. It was during one of these sessions I learned that he'd formerly owned a pawn shop.

I was intrigued by this fact, and upon my urging, Karl recounted a number of transactions involving people who were forced to swap their valuables in exchange for cash. He had lots of funny stories, but there were sad ones as well: women forfeiting their engagement rings to feed their babies, that kind of stuff. One Monday, after I'd been there two months or so and Karl had taken a liking to me, he said, "*Shatzi,*" (That's what he called me. It's the German word for *sweetheart.*) "how would you like to see some jewelry?"

Jewelry? Now there was the magic word. "Sure," I said.

Karl didn't need any more encouragement; he immediately invited me into his unit, and I readily obliged. Unlike my hovel, his place was neat as a pin. Once inside, he gestured for me to take a seat at his kitchen table, and I did as I was instructed. Karl retreated into his bedroom only to return toting an enormous wooden box. I was rapt. It was like a small pirate's chest except for the fact that the top was flat rather than rounded. Karl set the chest before me on the kitchen table and, with a flourish, produced a large ring of keys. He selected an ornate one, inserted it into the lock, and opened the box. My eyes nearly popped out of my head when I saw the contents. The chest was a treasure trove chock full of gold and platinum jewelry, brilliant diamonds, and sparkling gems of every hue. A lot of it was passé stuff of little value—cameos, onyx rings, that sort of thing—but there were some very high-quality pieces as well. I figured the lot was worth at least forty, maybe fifty grand.

Karl insisted I try on a few pieces, and I needed no arm-twisting. I was in heaven; it was like playing with my Nana's jewelry box, sorting her earrings and pearls, a delightful chore I'd performed as a kid. Once

I'd examined each bauble, Karl clapped his hands together.

"*Genug!*" he exclaimed. "*Was mochten sie, Shatzi?* What shall you have?"

"Oh no, Karl," I demurred. "I couldn't. It wouldn't be right."

"*Aber ja!* Take something!" Karl insisted magnanimously. "A pretty girl should have pretty things."

Suddenly, there was a heaviness at the back of my throat. It was the nicest thing a man had said to me in a long time. And Karl didn't want anything other than my friendship in return. My eyes brimmed with tears, but I had the good sense to select a gorgeous blue-topaz ring framed by pavé diamonds in an eighteen-carat-gold setting.

So, despite the sleaziness of the Velvet Pony, my stint there was not without its rewards. At least, that was my take on it. Silly, dopey girl that I was, I figured I'd landed right where I was supposed to be. Business was brisk, and the compensation generous, which was a blessing because my habit was becoming an expensive one.

CHAPTER SEVEN

Tango

ONE NIGHT, VINNIE APPROACHED ME AFTER MY SET.
"Hey, girl," he said. "You want to party?" I hesitated. The creep was
my boss. He was a seriously bad dude, and I sure didn't want to make
him angry. What I wanted to do was to go home—to Lyle's duplex, that
is—and crash. But Vinnie speared me with his crazed leer, and I thought
I'd better do what he wanted and avoid trouble.

That's not how it worked out.

"Sure!" I said. "Parrrty!"

And I was rewarded by what passed for a smile from that goon.
Thank goodness I'd only taken a few pills and was reasonably in control
of my faculties. Had it been otherwise, what next went down might have
meant the end of Miss Un Zapato.

In the dressing room, I quickly shrugged out of my stripper duds
and into a pair of denims and a tee. After flouncing into the passenger
seat of Vinnie's late-model Saab, the two of us tooled out of town for
parts unknown. I had no idea where we were going, didn't suspect a
thing until we ended up west of I-95 jigging down a rutted dirt road. It
was darker than dark, not a street light anywhere, and we were bucking
and rocking until my teeth felt like they were going to shake loose and
fly out of my mouth. Up ahead, a dilapidated building surrounded by
a razor-wire fence came into view, some kind of warehouse. The place
was lit up like a Christmas tree, so I guess someone was expecting us.

Vinnie was full of himself, acting cool and collected while giving me his macho-man act. But I wasn't fooled. I could see he was nervous, chain-smoking and jittery as a cat. He parked his sedan in front of the building right next to Ricco's BMW, and we hiked to the door. I stepped over the threshold and into a horror show.

The space was barebones and harshly lit by large overhead lights that cast shadows in grimy corners. But what immediately drew my eyes was the miserable creature who'd been secured to a chair and worked over. He was blubbering for mercy, a rivulet of blood oozing from his nose. Vinnie's brothers, Freddy and Ricco, were standing around shooting the breeze, seemingly without a care in the world. My eyes cut to the worn worktable before them, the gun that rested on its scarred surface.

I didn't want any part of this, and I started pleading with Vinnie to let the poor jerk go. "Come on, Vinnie," I said. "Let's get the hell outta here. Seriously. You guys have done enough damage."

I glanced at Vinnie's brothers. Freddy raised his eyebrows, shrugged. Ricco looked right through me, acted like I wasn't even there.

"This is a rite of passage," Vinnie said. I didn't know what he meant by that, but I was soon to find out. He strode to the table and palmed the weapon. Crossing the distance between us, he thrust the revolver toward me.

"Here," he said, indicating that I should take it from him. Freddy and Ricco snickered. They thought it was funny.

In the meantime, the floor show was really getting on my nerves.

"Vinnie, don't, I'm begging you," the unfortunate fellow pleaded. "Please! In the name of God, I never—"

"Shut your trap," Freddy bawled and cuffed him on the jaw.

"You're kidding, right?" I said, backing away.

"No. Not kidding. This weasel was holdin' out on me, doing a little business on the side. He needs to be taught a lesson, one that he'll never forget." And with that, Vinnie grabbed my hand and attempted to mold my fingers around the gun. "Pop him one in the kneecap, sweetheart."

A red-hot rage instantly boiled up inside me; it was as though someone lit a match in a tinderbox. I wasn't going to be part of this nasty business, and this goomba was not going to push me around! Who the hell did he think he was? I shoved the gun away.

"I'm outta here," I snarled, racing for the door. Once outside, I began to run in earnest. Even with two oxys in me, I was fast. But when I heard a shot ring out and then, in quick succession, another, I hightailed it lickety-split. I didn't know who the intended victim of this volley was. Perhaps they were merely wild shots meant to frighten me, but I wasn't about to stick around to find out.

The night was a thick black cloak, no stars, no moon. But my eyes adjusted quickly. Still, it's a wonder I didn't trip over a root and break a leg. I kept off the road, following along beside it, all the while checking behind me to see if there were headlight beams piercing the darkness. Sure enough, it was only a matter of minutes before I saw them, a pair of bouncing yellow eyeballs seeking me out.

I've heard that fear can lend a person superpowers, and I can tell you that happens to be true. I veered off into the brush with the speed of a cheetah and didn't stop until I found a big old cabbage palm to hide behind. Molding my back against that tree, I waited for my breathing to slow as Vinnie's Saab whizzed by. It wasn't until the Saab's taillights disappeared from view that I ventured forth, picking my way back toward the roadbed, not daring out into the open. Instead, I kept parallel to the pitted track, opting for the cover of bramble and bush. I wasn't too worried about Freddy and Ricco coming after me. I figured they'd be a while, had some cleaning up to do. It was Vinnie who was the problem. I wondered how long it would take him to realize I couldn't possibly have run so far and decide to swing back around to ferret me out. But I needn't have worried. He wasn't quick on the uptake, and he never did turn around.

Now I had other problems. I was a long way from civilization and not dressed for a hike in the wilderness. Thank goodness I'd exchanged my heels for sneakers; otherwise, I'd have never made it to this point. It had been a while since I'd done any strenuous exercise except for you know what. I was out of shape, but I still had legs and bull-headed stamina. The prospect of a long traipse didn't bother me. I was more concerned about the possibility of encountering wild hogs or a bear. It was February, cold and dry, and I was on high ground. I didn't think I'd be crossing any gator's path. But wild boars can be nasty creatures. I had heard they can kill a man, so there was a healthy dose of fear keeping me wide-eyed and alert as I stumbled through the night along that back road to hell.

Even though he'd warned me never to do so after working hours, I thought about calling Lyle. His wife was suspicious, had been giving him grief, pestering him about his whereabouts, who he was hanging with. He didn't want me rocking that love boat.

Eventually, I hit the highway. There wasn't much traffic at this hour. But after a couple of minutes, a tractor-trailer rig zoomed toward me, and I put my thumb out. What the heck? I thought. What worse thing could happen? Sure enough, the trucker stopped and picked me up, drove me straight to my little duplex.

I was exhausted, both mentally and physically. The unaccustomed exertion had sped up my metabolism so that now I was detoxing, and quickly. I popped some oxys, peeled out of my grimy clothing, and jumped into the shower. The hot water cascaded over me, cleaning away most of the nastiness. I was just beginning to feel like what had become my "normal" when a god-awful rapping on my door commenced, and I was delivered to hell's gate all over again.

I wrapped a bath sheet around me, quickly applied eyeliner and lip gloss, then dashed to the door. I knew, with a sickening finality, that it was Vinnie. Who else could it be at this hour? Perhaps I would soon be out of my misery, I thought.

I opened the door with a welcoming smile on my face, but there was no need. Vinnie was wasted; he peered at me as though I were an amoeba under a microscope.

"Vinnie," I said, struggling to keep the fear from my voice. "Come in."

He strutted over the threshold, all hopped up and jerky. It was plain to see he was flying on speed, which I thought could work either to my benefit or demise.

"Hey, babe! Why'd you cut out on me, huh?"

He was a lousy actor, but I was still terrified. I mumbled some answer and shrugged.

"You really think we were going to waste that guy? Come on! Gimme a break."

The oxys were kicking in, and my mind was becoming muddled. Did I really think Vinnie was capable of killing someone? I didn't know.

"You scared the hell out of me," I said accusingly. My heart was beating a staccato double time, and I figured I'd best play it cool and dumb.

"I guess I'm just a little fraidy-cat," I added, letting the towel slip a bit to afford him a look at my cleavage. "So you let that guy go?"

"Sure! We roughed him up a bit. That's it, I swear."

I sighed and made a show of my relief at this news.

"You wanna drink?" I asked, taking a new tack.

"Nah. I want you, girl. Come here," he said, pulling me close.

Just my luck, I thought. But it was a ten-minute one-man show and over before it'd begun. I made sure of that, and Vinnie was none the wiser. He left satisfied, and I was left thinking I'd dodged a bullet. But it was after that—after that night—that I started feeling conflicted, depraved even. I knew what I was doing was wrong. No matter how many pills I popped, I couldn't escape that fact. I'd been appeasing my conscience, telling myself that I was just making a living. But it was Satan, not Vinnie, who was knocking on my door, and I couldn't pretend otherwise—no matter how much I doped.

The next day, I didn't awaken until well past noon. When I did, I lie in bed pondering the events of the past evening and my present situation. It didn't take me long to figure out that I needed to put some distance between me and the Romano mobsters. And I had to face the fact that there was no future for me with Lyle. He'd made it clear he wasn't going to divorce his wife. I was just the girl in his duplex, some chick he could diddle whenever the urge came over him. It was demeaning. (What in my life wasn't?) I could well afford my own place. I came up with a game plan: I would bide my time, but as soon as the opportunity presented itself, I'd dismount the Velvet Pony and ride out of Sin City South on another horse.

That very night, I met Patrick and was delivered from the frying pan into the fire.

CHAPTER EIGHT

Jive

PATRICK WAS ITALIAN WITH THOSE SMOOTH, DARK LOOKS I'VE ALWAYS BEEN A SUCKER FOR. In hindsight, I can't imagine why I ever thought he might be *the one*. He would inflict the greatest trauma to my psyche, the most horrific physical abuse to my person of any of the abusers I have encountered in my to-date sorry existence. To add insult to injury, he was a small guy. In pumps, I towered over him. But what Patrick lacked in stature, he made up for in charm, and he was beautifully muscled with a disarming grin that immediately won me over.

When I slithered out to do my set that evening, Patrick's eyes locked on mine, and I knew without question I'd be seeing him in the VIP.

For all of his cockiness, there was something vulnerable about the guy; he was needy in a way I couldn't fathom. He brought out my mothering instincts. That man lapped up any affection I gave him like a cat does cream.

It was 2007, and Florida's building boom was at its peak. Patrick was a licensed contractor and a jack-of-all-trades. He could hang drywall with the best of them, even wire for electric if need be. Given his skills, he was much in demand. At the time I met him, he was supervising a construction crew working on a high-rise condominium. One night, about a week after he'd become a regular at the Pony, we were having a drink at the bar, and Patrick said, "Say, Meghan, how's about you come move in with me? The condo's cool. Great view of the ocean.

And you can't beat the rent."

"Yeah?" I replied, not really interested. "How much?"

"It's free," Patrick replied. "Like money in the bank, baby cakes."

At first I blew him off. What did I need with a contractor, a blue-collar worker? I was setting my sights a whole lot higher. A suit was what I wanted. An attorney would do, someone to take care of that DUI on my record. Better yet, a doc, I thought. How sweet would that be, to find someone who would not only allow me to retire but write my scripts in the bargain? But Patrick was so persuasive, and I had truly had my fill of Lyle and his bitchy wife. I decided this invitation was worth considering. I told Patrick I'd think about it, but that I'd have to see my future palace before making a commitment.

Later, when I arrived at the love shack, Lyle was waiting, and that really set me off. I was dead on my feet, would rather eat glass than party with him. But I sucked it up and smiled coquettishly at him.

"Hi, baby," I said, letting my bag fall to the floor as I covered the distance between us. "What's up?"

He was draped across the sofa, watching television on the new flat screen he'd recently installed, his signature bottle of Michelob on the cocktail table before him.

"Hey, doll!" Lyle exclaimed, drawing me down onto his lap and whispering into my ear. "I was thinking I'd like a little red-headed teen-ager tonight. Do you think I might find one around here?"

I pushed away, about to burst his bubble. But then I thought better of it. Lyle had been good to me. What would it hurt to let him down gently?

"Gee, I don't know," I replied in my little-girl voice. "Let me go see if there might be one hiding in the bedroom."

I disengaged and made a dash for my closet. It wasn't long before I located my auburn wig and varsity cheerleading outfit. I was back in Lyle's face before he had time to change his mind and decide he wanted a sultry Black Widow instead. Well, I cheered and I wiggled, and I took care of that adolescent fantasy real quick so I might have some peace. Lyle was gone in no time, having left with a smile on his face. I, on the other hand, had decided to split; I wouldn't be there when he came looking for a saucy French maid or some other incarnation.

The very next day, I was to meet Patrick at the apartment building to check it out and give it my "Good Housekeeping Seal of Approval" before moving in. We'd arranged for me to be there at one, but in my usual fashion, I'd gotten a late start and didn't make it until three-thirty. When I finally arrived, I could see that Patrick was pissed; he was stamping around, cussing like some bantam rooster whose hens had crossed the road to get to the other side. Well, excuse me, I thought, my dander up. Walk a mile in my shoes, mister! As usual, I tamped down the indignation, played it all girly-girly, which is what usually placates men. "Pick your battles," my mom always said. "Don't sweat the small stuff." Patrick was small, but I wasn't going there.

"Hey, sweetie," I cooed, wrapping my arms around him. In an instant, he was transformed into a boy wanting the approval of his mama. I should have known this guy was desperate for love, should have figured it out then and there. But I was in my drug-induced fog, and the writing on the wall was indecipherable. Let me tell you, that's a recipe for disaster:

Take (1) really needy, damaged man.
Mix with equal part clueless, dopey girl.
Simmer till near boiling.
And prepare to wipe the blood off the walls.

Oh, there'd be blood all right, and plenty of it. But the bloodletting wouldn't occur until much later. In those early days of our relationship, I conned myself into thinking I could manage the man-boy.

As usual, I was wrong.

At this point in time, however, it appeared as though I'd mollified

Patrick, for the next thing I knew, he was leading me to a bank of elevators. The doors whooshed open, and we were whisked from the cavernous, unfurnished lobby and deposited on the eleventh floor. Then, after traipsing down a narrow corridor, Patrick threw open the door to my new abode. Once inside, he waltzed about, pointing out the flat's most notable features: large squares of travertine tiles splattered with grout, floor-to-ceiling windows covered with drywall mud, a kitchen with no appliances. I smiled brightly as my mind recoiled in horror. The place was nothing more than a construction site, hardly suitable for habitation! At least there was electricity; we wouldn't be in the dark at night. But there was no air-conditioning, and I was already starting to wilt. We're talking Florida in the spring: it's hot and only going to get a whole lot toastier. Still, once I got past my initial shock, I wavered. On one hand, I was far from desperate. On the other, I needed to put some distance between Lyle and yours truly. I gazed about, pausing to weigh the pros and cons, and then came to a decision.

"Here's the deal," I said, grabbing Patrick by the arm and pulling him to me. "If you can get the appliances installed and the A/C up and running, I'll have some furniture delivered."

Patrick replied with one of his favorite expressions: "Yeah, baby!"

Two weeks later, I moved out of Kyle's duplex into the Daytona Beach Riviera, a hard-hat zone with a great view, totally illegal and rent-free.

Which is how I learned to hang drywall.

The condo offered a truly stunning view of the Atlantic. On the flip side, we were treated to laser-like sunrays from about 7:00 a.m. until noon, which didn't adversely affect Patrick because he was an early riser. Not so for me. Working nights at the Velvet Pony, I seldom hit the sack until after 2:00 a.m. Who could blame me for wanting to sleep late? Soon, like Patrick, I was up at the crack of dawn, the only difference between his situation and mine being that he had a full day ahead of him while I had nothing to occupy me until late afternoon. After complaining about this for quite some time, I decided to tell Patrick about an idea I had.

"I think I'll buy a computer," I yammered to him one morning over coffee. "Take an online class or something."

But before I could expound upon my plans, he cut me off, saying "Damn it, Meghan! I can give you something to do, and I'll pay you good money for it, too."

"Like what?" I asked, thinking he wanted a special "party" or something equally distasteful.

"Sweetheart, I'm way behind schedule, and I keep losing my guys to bigger projects . . . or dope . . . or booze. You're always going on about how strong you are, how you can best any man. Well, here's your opportunity, babe. You can start today."

"Doing what?" I asked, still suspicious.

"Hanging drywall, baby. But let me warn you, it's a rough business."

Well, those were enticing words to a girl who thrives on competition. Suddenly, Patrick had my full attention. How tough could it be? I wondered, thinking about the rigors of my current profession. My athlete's body ached for the challenge, and my devil-may-care attitude surfaced right on cue.

"You're on!" I exclaimed. "But I can only work till 3. After that, I'll need to shower and perform a miracle to transform myself from day laborer to harlot. There's no way you can pay me enough to give up my night job."

I was soon to learn that hanging drywall is not for the faint of heart. Think about it: Have you ever seen a fat drywall guy? The process involves a great deal of bending and stretching. It's an exercise akin to Pilates, but much more difficult. I'd hold those panels of sheetrock before me and think of Jesus on the cross. My arms wanted to fall off, but I just kept on nailing sheet after sheet like an automaton and—What do you know?—I'd forget to take a pill! Day by day, my head was becoming clearer, and I was seriously buffing up. I discovered there was an almost irresistible rhythm to hanging drywall. I'd turn on my MP3 player and jive to the beat, sweat pouring off me, and feel . . .

And that's precisely what ricocheted around my empty noodle: I started to *feel*—almost normal, almost happy. Once the sheets were all nailed up, we'd tape them one to the other. And there was an art to that, too, believe it or not, to get the tape perfectly smooth with no humps or creases. Then we'd spackle, which is the part I liked best. Trowel in hand, laying on the spackle, feathering, feathering, creating a seamless seam. I'd step away and view my creation with a critical eye. Then we'd sand the dried mud, finessing, finessing.

It's lovely work. I have a new appreciation for walls, can't walk into a building without checking out the walls to see if I can detect any seams. Pretty funny, huh?

Well, if you think that's funny, here's another one for you: all the while I was working like a serf hanging drywall, I was piecing together my own psyche, taping one bad memory to another, working through the pain, and getting a clearer picture of who I was and what I was put on this earth to do. I came to the realization pretty darn quickly that it sure as heck wasn't dancing, and it wasn't hanging drywall either. I was doing some serious soul-searching. That's what physical exercise can do for the mind. But I was still lost and didn't trust myself to stand on my own two feet. So I deceived myself into thinking that I was in love with Patrick. In return, he opened up to me, recounting his sad little history, personal demons and all.

Patrick and his little brother, Tommy, had grown up on the Jersey Shore. (Hence, moy poifect Snookie accent.) Patrick's father, Sol, was a Teamster, not well positioned in the organization but pulling a little clout nonetheless. The Teamsters weren't, and still aren't, Boy Scouts, and when Sol's local chapter needed a bit of dirty work done, his name was at the top of the list. Like Patrick, he was squat and muscular but more powerfully built. And he was always ready to mix it up, whether at the voting precincts, where he might be called upon to dissuade conservatives from casting their votes, or on the strike lines, where he willingly roughed up any scab who was foolish enough to dare cross over. Where he wielded absolute power, however, was in the miserable little walk-up flat over a pastry shop that his family called home. Suffice it to say, Sol was not in the habit of displaying affection. He was, however, quick to show his ire, cuffing the boys if they didn't hop-to when he made a demand—"Bring me a beer," "Get me the paper." But it was Anna, Patrick's mother, who took the full brunt of Sol's smoldering anger. Soft-spoken and unassuming, she'd never worked outside the home, and she was completely dependent upon Sol for her livelihood.

Weekends were the worst. Friday nights, Sol would get softened up in the saloon before coming home for dinner. By the time he climbed the back stairs to the flat, his alcohol-induced good humor had evaporated, and his black mood set in. Sol would continue drinking throughout the meal, getting meaner and uglier by the minute. Anna and the boys would shrink from him, trying to avoid his wrath, but by ten or eleven o'clock, the beatings would commence.

When Patrick was nine, his mother committed suicide, a great defense mechanism if ever there was one! One weekday, after Sol had left for work and the boys were off at school, Anna did the breakfast dishes and cleaned the kitchen, taking extra pains to assure that all was neat and orderly. Then she veered from her usual routine, treating herself to a long hot bath in the big claw-footed tub. Afterward, she carefully made up her face before donning her Sunday best. Dressed to the nines and with nowhere to go, she ferreted out Sol's bottle of whiskey and poured herself a water glass, neat. Anna was hosting her own going-away party, doing it up in style. She sat at the kitchen table, smoked five Lucky Strikes, and nearly finished the liquor before crossing to the oven and turning up the gas. The result of her exit was that Patrick and Tommy were left in the care of that Neanderthal, Sol. No wonder the boy was damaged. Who can blame him for wanting a mama to nurture him?

Unfortunately, I wasn't up to the task. But that didn't stop Patrick and me from adding to our family. We both desired a sweet ball of fur to cuddle. So, on one of my days off, we headed out to the local pound to adopt an orphan. From the moment I set eyes on Bentley, I knew he was destined to be my darling boy. Equal parts Chihuahua and dachshund, the diminutive mutt was a Chi-wiener! He looked like baby Snoopy, all white with black spots and limpid brown eyes that could persuade Dracula to turn vegan. I wanted to take him home immediately but was told I'd have to wait four days for him to be neutered and heal, poor thing.

When we finally brought him back to the condo, the little guy took to it like a dung beetle to poo. I'd worried that he wouldn't be able to navigate the stairs, but his pluck and stubby little legs carried him up them effortlessly. He was exactly what I'd been craving, a sweet little bundle of joy who never tired of slathering my face with doggie kisses. Patrick was smitten, too. We both fell head over heels for that dog.

Bentley was good for me in a number of ways. One, I really cut back on the pills. Bentley's high energy and sunny disposition were infectious, and he was always up for a walk in the park or a romp on the beach, which got me out in the fresh air. Two, he was completely dependent on me. Suddenly, I had a responsibility to someone other than myself; it was a commitment I didn't take lightly.

For a while, life was good with Patrick, especially after Bentley became part of the equation. In June, before the heat got really wicked, Mom called to announce that we were taking a vacation in Key West. She'd planned it and paid for the whole thing. All we had to do was come along for the ride. Mom had booked rooms at the Pier House, a plush, dog-friendly hotel with beautifully appointed suites and its own spit of beach for the kids to frolic on.

We did all the usual touristy things, charging around the quaint streets of Key West on moped rentals, whooping it up and having the time of our lives. A side note about my family: they're very embracing. True to form, everyone accepted Patrick hands down—from Mom, to my normally wary brother, to Mary and the kids. And he, in turn, wallowed in all the affection flowing his way. He was so needy. The writing *was* on the wall, as hard to ignore as graffiti. I just couldn't see it.

Four days flew by in an instant, and we were headed back to our respective haunts, tanned and rested, perhaps a few pounds heavier. But Patrick had acquired something else on his holiday: he had a new family.

My life fell into a pleasant routine. I continued helping Patrick until midafternoon, sweating buckets while I accomplished the work of three men and a boy. After which, I turned up at the club, all clean and shiny, prepared for another kind of workout altogether. In my spare time, the all-American girl exercised with Bentley, taking long walks and running the beach. I was lean and mean and curvy in all the right places, arguably in the best shape of my life. And hardly using to boot—just a couple of pills before work. I simply couldn't face the sordidness of the Pony without them. But I was more lucid than I'd been in a long time, and things that I'd formerly let slide suddenly bothered me. I picked up on more shenanigans going on at the club than I wanted to know of.

Better to be clueless than dead, I'd always figured.

CHAPTER NINE

Slam Dancin'

JUST AT THE TIME **I** WAS GETTING MY ACT TOGETHER, **P**ATRICK WAS IN THE PROCESS OF LOSING HIS. The two of us had worked with such efficiency that the project was nearing completion. We didn't realize it then (no one did), but we were all tottering on the precipice of an economic brink; Florida's building boom was going bust. Without enough work to go around, laborers who'd been worth their weight in gold were suddenly a dime a dozen.

Patrick hadn't needed me to help out for a couple of months, and I was okay with that. It was nice to grow fingernails again, not to pluck slivers out of my knees or have to wash drywall spackle from my hair. Then one day, Patrick didn't pop out of bed to go to work.

"Nothing to do," he muttered when I shook him awake. "The painters are coming in today, and then the carpet installers."

He tossed to his side and pulled up the covers as if to shield himself from the world at large. "My job is done."

"Great," I said. "You've worked really hard, baby. Take some time off."

"Yeah," he mumbled. "Don't worry. I'll find another job."

"Sure you will," I reassured him. I wasn't concerned. I made enough at the Velvet Pony for the both of us and then some. As it turned out, that wasn't the problem. When I arrived home that evening, Patrick was plastered, and I don't mean with a trowel. He was passed out and snoring on the sofa. I figured it was a transient indiscretion. I shooed Patrick off to bed, fed Bentley, and then took him for a long walk before turning in myself.

The next night when I returned from work, it was déjà vu. Patrick was fast asleep in front of the TV, empty beer bottles scattered on the coffee table. Worse yet, not only had Bentley not been fed, he'd also had an accident on the floor. Patrick had failed to walk him. Things were falling apart quickly here, and I didn't know what to do about it.

With nothing to occupy him, Patrick had taken to sleeping late. I had my own crazy life at the club, which didn't allow much time for intimacy between us, and we saw less and less of each other. I guess I was an enabler, because it took a while before it finally occurred to me that Patrick had either become a changed man or, worse yet, had reverted to type. As far as I was concerned, neither scenario was acceptable.

I kept trying to light a fire under Patrick, but to no avail. It was shades of Derrick all over again, and I was becoming increasingly disenchanted. What the heck did I need with a lush to support? I asked myself. Suddenly, I was totally fed up with the whole situation. Patrick seemed disinclined to do a darned thing other than drink and fritter his life away. To add insult to injury, he announced that we either had to move out of the apartment or start paying rent. No more free ride for us; the condo was about to receive its certificate of occupancy, and the owner was preparing to lease units. We weren't talking chump change either. Though, heaven knows, I could have afforded the rent. What happened as a result of this situation was I did some serious stocktaking. Did I want to carry Patrick the rest of my life like Mom had carried Dad? Like Nana had supported Papa? The obvious answer was no! So I stiffened my resolve, packed my suitcase, and moved in with Storm.

Apparently, it takes only a few pills a day to alter one's perception because I never anticipated any repercussions. Patrick was so in the bag most of the time I figured he wouldn't much care that Bentley and I had abandoned him. But I underestimated him. Almost immediately, Patrick began calling me non-stop. I simply put my cell on vibrate, got in the habit of checking the display to see who was calling before answering, and managed to avoid him for a few days. But one night, after I'd taken a pill to relax, I foolishly accepted his call. I'd been curled up on the sofa at Storm's apartment, trying to concentrate on some reality show, and a wave of pity washed over me.

"Meghan." His voice accosted me. "What's going on?"

"It's over Patrick," I said. "I'm sorry."

"Over?" he cried. "Since when? I thought we were happy."

"Come on, Patrick," I tried to reason with him. "How could I be happy with things the way they were? You, drunk all the time, not working."

"You're one to talk," he hurled back at me. "Pill head!"

The moniker was apt, but his comment really burned me. "I work, Patrick, and I make good money. Can't say the same for you."

"Meghan, I love you!" Patrick lost it, began blubbering. "You can't leave me, baby."

"I can and I have," I said dispassionately. "We had some good times, Patrick. But it's time to move on."

"No, no!"

I powered down the cell phone, prayed I'd heard the last from him, and put him out of my mind.

I thought I was on to the next chapter until a few days later when Patrick showed up at the club. He was all boozy and full of his cocky self while I was zoned out and making love to a steel pole. When I heard him holler "Meghan, get off of there and get your ass over here," I was knocked out of the zone pretty quickly. Someone cut the canned music, and Lonnie and Tony materialized like vampires out of thin air. Lonnie clamped a hand over Patrick's mouth, and the two bouncers unceremoniously escorted the loud-mouthed pipsqueak outside. I finished my set, not thinking much of it, popped a few oxys in the dressing room, and the drama retreated to a manageable distance.

We were changing into street clothes when Storm announced she was going to Club Rain to meet her boyfriend.

"Why don't you come along?" she asked. "Kick back, have some fun?"

"Nah," I demurred. "I'd just be a third wheel. Besides, I'm beat."

"Have it your way, party-pooper," she said, tossing me the key to her Sheffield Arms apartment. "Just go on home then."

"Thanks, Storm," I replied, wanting nothing more than to soak in a hot tub and have a Xanax nightcap.

I did that very thing, changed into sweats and a tee, and settled in with Bentley to watch some television. I was just beginning to nod off when Bentley leapt to his feet, growling menacingly. In the next instant, there was a horrific pounding on the door.

"Who's there?" I asked, attempting to shake off my lethargy. Bentley jumped to the floor, barking frenziedly, and lunged at the door.

"Let me in, Meghan," Patrick demanded.

"Go away," I cried. But the battering on the door only intensified. By this time, I'd gained my legs and had come to stand before the door. I peered at the lock, making sure the deadbolt was fastened. But the lock was superfluous; in the next instant, the hollow-core door exploded, and Tommy, Nick's brother, pushed through the opening. Bentley came to my defense, snarling ferociously, only to be delivered a swift kick. Yelping in pain, my sweet puppy skulked off to the far corner of the room. With more sense than I, he remained there, out of harm's way.

"Bentley!" I screamed as my blood began to boil. I backed away, instinctively searching for a weapon.

"Leave the dog alone!" Patrick bellowed, following on the heels of his kid brother. Behind him was a third Cro-Magnon type and, despite the fact that I was dopey and underwater, I pegged him for one of Patrick's subcontractors.

This was no social call. But did I rush to the bedroom, lock the door, and dial 9-1-1? Not this girl! Instead, I hurtled toward them, actually believing I had a chance against those three cretins. On the way, I palmed a heavy cut-glass ashtray from an end table, thinking it might inflict some damage. But I was no match for them. Tommy charged, head down like a linebacker, smashing into me and knocking me off my feet. That was all the advantage the other two needed. Cro-Mag Man hoisted me up, throwing me over his shoulder like a rag doll. The ashtray fell from my grasp, shattering into a zillion pieces on the tile floor.

"Lee, Tommy, come on," Patrick commanded breathlessly. "Let's get her the hell outta here before somebody makes us!"

Once outside, Patrick threw open the back door of an older Chevy, and Lee muscled me in. I skittered to the far side of the car, cringing. My mushy brain could hardly wrap itself around this bizarre chain of events. I was being kidnapped! What were they going to do to me? I wondered. The obvious answer to that question was not reassuring. Tommy slipped behind the wheel, and Patrick shoved into the passenger seat, ordering him to "Drive, drive!" Obligingly, Tommy stomped on the accelerator, and my head snapped back. I scrambled to find some way out of this desperate situation. But my prospects looked grim.

"Never let someone get you in a car and drive you to another location. If you do, your chances of survival are greatly diminished." That's the advice I'd heard on an Oprah rerun. Yet I'd done that very thing. I was ruing the Xanax I'd swallowed earlier, but I took some small comfort in the fact that the three stooges weren't in the best of shape either. I could smell the alcohol on them. They'd probably heavily fortified themselves before embarking on this ill-conceived mission. One thing was for certain: I wasn't going to overpower them. Still, I figured I might have a chance of outwitting three morons with more brawn than brains.

As the car peeled away from the curb, I was entirely forgotten. I'm sure my captors assumed I was incapacitated, still reeling from the force of Tommy's tackle. And I was. They were yelling directions and swearing at one another, all jazzed up like naughty brutes at a frat party. But as we sped off into the night, I'd recovered enough to realize this might be my window of opportunity; now was the time to make my move! I yanked upward on the door lever and launched myself out of the moving automobile, rolling when I hit the pavement. So help me, I don't know why I knew to do that, but I guess it was the right thing. My knees were scraped raw in places, but I scrambled to my feet, singing silent praises to God for not having broken any bones.

Adrenaline coursed through my body, infusing me with a false sense of power. There was nothing for it but to run, and run I did, blindly sprinting down the unpaved road. In the next instant, I heard the Chevy behind me, rubber tires squealing, as Tommy cut a sharp turn and headed in my direction. In front of me, I could see my own shadow silhouetted in the glare from the headlights. I bolted into the tree line, where I had to slow my pace while dodging limbs and branches. I picked my way through the forest, my runner's legs holding me in good stead. It wasn't long before the sound of the car faded and all I heard was my labored breathing and thudding heart.

Somehow I managed to find my way back to the highway. Keeping well off the road, I headed in the direction of Sheffield Arms, thinking I'd dodged another bullet.

I pounded up the metal stairway, but even before I reached the landing, a car screeched to a halt in front of the building. I was acquainted with a few of Storm's neighbors, and I banged on their doors and frantically stabbed doorbells, all to no avail. Who was going to look trouble in the face at three-thirty in the morning? I flew from one door to the next, desperately beating my fists against them, screaming for someone to come to my aid.

"Help! Help me, please!" I begged. But no door opened; no one took me in, though I'm sure more than one coward peeked out from behind partially closed blinds, loath to get involved.

The sound of my pursuers' footfalls thudding on the metal stairway echoed hollowly throughout the corridor. I raced around the building, thinking I could lose myself in the shadows. Seemingly out of nowhere, Lee and Tommy appeared. They pounced on me and held me fast. I screamed as I thrashed, eventually managing to slip from their grasp and hoist myself up and over the railing. It was a twenty foot drop, and I landed akimbo. In the process, I twisted my ankle, but that wasn't enough to stop me. I hobbled to my feet and cut across the yard before being tackled from behind. I toppled to the ground in a heap as a freight train hurtled through my head.

I guess I'd been knocked unconscious, for the next thing I knew, I was back in the car with Lee. It was like experiencing a recurring nightmare, only this time, the danger level had ramped up considerably. My hands and feet were bound, and a quick glance around told me the doors were locked, too. My predicament appeared direr with each passing moment.

Blood was seeping from my suddenly swollen, stuffy nose, and my ears were ringing. It didn't take a rocket scientist to figure out that I'd been given a pummeling, but I had no memory of it. I shook my head, hoping to clear it, but the clanging in my belfry was making it difficult to concentrate. My eyes fell on the bed sheet lying balled up on the floorboards, and a stunning realization struck me: I was not long for this world! These bozos weren't just planning to rough me up a bit, they were going to kill me! Why else a sheet? Patrick was going to punish me for not loving him, thereby depriving him of my family. Furthermore, he was hell-bent on ensuring that no one else would ever have a crack at me either. My head cleared rather quickly. I knew I needed to be ready to move at the next opportunity. But first I had to loosen the bindings on my hands and feet.

People always tell me I have a lousy poker face. I just can't seem to keep the elation from my mug when my hand is full of aces. Not this time. I played dead like no possum ever had while struggling to make sense of my captors conversation. Fragments came to me.

". . . really fucked that up, Patrick," Tommy's voice, haranguing his older brother, ruing the fact that he'd ever agreed to this diabolical scheme.

"The hell we going to do with the fuckin' body?" Lee asking darkly.

"Guys, guys!" Patrick's voice, high-pitched as he attempted to mollify co-conspirators, who'd finally come to the realization that they were in over their heads, particularly given the fact that I'd been screaming at the top of my lungs at the Sheffield Arms apartment building. Surely someone had taken notice.

The three of them were jabbering away at one another, paying me no mind, and I used this opportunity to work at my bindings. It wasn't long before both hands were free. I slid my hands down to tackle the knotted rope around my ankles, all the while keeping my ears tuned, praying I'd not be discovered.

"No, no," Patrick cried. "You missed the turn!"

"What the hell?" Tommy exclaimed. "I can't see a fuckin' thing!"

"Turn around. Turn around, damn it," Patrick commanded. And, I swear, the car took the curve on two wheels, skidding along on its side before regaining all four tires.

"Jeez!" Lee cried. "Get a grip, Tommy!"

As we bounced and rocked down a dirt track, I told myself it was I who had to get a grip. I needed to concentrate on the business at hand, stay sharp, and be ready for action.

We were in a wooded area, a wildlife preserve maybe. It didn't matter. I knew what I had to do. My kidnappers were unarmed and blurry-eyed drunk. The only advantage they had over me was the fact that there were three of them to one little ol' me. But I was becoming more clearheaded every minute, and I was seething with anger. These bozos had underestimated me. I hadn't taken karate lessons with my big brother and learned to tie all those knots he mastered during his scouting days for nothing!

I left the rope in a tangle around my ankles, but I could break away at any moment—at least, I hoped so. In my mind's eye, I tied the knots that I'd need to fashion to execute my little plan. My senses were heightened. Any vestiges of the Xanax in my system had been overridden by the adrenaline pricking my heart as it imbued me with courage and superhuman strength. The fact that I'd called upon Jesus, His Blessed Mother, and all the angels and saints to deliver me from this horror movie I found myself in probably didn't hurt any either.

"Slow down and pull over," Patrick commanded, and I prepared to give it my all or die trying. I moaned and, sure enough, Lee suddenly remembered me. He put his face in mine, trying to assess the damage, which is exactly what I'd hoped he'd do, and it gave me the advantage I needed to deal him the double whammy I'd planned. I crashed my forehead into his, all the while imagining mine encased in steel. I followed the head butt with a noose around his neck. He never knew what hit him. I moaned louder to cover his retching and pulled the rope taut. Lee's eyes rolled to the back of his head, and I looped the ends of the rope around the door lever.

It was black as pitch. Patrick and Tommy were blathering away at one another, none the wiser. The car skidded to a halt, and Tommy jumped out and opened my door. I was ready for him. I smashed my right foot into his groin with as much strength as I could muster, which must have been considerable as the maneuver brought that big guy to his knees. Patrick tugged at the other door handle. Given my rope ministrations, the lever refused to release. I have to hand it to him; he was fast. In the next instant, he'd rounded the vehicle and was dragging me out of the car. I struggled, flailing at him, and his grip loosened on me. My head hit the ground. And wouldn't you know? There was a little pointy rock just waiting for my noggin to make contact. I saw stars, just like they say you do. As I began to lose consciousness, all I could think was it couldn't end like this. The Little Caesar wimp was going to do me in? Come on! It was embarrassing.

As my eyes began to lose focus, they were full of the sky. But there were no stars, only a whisper of a pale white crescent, and it shed no light. Great, I thought, not even a falling star or a humongous moon to mark my passing. When I heard sirens, I snorted through my recently flattened nose, which was as near as I could come to a laugh. Someone at the Arms had called the cops!

Next thing I knew, I was on the lacrosse field—running, running, running. I cradled the ball in my wicket and charged toward the goalie. I had a clear shot, flung my stick, and the ball socked into the net. Whoohoo! I scored.

I woke up in the hospital. And the good news was: I woke up.

I'd been badly beaten, but I'd done my share of damage. Come to find out, I hadn't killed Lee, which was probably the Holy Spirit looking after me because, in the end, I don't think I could have lived with that. The creep wasn't incapacitated too much either, just had a little raspy voice to show for his encounter with yours truly, which he could lie about if he was ever called on it. After he'd done his time, that is. I guess when one is in his sixties, his voice gets a little raspy anyway, wouldn't you say?

The court appointed an advocate for me, a plump lady with a sweet disposition and really good clothes. I figured her for a divorced socialite, well educated with too much time on her hands, and I found out later that I'd nailed her. I really took a shine to Darla and she to me, and my mom absolutely adored her. In fact, the two of them still keep in touch, exchanging greeting cards on holidays. Darla helped me navigate the court system. Tough as I am, I couldn't have done it without her. When my lawyer said I could help determine Patrick's punishment, whether it be severe or lenient, I got all soft and regretful, thinking I should let him off easy given his miserable childhood and all. But no! Darla was a stickler. She said, "That boy needs to be punished for what he did. Hell! He was going to kill you!" I let that roll around in my hollow mind for a while, finally coming to the conclusion that she was right. I testified against the three of them, Patrick, Lee, and Tommy and I put them away for a very long time.

There was no satisfaction in it. The court proceedings were grueling. I had to relive the horror over and over again at each retelling. And the fact that I put a former lover behind bars didn't sit well with me. To this day, I fear him coming for me.

I'd like to tell you I walked out of that courtroom healed, drug-free, and ready to jump-start my new and better existence. But that was not to be the case. I slid right back into my old unsatisfactory patterns, and the emotional baggage kept piling on. Like a cat, I'd eluded death a number of times. But I reckoned I had several more close-encountersof-the-dopey-girl kind to go before I was toast.

Darla assured me I could stay as long as I wished, and it was like a vacation for me—chilling at her pool, getting in a game of tennis at the club. But it wasn't long before I got the itch to strike out on my own. Like a migratory bird, I returned to my old haunts, Daytona and the Velvet Pony. But I had no place to hang my hat—or wigs, as the case may be—and couldn't keep sponging off Storm, although she swore she didn't mind the company. I ended up camping out at a hotel just off the turnpike, a stopgap measure at best. But I was too busy dancing at night and too tired during the day to arrange for other lodgings.

CHAPTER TEN

Tap Dancing

**AFTER MY DAY IN COURT, RETURNING TO THE PONY WAS LIKE COM-
ING HOME.** I know that sounds strange, but it was. The money flowed
freely, and the work wasn't too taxing. But I was more clearheaded than
I'd been in a long time, and I started picking up on some bad vibes.
For instance, one day I overheard Vinnie spouting off about one of the
bouncers.

"He knows too much," he said. "I don't trust him."

"Whataya mean?" Freddy countered. "He's a jerk, but he's got our
back. Tony would never cross us."

"Like hell he wouldn't. He's got a loose mouth. I want him gone."

The next day, Tony didn't show up for work.

The Velvet Pony was no different than a thousand other strip joints.
The girls were from all walks of life and of every nationality, all of them
beautiful yet damaged. Like me, they'd found themselves descending
into a netherworld of immorality, a path they'd never imagined traveling. The money was like a narcotic, highly addictive, and we all made
excuses for our debauchery. It's a stage girls in the sex trade go through.
One rationalizes, "It's so easy. I need the money," that kind of thing, to
ease the conscience and sleep at night.

My mental faculties were keener, and I noted things I'd only been
peripherally aware of: people disappeared; girls came and went. That
was the nature of the business. But occasionally someone just fell off

the planet. Cops would come around, investigate, but nothing would ever come of it. The unfortunates who went missing were of little consequence.

Ever since Storm had been a little tyke, she'd wanted only one thing: to dance. She'd pestered her folks for lessons, and she'd done it all—ballet, hip-hop, jazz, you name it. When things were slow at the club, she'd crack us up performing a striptease while tapping to "I'm a Yankee Doodle Dandy."

I'd been back for almost a week, still bunking at the hotel, when I complained to Storm. "I can't live at the Days Inn for the rest of my life. Gotta find a place to crash. Any ideas?"

"Move back in with me," Storm said, carefully feeding her toes into black, fishnet hose.

"No. I love you, but no." I shrugged into one of my slinky Fredericks of Hollywood sheathes.

"Not up to your standards, huh?" Storm drew the hose up over her shapely legs and then turned to me.

"I need my own place."

"I get it. Um . . . Let me think." Storm paused and then snapped her fingers. "Oh! You know what? You're in luck! A friend of mine has a house he wants to rent. It's in the boondocks, between here and Sanford. Would a house be too much for you?"

"Heck no! I just want a place of my own. A house would be great."

"I'll forward you his contact information. You can call him and work out the details."

I got lost trying to find the house. When I finally located it, it was love at first sight: a white stucco bungalow on a tree-lined street in a quiet middle-class neighborhood. It looked like a little wedding cake set amid a lush, green, well-tended lawn. It boasted three bedrooms and two baths, an eat-in kitchen, and a fenced-in backyard. Everything was orderly, neat, and clean. It was worlds away from the wild nightlife of the strip and the thundering roar of the bikers as they wildly rocketed about in their insatiable quest for pleasure.

This was exactly what had been missing from my life, I told myself. Maybe here, in this tranquil setting, I could finally begin getting my act together.

After the Patrick fiasco, I cut back on the pills. But it was just a matter of time before I upped my dosage. Constantly under the influence, it's no wonder I was a little spacey. But I was still functioning at about eighty percent. I could manage most things, but details had long since become unimportant. I simply couldn't focus on them before my mind veered away. It wasn't long before the well-maintained property I'd leased became an eyesore. I had more than enough money to hire a lawn service, but it never occurred to me to do so.

I really didn't notice when, over the course of several months, the grass turned to an unsightly tangle of weeds and uncollected newspapers and fliers littered my driveway. In the beginning, my neighbors offered mild suggestions about lawn care, upkeep, that sort of thing, and I would resolve to remedy the situation, but I always forgot to follow through.

In the first weeks after my move to Sanford, I purchased a few basics. A pillow-top Tempur-Pedic adjustable king-sized bed was my first acquisition, and I gladly dropped three grand for that luxury. But I quickly lost interest, and my house was sparsely furnished. One day, I got it in my head to call my mother, have her drive up to see my place. I thought it would be great fun to go shopping together, pick out some furniture, and do lunch. I informed Vinnie that I'd be taking the weekend off, and he went ballistic. But he sure as shooting wasn't going to fire me, and we both knew it.

Mom arrived on a Friday afternoon, and she had barely made it through the door before she began asking questions like when was the last time I vacuumed the carpets or scoured the bathrooms. When she pointed these things out to me, I felt bad, suddenly realizing I'd let things slide. Almost immediately, she set to work cleaning the pigsty I'd been living in. At one point, she asked me where she was to sleep, and I realized there was no bed for her, another detail I'd overlooked. We drove to a big-box store and picked up an air mattress and, at Mom's insistence, a slew of household supplies.

I awoke the next morning to find that Mom had cleaned out the refrigerator and was in the process of mopping the kitchen floor.

"Honey," she said. "You really need to get a routine, you know? Do a chore every day, and the housework won't get ahead of you."

"You're right, Mom," I replied, resolving to do just that. The place certainly did look better, and it smelled lemony and fresh.

"I was going to make some breakfast," Mom said, "but there's nothing but junk food, chips, moldy cheese—"

I cut her off. "That's okay. I'm not hungry." I lit up a cigarette, my typical breakfast.

"Meghan," Mom said, waving a hand in the air to dispel the smoke. "Come sit down." She wrung the damp mop into a bucket of sudsy water and leaned it against a kitchen counter. "I'm worried about you," she said, motioning to the living room and the only two chairs in the place. "Why are you living like this?"

I was immediately on the defensive. "What do you mean? I thought you liked the house."

"The house is fine. The fact that it's filthy and you have no food or cleaning supplies is not." Mom leaned forward in her chair, eyeing me critically. "What's going on with you?"

She had no idea that I was dancing in a strip club or that I was addicted to pain medication.

"You're such a clean freak!" I exclaimed. "This is how the other half of the world lives."

"No, it's not. You weren't raised this way."

"Mom! Don't start. I'm really busy, you know? I'm tending bar till two in the morning six nights a week, doing a little modeling on the side. Hey!" I jumped to my feet and went to stand before Mom. "I just signed a contract with PC Street. I'm going to be their girl. I'm exhausted, that's all."

"Then hire a cleaning service, sweetie. And a lawn crew, too, while you're at it."

"You're right, Mom," I said. "I'll do that. Come on." I took Mom's hand and pulled her to her feet. "Let's get dressed and go to lunch!"

After lunch, we drove around town checking out furniture stores and consignment shops. Mom bought me a pair of leather sofas, a few occasional tables, and some bed linens. "A little housewarming present for my girl," she said. And it wasn't long before I caught the retail-therapy fever and was swiping my credit card for a dinette set, framed prints, lamps, and some jazzy pillows. Later that afternoon, our purchases were delivered, and Mom and I had fun arranging furniture, hanging pictures, and making the place look like a bona fide home.

Afterward, I treated us to a nice supper at one of the few fine-dining establishments in Sanford. I was feeling happier and more normal than I had in a long time. Mom downed two glasses of wine with dinner, which did much to improve her mood. She asked why I didn't join her. But I begged off, saying I was sick of the stuff, slinging drinks six nights a week as I did. In fact, I was chilling to my elixir of choice, an oxy cocktail.

Mom left in the morning, and I was both glad and sad. Her presence had served as a reminder of how far from the righteous path I'd strayed, which left me feeling . . . And there it was again: I was *feeling*, the very thing I'd been so studiously avoiding. I downed some pills and toddled on to the Pony, my earlier misgivings forgotten.

It was Monday, my day off, and I'd slept in past noon. After haphazardly making an attempt to tidy the squalor that my kitchen had again become, I decided to drive down to the river and take a walk in the park with Bentley—commune with nature for a change. It was one of those gorgeous Flori-days. The sky was sapphire perfection with only a few wispy clouds, a gentle breeze blowing in from the west bringing with it the scent of orange blossoms. I suddenly felt giddy with happiness and on top of the world. I had plenty of money—more money than I knew what to do with—a precious doggie who adored me whether I remembered to feed him or not, and a cool little house to come home to after a wild night at the Pony. The only thing missing in my life was a man.

But hey, I told myself, given what I did for a living, did I really want a guy to lord it over me twenty-four seven? Well yeah, was the answer that came to me. I think I did. Chalk it up to hormones, but an undeniable yearning suffused me nonetheless.

Bentley and I frolicked in the park. That dog chased every squirrel that crossed his path only to promptly lose them once they'd scurried up a tree. He'd sniff around the tree trunk, mystified, wondering how that darned critter had disappeared. Bentley hadn't mastered the concept of *up*, and I can't say he ever did. As low to the ground as that dog was, it's no wonder.

I didn't love him for his brains.

Eventually, I headed in the direction of the river, thinking we'd stroll along the water's edge where Bentley could ferret out crabs and lizards. Even though it was Monday, there was plenty of action on the water. Fishermen thronged the pier, angling for dinner, and jet skis sliced through the water with an annoying buzz. In the distance, larger vessels divided the steel-blue expanse, sailboats with their sheets unfurled, speedboats trailing wake-boarders or water-skiers. I paused and took it all in, thinking it had been too long since I'd been on water skis. A male voice interrupted my reverie.

"Well hello, beautiful."

I whirled around to find a deeply tanned, brawny fellow ogling me from the base of the pier. What else is new? I thought.

"Hello yourself," I said, taking in the watercraft rental stand and not thinking much of it.

"Want to take a spin on the water?" He nodded toward the dock where several jet skis were moored.

I realized this was his little enterprise. The guy was either leasing space or, better yet, owned it—a parcel on the riverfront, no less! Apparently, he'd been doing a brisk trade renting out jet skis, paddle boards, kayaks, and stripped-down motorboats to tourists on holiday. I gave him another once-over. I was a little interested, but "I'll pass" is what I said, thinking it high time I got back home to shower. Storm and I had big plans. We were going to go out for an early dinner, gorge ourselves on lobster at a new seafood joint she'd gotten wind of, and then watch a romantic comedy featuring dreamy Jude Law. That's the kind of excitement exotic dancers look forward to.

In the meantime, Bentley was all over this fellow, licking his Docksiders, piddling at his feet. It was as though he were bonding.

"I love animals," the guy admitted, giving me that puppy-dog look large men can get away with. He winked at me and said, "Too bad you're in a hurry. I think I've got your number."

"You'd better stand in line, sweetheart," I said. "Come on, Bentley."

I turned and sashayed away, fully aware of the fact that his eyes were on my backside. As I drove off in my Benz, the entire incident was forgotten.

But it would come back to haunt me.

CHAPTER ELEVEN

The Freddy

IT WAS LATE, AND WE WERE CLOSING UP THE PONY WHEN VINNIE SAID,
"HEY, DOLL, YOU WANNA GO GRAB A BITE SOMEWHERE?"

It was the last thing I wanted to do. But I said, "Sure!" Have to
keep the boss man happy, right? Still, my defenses were up. I'd done
this kind of thing before, and with disastrous consequences, so I was
wary. As we stepped out into the parking lot, Freddy appeared, and my
heart dropped to my heels. Nothing good was going to come from this,
I thought. But I put my misgivings on the back burner, thinking I'd just
go with the flow. What else could I do?

We tooled out onto the strip, and I realized in an instant that Vinnie
was on a planet called Oblivion. The radio was cranked up full blast,
and he was beating time on the steering wheel like some crazed drum-
mer. Coked up and wired, he was the total opposite of me; whereas I
liked to slow things down, Vinnie preferred "speeding." As for Freddy . . . I never could figure what made that weirdo tick. I think maybe
he was just evil, pure and simple.

"So where you wanna go?" Vinnie asked.

"I don't know," I said, wishing I had the perfect answer that would
assure this night ended on a happy note.

"Hey, isn't that Lamont?" Freddy said, pointing toward a high-
rise hotel.

I cut my eyes to the place where Freddy was pointing and took in the handsome black dude ducking into the alley.

"Yeah, that's him!" Vinnie cried, yanking the steering wheel to the left. "That bastard owes us!"

"Damn straight! He's been holding out," Freddy agreed.

I was beginning to realize how this all worked. Vinnie and Freddy were out for blood. This was their idea of fun. Vinnie wheeled off the highway and turned into the alley, tires squealing. He put the car in park, the headlights illuminating the dark corridor where Lamont had hoped to lose himself. Vinnie and Freddy jumped out of the car and jack-stepped toward the poor guy. Trapped, he turned to face the pair of hoodlums. He raised his palms as if to show them he was unarmed, then quickly dropped them and affected a nonchalant pose. He was one cool drink of water.

They exchanged words, but I was still in the car and couldn't hear what was being said. Lamont shook his head as if to say no. Next thing I knew, Vinnie and Freddy were on him, pummeling him in the gut and about the head. It was hardly a fair fight, two against one. Lamont didn't have a chance. When he finally went down, Freddy began kicking him viciously, over and over again. Lamont covered his head with his arms and curled into a ball, taking the beating. Eventually the brothers seemed to tire of their sport and sauntered back to the car.

Vinnie backed out of the alleyway, and neither he nor Freddy said a word about what had just gone down. It was nothing to them. Somehow, I got through the rest of the evening—morning, actually. We went to a club, and I knocked back a few Cosmos, which helped to keep me from dwelling on what I'd just witnessed. It was nearly three by the time Vinnie dropped me back at my little house. All I wanted was to sleep for a very long time and wake up to a new reality. I needed to get out of there, away from the likes of Vinnie and Freddy and Ricco, far away from the Velvet Pony. If I didn't, I just might end up like Tony, vanished and forgotten, or like poor Lamont, beaten senseless and abandoned.

In the morning, I packed up what few possessions I had, grabbed Bentley, and hitched a ride to the Velvet Pony. I didn't relish leaving the furniture Mom and I had purchased. But except for my Tempur-Pedic, there wasn't much of anything worthwhile. The leather sofas were in shreds from Bentley's nails and singed with burn holes, telltale reminders of those times I'd fallen asleep with a lit ciggy in hand. Let the landlord have it or haul it off, I thought.

Although I was returning to the Pony, I had no fear of running into Vinnie or the other thugs. Given the events of the previous evening, I figured they'd sleep till midday. And, just as expected, the place was locked up tighter than a loony in a straitjacket, which was too bad because most of my makeup and all of my wigs were inside, to say nothing of my Fredericks of Hollywood stripper duds. But my gorgeous Mercedes was parked in front, just where I'd left it. I slid behind the wheel, never so happy to be driving away from another bad chapter in my life. As I drove out of town, passing the great ugly racetrack, a herd of bikers, festooned with their leather chaps and bandanas, was just stampeding in from I-95, eager for booze and girls and a good time. I cried, "Adios and good riddance," raised my hand, and waved bye-bye to Sin City South.

CHAPTER TWELVE

Square Dancing

I ENDED UP IN A SLEEPY LITTLE BURG CALLED EDGEWATER. IT WAS EX-
ACTLY WHAT I WAS LOOKING FOR, AS DIFFERENT FROM DAYTONA AS POP-
CORN TO PUDDING. There were no strip joints in Edgewater, so I was
going to have to find other means of employment. As was my custom,
I found temporary lodgings in a hotel off the expressway.

It had been several days since I'd shown up for work at the Pony,
and I needed a paycheck to pay for my pills. I was accustomed to pulling down one to two grand a night, so retail was out of the question.
In my travels to the grocery store, I discovered an inviting-looking
bistro, strategically located at a busy intersection—busy for this boon-
dock, anyway. I figured it was as good a place as any, parked the
Benz, and sauntered on in. Inside, it was like every other brewpub,
nondescript except for the fact that it hugged the shore of a marshy
little lake, which explained the sign proclaiming, "Waterfront Dining." It didn't take but a minute to ascertain that the nerdy kid with
lank hair and Coke-bottle glasses was the man in charge.

"Hi!" I said, flashing him my pearly whites. "Looks to me like you
could use a real bartender."

I gazed pointedly toward the bar where a few patrons were seated
on bar stools and raised my eyebrows.

"Huh?" he said, fixated on my chest.

"Listen. I'll make you a deal," I said. "Give me a shot at the bar, and I'll double your take on Friday."

"Uh . . . Why not tonight?" he asked.

"I need the weekend. You won't be sorry."

"Okay."

I showed up at four o'clock on Friday wearing black short shorts and a teensy red tee that left little to the imagination.

"Hello again," I said, putting my face into the kid's and extending my hand. "I'm Meghan, and you are—"

"Garth. Garth Stone," the kid said.

"Great name," I said, slipping behind the bar. I did a mental inventory as I assessed the setup. Easy breezy, I thought, taking in the well brands and the premiums, the beer on tap, and the house wines. I turned toward the kid, saying, "So, Garth, what can I get ya? Coffee, tea, or me? Ha, ha!"

The kid was too dull to get the joke. He just stood there wondering if he'd made the mistake of a lifetime as the day laborers started trickling in. There was no more time for small talk. I was all over the bar, and in the back of my brain, it registered: I've always loved this work. Given my ADHD, it was ideal—fast-paced and instantly rewarding. I was grinning from ear to ear, showing my big white teeth as I flirted, filled orders, and made an impression. And I was having the time of my life. Why had I ever strayed from this?

Early the next evening, a strapping specimen came strutting into the bar. Dirty-blonde hair ringing a pink pate, cowboy boots up to his waist . . . He was a country boy, but moneyed, I could tell. And there was something familiar about him. I couldn't help but notice he was sporting Hilfiger. True to form, I was so gullible, I figured him for a harmless teddy bear. And after the likes of Vinnie and his brothers, I guess you could say he was.

Zane took a shine to me right away. Most men did. I just never seemed to pick the right ones out of the lot.

"Well, if it ain't you!" he announced, bellying up to the bar.

"And if it ain't you," I replied, clueless. "What'll it be?"

"How's about you on a stick?" He smiled, looking around to see if anyone else got the joke, smug as can be at his poor attempt at humor.

"Not on the menu, hon," I answered.

"Well, it should be. I believe I could eat you up!"

"And I've heard it all before. Don't have all day, though if I did, I'd be happy to just stand here and shoot the breeze . . ."

I gave him a hard look, raised my eyebrows, and he finally got it.

"Um . . . What do you have on draft?"

"We got Miller, Miller Lite, Bud, Bud Lite, Michelob . . ."

"I'll have a Bud Lite, sweetheart!"

"Ooo!" I widened my eyes. "Big spender!"

I sauntered down the length of the bar, pulled the draft, and then gave it a shove, sending it his way with an attitude.

"There you go, *sweetheart*," I added, figuring he was smart enough to get my drift. Meanwhile, it had started to pick up. The locals were getting off work, stopping in for a pop to unwind before facing the wife and kids. Later, the serious drinkers would congregate, foregoing dinner for liquid fortitude. But at this point, it was mostly a younger crowd, and they were boisterous and thirsty. So I was slamming just the way I liked it, mixing drinks double time and keeping up a running commentary with the regulars, all the while flashing my million-dollar smile and shaking my booty for tips.

Soon the rush was over, the construction workers and clerks having left for hearth and home, and there was a lull before the dinner hour. I was getting my second wind, feeling pretty full of myself. Zane was still at the bar, and I figured it was time to give him a little attention. I wandered over and stood before him, bent to wash a glass, making sure he got a good look at my cleavage. When I straightened, I could see the ploy had had its desired effect. The man was fixated. Why did I do this? I wondered. I wasn't even interested in this guy, and here I was playing that game again, thinking to myself it was high time I got me a new boyfriend. And why did I always need a boyfriend? You'd think I'd know they were nothing but trouble. Sure enough, Zane would prove to be no exception. But ignorance is bliss, and hope springs eternal and a thousand other inane platitudes we spout to explain our shortcomings and foibles.

He showed up the following night and resumed his seat at the bar.

"You don't remember me, do you?" he finally asked.

"Can't say as I do," I replied, searching my memory bank for that bit of information.

"I saw you down by the river a while back. You were walking your dog."

Realization came flooding over me: he was the guy with the watercraft rental. "Riiight! You offered me a ride on a jet ski."

"Offer still stands," he said, smiling rakishly.

It went on like this for a week, the two of us gradually getting acquainted. One night I happened to let slip the fact that I was darned sick and tired of shacking up at the Motel 6. Zane seemed truly incredulous.

"You're kidding me," he said. "A girl like you living like that? Why don't you come home with me? I got a nice place on a lake. You could have your own private suite, bedroom and bath . . ."

"Yeah," I said, "and what's the rental fee? Me?"

"No!" he said as if there could be nothing further from the truth. "I mean it. You could have your own space. I wouldn't bother you."

"How do I know you're not an axe murderer?" I asked.

At that moment, Gena, one of the middle-aged waitresses who'd been working there forever, happened to be passing by, a carafe of coffee in hand.

"Hey, Gena," Zane bellowed, and she turned and headed in his direction, a question on her face.

"Yeah, Zane?" she said.

"Gena, tell Meghan I'm not an axe murderer, will you?"

"Okay. Meghan, he's not an axe murderer," she said, a weary smile tugging at her lips. "At least, not that I know of. He's got a big spread. Maybe that's where he buries the bodies." Gena chuckled at her own joke before trotting away to her tables.

Later I would recall this exchange and marvel at the irony of it.

"Niiice, Gena," Zane said. "Thanks a lot, girlfriend." Zane was so crestfallen I couldn't help but feel sorry for him.

"Okay," I said, "I believe you. But I want to see this place—my digs—before I make a decision. Fair enough?"

"Sure, sure," Zane said, relief washing over his face.

The next day was Monday, and Bentley and I headed to Zane's place. It was west of I-95, which in those parts is cattle country. I found the oversized mailbox he'd told me to look for and the metal signpost beyond proclaiming, "Hendry Ranch." I left the highway for another rutted dirt road, the likes of which I'd hoped never to see again.

The house was nice for a bachelor pad, spacious and clean. I found the plethora of taxidermic deer and bear mounts, with their unseeing eyes staring down at me, a bit creepy. But true to Zane's word, there was a pretty little lake out front. And in the back, a large screened enclosure housed a blue-tiled swimming pool ringed by teak deck chairs and chaise lounges. My initial estimation of Zane proved correct; he'd obviously come from money. Granted, it was redneck money, but there was plenty of cash in the coffers. He didn't have any taste to speak of, but he could afford to develop some if someone would just show him the ropes. Maybe, I thought to myself, I could do that little thing, teach the big lug how to do things right.

Was I wrong.

I settled in to life on the ranch, and it was a surprisingly comfortable existence. Zane was guileless, like an open book. At least that's what I thought. He had boundless energy, was always insisting I take a swim in the pool or go fishing or hang with him at the watercraft rental. It'd been too long since I'd used my body for anything other than you know what, fresh air and exercise having been sorely lacking in my daily regimen for quite some time now. (Pole dancing didn't count, nor did the gymnastics I'd performed in the VIP.)

Once again, I was cutting back on the pills, beginning to feel as though I was finally getting a handle on my life. I had no desire to return to the Velvet Pony, although I did miss shooting the breeze with Storm, our late-night girl-talk sessions and the easy camaraderie we shared.

Those first few weeks on the ranch, Zane honored our bargain; I slept alone in my own bed in my own room. Of course, that didn't last forever; eventually I moved my things into the master suite. But almost from the moment I arrived, I began to feel safe, as though this arrangement might possibly work.

The Hendrys had made a killing selling off their many acres of land to the state of Florida for nature conservancies. The cattle business had been reduced to a mere sideline, more set dressing than anything. Still, raising cattle was in their blood. Old man Hendry's place was a rambling two-story house with an enormous Olympic-sized swimming pool and numerous outbuildings. In 2004, he retained an interior designer hailing from Palm Beach to renovate the original structure, spent a cool million to update it and bring it into the twenty-first century. And it was *done*. State-of-the-art everything, but with a restrained hand and not glitzy, which is not to say any expense had been spared. Scads of Ralph Lauren print and plaid fabrics in a variety of textures were intermixed with butter-soft leather upholstery and elegant wood furnishings that had been distressed, waxed, and sealed so the men could scuff their boots on them and do no harm. It was my kind of place. But the Hendrys didn't seem to have a great appreciation for the finer things. They were into the land, the cattle, the groves.

The ranch was pastoral, a little Eden. Mornings I would wake to the sound of birds singing their hearts out. I'd look out my window at the lake, and there would be ducks floating on it, so unperturbed and serious-looking; a pair of ibis in the reeds working the perimeter, spearing the muck for their breakfast; occasionally, an otter stitching his way in tight loops across the silvery surface, causing fish to fly in a vain attempt to elude him. And I would think maybe I should tamp down my dreams, exchange my *Glamour* subscription for *Field & Stream*, live a quiet life out there with Zane and his clan. I would never want for anything.

Maybe God put me there to get some perspective, I thought. But I was still handling my little problem, just couldn't seem to get through the day without five or ten oxys. I'd pace myself, try not to take one until noon. But by five, I really felt I needed an oxy cocktail, and I usually downed three while everyone else was delighting to the cheery sound of ice tinkling in their glasses. Zane wasn't any help. He believed every lie I told him, how I had a back injury from playing soccer, and let's not forget my poor pulverized tailbone from being body-checked in lacrosse, and . . . and . . .

Heck, he'd drive me to the doc and pay for the prescription. It was so easy. It's the pretty-girl thing and having the benefit of a good education and great teeth. I never had a doc question me either. I was an athlete, a bit of a girl, but strong. Of course, I got smacked around playing with the big boys, had lots of aches and pains. "Perhaps you should take up tennis," they'd say as they were writing my scripts. "Golf maybe." Yada, yada. Maybe you should spend a night at the Velvet Pony in the VIP, I thought, or with Vinnie or Patrick out for blood sport. Now there's some pain!

I was just one big festering sore. How had I been reduced to this? I wondered. But I kept on pretending that everything was okay, that I was rebuilding my life, when deep down inside, I knew I was just kidding myself. Sure, I could have a decent future with Zane. Except for one thing: *I didn't love him!* Well, lots of women have *settled*, I told myself. It's hardly a new concept. I'd made a mess of everything else. Perhaps I could be a really good settler, a pioneer. But in my heart, I knew it was never going to work, that I was just keeping time, waiting for the coda and the crashing grand finale.

When I look back on my life with Zane, I almost wish that he'd been what he appeared to be, that I'd been clean, and that we could have given it a go. But he wasn't, and I wasn't, and it never would have worked anyway. In all honesty, I think I fell in love with his family more than with him. They were just so uncomplicated and easy to be with, no ulterior motives, no backstabbing. All that was required of me was to show up on Zane's arm once in a while and care for his son, Jamie, when he had him for the weekend. And I welcomed that task. Jamie was a precious child, and I fell for him like I hadn't fallen for his dad.

I'd long since stopped having my periods, probably due to my pill consumption. But my hormones were all over the place. Just about the time I resigned myself to the fact that I'd never have kids of my own, one darling boy dropped into my arms, and I thought God had sent him to me special delivery. I adored that child and never regretted one minute of the time I spent caring for him. Jamie was the one thing that filled that big hole in my heart. But I was in denial, clinging to the belief that we were one big happy family.

Zane's half brother, Matt, was a sweet guy and gorgeous to boot. In fact, I had a little thing for Matt, but he was honorable and wouldn't dream of making the moves on his brother's girl. It's no wonder I started to let my defenses down, to think that I could actually be a part of this wholesome picture. And that's precisely when disaster struck, and I got smacked back to reality real quick.

Zane and his cronies—a few fellow ranchers, some former pro ballplayers, all of them high rollers and flush with cash—got together once a year to hunt. It happened to be Zane's turn to host, and he'd been giddy with excitement while making arrangements for the upcoming event. In addition to hiring a cleaning company to spiff up the place and having the carpets shampooed, he'd restocked the bar, loaded the refrigerators with beer, and crammed the freezers full of prime cuts of beef. Although it was Zane's weekend to keep Jamie, he'd arranged for him to stay with his mom.

As the date for the hunt approached, Zane became more animated.

Even in my dopey state, I sensed something afoot. I'd hear Zane on the phone, laughing with one of his hunting buddies. If I sidled near, he'd hush up and rearrange his face. Something just didn't feel right about the whole setup.

One night, Zane's brother stopped by. I was in the family room watching television when I overheard the two of them discussing the upcoming hunt. Curious, I ambled into the kitchen and opened the refrigerator door, pretending to search for something to nosh. What I really was doing was eavesdropping. By this time, Zane's family was on to the fact that I had a little problem. They didn't care. They genuinely seemed to like me, but they didn't take me too seriously either. Zane had taken a fancy to me, so they accepted me and my addiction as a package deal. I realized that, and at times like this, it worked to my advantage.

"I don't want any trouble," Matt hissed. "Keep it on the up-and-up!"

"What are you talking about, trouble?" Zane shot back. "Has there ever been a hint of a snag? No! So don't give me that, Mr. Goody-Goody!"

Matt leaned forward, put his head in his hands, and said nothing. I cut my eyes to him. I thought he looked weary and irritated. But what did I know? Later on, when it all became clear to me, I would remember this moment.

I scrabbled through the fridge and palmed a yogurt cup. After snagging a spoon from the utensil drawer, I ambled into the family room and plopped myself down on the sofa next to Zane.

"Hey, Matt!" I peeled away the cup's foil top, making a show of licking the underside before depositing it on the coffee table. "What's happenin'?" I spooned a dollop of yogurt into my mouth, then turned the spoon upside down and slowly drew it from between my lips. What a hussy I was! But I felt like Mata Hari, a spy in an enemy camp, and for the first time in a long time, alive.

"Hi, Meg," Matt said, rising from his slump. "You sure look pretty tonight."

"Yeah, right," I said, knowing full well I looked a mess. But I couldn't stop putting out those vibes; the response they produced was the one thing I could count on to bolster my battered ego. Girls like me, who had danced—we were damaged goods.

Zane sized me up, glanced between Matt and me, and narrowed his eyes. I sensed it would be counterproductive to get Zane's dander up, so I took a different tack. I leaned back on the sofa and eyed Zane.

"Hey, baby," I said. "Open up."

His expression softened, and Zane did as he was told. I spooned a dollop of yogurt into his craw and finished with a baby kiss to his sun-chapped lips, and he became as docile as a lamb.

Men!

"Say," Zane said, "I got an idea! Meghan, with your connections, I bet you could invite a bunch of girls to join us on the hunt."

"Sure," I said before really thinking it through. My mind glommed onto the idea, and I was already making a mental list of possible candidates.

"What we're really looking for are Russian women," Zane said. "Slavs, girls here illegally with no papers. Know what I mean?"

"Of course," I said, my mind racing. I knew lots of girls who would fit that bill. And they all needed work. I wasn't exactly clear on what the gig entailed, but I figured it was the usual VIP stuff. And they, *we* were all up for *that*. Take a chill pill, and it all recedes to the edges of consciousness.

I recruited half a dozen working girls, all of them attractive, all in the States illegally. How was I to know Zane was up to no good?

"What exactly are you hunting?" I asked one evening over a dinner Zane had prepared. In my drug-altered state, I couldn't cook. (Even sober, I had a hard time following directions.) But Zane didn't seem to mind. I imagine he'd been cooking for himself for so long he didn't require anything more than a comely face opposite his at the table, which was a good thing. Otherwise, we'd have been living on frozen pizzas, cold cereal, and hotdogs—the sum of my culinary expertise.

"Oh, you know," Zane equivocated. "Deer, pheasant—the usual."

He laughed, but it wasn't his normal laugh. There was something strange about it, and my antenna shot up. He was hiding something.

CHAPTER THIRTEEN

The Stomp

THE NEXT MORNING, MEMBERS OF THE HUNT CLUB BEGAN ARRIVING FROM AS FAR AWAY AS TEXAS. Zane had asked a few of them to join us for drinks and dinner that evening. At his suggestion, I'd also invited Storm, Tina, Gigi and Giselle. Zane threw some rib-eye steaks and Idaho bakers on the grill, and the girls and I fixed a big tossed salad. After we'd eaten, the guys congregated around the pool with drinks in hand while we women loaded up the dishwasher. Once we'd cleaned up the kitchen, one of the men suggested we drive into Daytona for some action. Zane looked to me.

"Where should we go, Meggy?" he asked.

I didn't hesitate. "Rain," I said.

Zane wasn't much of a drinker, but once he started in, he usually got wasted. Normally, I'd have been worried. But I figured someone in our group would be capable of driving if Zane were in no condition to do so. It was an opportunity to get dressed up, to see and be seen, and I jumped at the opportunity. The girls and I styled our hair and reapplied makeup before heading off to the city.

We took two cars. Zane piloted his Range Rover, and I sat up front with him. Storm was in the back with one of the pro ball players. Tina had hooked up with a garrulous realtor from Palm Beach, and he drove a Hummer, chauffeuring the blokes who'd paired with Gigi and Giselle. It was after midnight when we pulled up to Rain, the one and only high-class club in Daytona. Management immediately rolled out the red carpet to welcome me, the minor celeb. "Hello, Meghan," the bouncer exclaimed. "Long time, no see! You'll be wanting a table upstairs in the VIP?"

I flashed him my dazzling smile.

"Perfect," I said, not allowing the disappointment I felt to creep into my voice. Zane and his cronies had never experienced Rain's VIP, and they were willing to pay for the privilege. But I'd been out of circulation for so long, all I wanted was to party downstairs with the younger set, mix it up with some cute guys, and feel like my old self way back when in another lifetime. Instead, we wove through the throng of gyrating bodies pulsating with slashes of color from the strobes and made our way to the back elevator. Danny pressed the up button, and the metal doors whisked open. Silently, he motioned us inside and we complied.

"Can you send over a couple bottles of Cristal?" I asked as we were shuttled to the second floor.

"Already on their way," Danny said.

The champagne arrived, and we polished off the first two bottles in no time. The guys switched to mixed drinks, but we girls kept quaffing the pricy elixir like it was soda pop. We were all pretty lit up, I can tell you. So it wasn't surprising when the men started letting comments slip about the upcoming hunt. When the former jock said, "Gonna get me some Bambi tomorrow," Zane and the other fellows guffawed.

"I love venison," Storm said, trying to make pleasant conversation. But her comment had an unusual effect on the guys: they roared with laughter.

I turned to Storm and shrugged my shoulders.

"I think I'll go powder my nose," I said, rising from my chair.

"I'll join you." Storm pushed away from the table and followed me to the loo. Once we reached the relative safety of Rain's opulent ladies' room, Storm said, "I gotta tell you, I'm not too keen on your boyfriend or his pals."

"Zane's not usually like this," I explained. "He's all wound up over the stupid hunt, is all."

"Well, they give me the creeps," Storm said. "I think I'm gonna cut outta here, go downstairs and find me some action."

I sighed, withdrew a lipstick from my purse. "Can't say as I blame you."

"Come with me," she said.

"Nah."

"Why not? He doesn't own you."

I shook my head no. "Zane's been good to me. I don't want to tick him off."

Storm scrutinized her features in the mirror, made a minor adjustment to her hair. "Slip out for a dance, at least. Come on!"

"Okay," I agreed, feeling reckless. We stole downstairs, joined the mob of roiling dancers, and lost ourselves in the mindless, throbbing beat. I don't know how much time elapsed. One minute I was shaking my booty with abandon. The next, my upper arm was clamped in a vice-like grip and I was staring into Zane's angry mug.

"The hell you doing?" he bellowed, looking around for some chump to deck. Storm had vamoosed, and the former pro was standing in the wings, ready for action should it be called for. The other revelers backed away leaving Zane and me in the center of the dance floor. Out of nowhere, Danny appeared, and tempers diffused like fog in sunshine.

"Okay, guys," Danny soothed. "Take it outside, why doncha?"

Then we were all out in the parking lot, climbing into cars—Gigi and Giselle and the rest of the men—all of us liquored up. But hey, it was Daytona! Zane was soused and weaving all over the road, but somehow we managed to make it back to the ranch without mishap.

Morning dawned—the day of the much-anticipated hunt—and I was sent packing. Never mind that the two Gs were staying, to say nothing of the fact that the other girls I'd enlisted for this enterprise were set to arrive at noon. I wasn't clear on this. But then I hadn't been clear on a lot of things for quite some time, so I didn't question the logic behind this decision. I breezed off in my Benz, happy for the break. I planned to spend a few days with Mom in Vero Beach and return once the whole crazy hunt business was history and Zane had returned to the normally sober, affable fellow that I thought he was.

As usual, Mom was happy to see me, although a little perplexed at how dopey I appeared. "You're so thin," she commented, pouring me a big glass of orange juice. "You're not eating, are you?"

"I eat."

"Are you throwing up again?" She eyed me critically.

"Mom! I'm fine. I just need a little rest. Cut me some slack, okay?"

"Okay, sweetie," she said. "Shall we go out for an early dinner?"

"Yeah, great!" I said. "The Driftwood?"

"Are there any tables outside?" I asked, thinking I could light up and the smoke wouldn't bother anyone.

"Follow me," the hostess said, leading the way. We wended through the historic grillroom festooned with salvaged metalwork and fascinating artifacts and out the back door into a balmy Florida evening. The sun was low in the west, and there was a soft breeze coming off the ocean, whispering through the myriad palm fronds. A three-piece reggae band was making music on the deck, and I felt as though I were a million miles from Daytona, the cattle ranch, and weird boyfriends.

"Gosh, this is so great!" I said.

"I know," Mom agreed. "It's like being on a minivacation."

I settled back in my chair, took a deep drag of my cigarette, and my eyelashes fluttered.

"Meghan," Mom cried, suddenly alarmed. "What's the matter with you?"

Guiltily, I remembered the three oxycodone I'd tossed down my gullet before leaving the house. But it was impossible to harbor negative thoughts in my present condition. The pills were kicking in, and I was feeling delightfully drowsy.

"Nothing," I said, rousing myself in an attempt to allay Mom's concerns.

I relished my meal with a drug-induced languorous sensuality.

"This is delicious," I said, digging into my fish taco. My coordination was off, and bits of grouper and diced tomato fell on my lap.

"Close your mouth when you chew," Mom said.

When we rose to leave, I stumbled, and Mom rushed to my side to steady me. I staggered to the parking lot, happy as a clam. Not so Mom; she was freaking out. "What the heck is with you?" she demanded once we were in the car and away from prying eyes.

I could barely keep my own eyes open. "I just need some rest."

"I guess," Mom said, unconvinced. She pulled out onto Ocean Drive. "And I'm going to make sure you get some proper nutrition. I know you haven't been eating right."

The weekend passed uneventfully. Mom washed my clothes and fed me regularly. Somehow, I managed to con her yet again. But from time to time, I'd catch her eyeing me suspiciously.

"You haven't worked out since you got here." Mom hovered over me as I knelt on the floor packing my suitcase.

"Haven't even taken a run on the beach," she said.

"Yeah," I agreed. "Getting lazy in my old age."

"That's not like you."

Her words penetrated my fog. She was right. It wasn't like the old me, the girl who'd always been up for physical activity of any kind. Suddenly, I wanted to be that girl again. But who was I kidding? All the while, the Devil's voice shrieked inside my head, "You're hooked! You'll never be that girl again." And he was right. I welcomed the numbness, being separated from everyone and everything that could wound.

So I kissed Mom good-bye and headed north to Sebastian and State Road 512. In a few short hours, I was back at the ranch—home sweet home.

I arrived to a nightmare. Pulling into the long drive leading to

Zane's house, I immediately sensed something amiss. I was glad for having swallowed only one oxy before leaving Mom's place; I was ready to bolt if need be. Sure enough, as I rounded the bend where two enormous oak trees forced the driveway to curve to the right, Zane's spread came into view. I slammed on the brakes and briefly considered shifting into reverse and hightailing it out of there. When reason returned, I slowly coasted into my new purgatory of the moment.

One ambulance and two police cruisers, with their bubble lights on, were parked in the driveway. The beams those lights cast created an eerie strobe effect as they bounced off the trees lining the drive. My mind seesawed off to another rutted road, another horror. I willed myself back to the present. After putting the Benz in park, I climbed out and steeled myself for the worst. A cop materialized out of the gloom, blocking my path.

"You Meghan?" he asked with a snarl.

"Who's asking?" I said, giving it back to him in spades. I realized PDQ this guy had no sense of humor. Worse yet, my feminine wiles were getting me nowhere.

"What the hell's going on here?" I asked. But before the cop had time to reply, he was being elbowed out of the way by a stocky, barrel-chested fellow. Right off, I figured this character for a sot. What other explanation could there be for that roadmap of red veins crisscrossing his wide nose and ruddy cheeks?

"Captain Morrissey," he growled, as though the two of us were going to embark upon a forbidden tryst or something. He gave me the once-over, then favored me with a smile that made me feel like the plastic prize at the bottom of a Cracker Jack box. He liked me! And I immediately took a liking to him. My defenses crumbled. The guy was full of blarney, but genuine all the same. Morrissey took me under his short, squat wing, and I was glad for the protection.

"Okay, it's like this," he said, hustling me away from the lieutenant's elephantine ears. "We got ourselves a *situation*."

"A situation?" I said. "What do you mean?"

"Calm down," he answered, but it sounded like, "Com dawn." His voice was full of Brooklyn, which I can relate to. I can't help myself; I love dos guays, and if dey happen to be Italian, all da betta. But Morrissey was Irish, and I have a soft spot in my heart for that tribe as well, so I was listening.

"Do you mean to tell me you don't know what went down here, sweetheart?" he asked.

And there it was: the "sweetheart." I breathed a sigh of relief, knowing I was home free.

"Morrissey," I said, looking him square in the eye. "I have no idea what it is you're talking about. All I know is that I've been three hours on the road, and I want nothing more than a hot bath and bed. Can you please tell me what gives?"

In the next instant, a pair of paramedics came trotting down the drive, a gurney between them. I cut my eyes to the portable cot only to see a slender white arm dangling off the side. The EMTs passed me by, and I caught a glimpse of a red heart tattoo on the inside wrist of that pale limb. Then my own heart contracted, for I knew without question it was Giselle on that stretcher, and that she had been injured. My ears were full of a pounding tide emanating from my chest, and my knees buckled. Morrissey steadied me, and I leaned against him, grateful for his bulk and solidness. In the back of my squishy brain, I realized I'd always had suspicions about the hunt. But now I was confronted with the reality of it. Bad, bad stuff had gone down here, and my sweet Zane had been the depraved mastermind behind it.

Morrissey clapped a meaty palm on the small of my back, directing me toward the house. I allowed myself to be manipulated, for I had shut down; my circuits had come unwired. In the next moment, I realized why Morrissey had drawn me to the sidelines. Shuffling down the pathway between two uniformed cops was none other than my own true love. His chin was on his chest, his wrists cuffed around his back, and he looked totally dejected.

"Zane," I cried. And the big oaf raised his shaggy head and met my eyes as he passed in front of me. Still, my brain refused to work; I couldn't wrap my mind around it. "Morrissey," I hissed, turning toward him. "What happened?"

Part of me simply didn't want to know, didn't want to hear the damning words. Morrissey shook his head and gazed into my eyes with such compassion something inside me cracked open. I was sobbing, snuffling like a two-year-old, dashing tears away with my knuckles. But the waterworks continued to course down my face. For the life of me, I couldn't seem to stop them, a phenomenon that seemed to endear me all the more to my newest champion. But at that point, I was so overcome I didn't care what the man thought of me.

When my tears finally subsided and I reined in my seesawing emotions, Morrissey reverted to type. "I'm going to need to take you down to headquarters," he announced gruffly. I was still incapable of speech, so I merely nodded my head. Although the thought of staying up all night with no oxys to keep me company was a dismal one, I was resigned. Some small part of me knew that I had been fooling myself, thinking this idyll with Zane would end well. It hadn't. And now it was time to pay the piper. Ever the cock-eyed, dopey optimist, I tried to put a positive spin on this latest calamity. I told myself maybe, just maybe this episode would mark an end to the train wreck my life had become, an end to bad boyfriends, poor choices, dancing, and drugs.

But of course, there was no end in sight for the addicted girl, only minor interruptions.

In case you haven't figured it out, I'll let you in on what had been going down at the Hendry Ranch. Entrepreneur that he was, my man, Zane, had been offering the wealthy, jaded hunter an opportunity to stalk super-exotic game. The quarry: Bambi. If you're still in the dark, I'll spell it out for you: G-I-R-L-S. For a fee, a guy could hunt them down and do with them what he would, have sex with them as rough as he liked. The girls were disposable.

Apparently, this kind of thing had been going on for quite some time. There was a lucrative market for it, and the hunts probably would have continued indefinitely had it not been for the fact that Zane's half brother, Matt, was possessed of a conscience. For the last six months, he'd been feeding information to the Volusia County Sheriff's Office, and the investigators had been in the wings, just waiting for it all to go down. But the cavalry hadn't arrived in time to prevent Giselle's battered face and broken arm, injuries that temporarily closed the curtain on the G sisters' twosome act. I still feel responsible for that. I'm not saying I cared much for Giselle, but no one deserves to be treated as she had been.

I didn't stick around to find out how the dust settled. A pair of deputies accompanied me when I went back to clean out my stuff. There wasn't much to collect: some clothes, a few pieces of jewelry. Coating my regret with oxy sugar, I kept self-recrimination at bay. I did feel a twinge about leaving Jamie. I would truly miss that angel boy; he'd gotten under my thick skin, and I figured he was the closest thing to my very own baby I'd ever have.

I comforted myself with the fact that I still had Bentley and drove away from the Hendry ranch right back to the Velvet Pony and Sin City South. I was broke and I needed money. What else could I do?

CHAPTER FOURTEEN

The Shag

THE NEXT DAY, I SAUNTERED INTO THE PONY LOOKING TO RESUME MY POSITION AS QUEEN BEE, JUST PICK UP WHERE I'D LEFT OFF. I'd led a charmed existence up to this point, didn't feel my luck had changed. And I was right. My luck hadn't changed. I had.

Over time, drugs work on a person, altering her consciousness and perception. When one is in the drug, she starts living an alternate reality. Her brain isn't functioning properly, but the ego is still in its corner, telling her everything she does makes sense and is okay when it doesn't and it's not. At the same time, that old trickster Devil is prodding her, chattering in her head, making her even more anxious and paranoid.

I believe the Devil is always seeking a means to insinuate himself into a person's psyche. Drugs and alcohol help ensure his success. They erode one's morals, allowing the door between good and evil to be pried open a crack. That's all Satan needs to gain a toehold. And every time one falls back into the addiction, that door opens wider and more demons enter in until they're partying inside one's head, making her do crazy things she'd never in a million years consider while sober.

I arrived to find big changes at the Pony, too. The G twins were history; Giselle was recuperating while Gigi attempted to reinvent herself as a solo act somewhere out in the heartland. And after Zane's arrest, Storm vamoosed too. I imagine she didn't want to get involved, and I can't say as I blame her. Another surprise was to find that three Ukrainian chicks had replaced Gigi, Gisele, and Storm. But I should have seen it coming: a wave of immigrants flooding into Florida's sex trade.

Vinnie, Freddy, and Ricco were gone, too. I'm not exactly sure what prompted their exodus. I imagine the syndicate, that is to say, *the mob*, wasn't happy with the slipshod way things had been run or the ensuing media frenzy unleashed by Zane's debauched entertainment that subsequently cast a light on the Pony. Although I've heard it said that "all news is good news," in this case it wasn't. Prurient sex clubs like the Velvet Pony endure only so long as they stay under the radar. A little payola and the law turns a blind eye. Notoriety, on the other hand, is a no-no.

The biggest surprise of all was to find that the Romano brothers' successor was a hard-headed Russian. I'd thought it would be a piece of cake to take up where I'd left off and resume my former position. I'd simply bat my eyelashes, show a little bosom, and the boss man would be eating out of my hand. Sergei Kozlov was not so easily swayed.

"Vat you vant," he asked, "come bok here after da mass you mad?"

"Me? I didn't do diddly squat," I said. "How the heck was I supposed to know? I wasn't even there when it went down."

"You trauble. Don't vant no trauble."

"I'm the best thing that ever happened to this place. You'll see. Just let me dance, why doncha?" I was practically pleading with the guy. "Whattaya got to lose?"

Sergei thought about it for a full minute, then got back to me. "Da. Okay. Got dressed. Ve see."

I was back in!

My next hurdle was to win over the new girls. I had none of my sleazy polyester gowns, no seven-inch Lucite heels, and nary a wig. But I've always been able to coax exactly what I want out of any unsuspecting fool, be they male or female. And this time proved no exception. I made friends quickly.

I was dancing as though nothing had changed. I'd pop a few Oxy-Contin before my set, and the self-doubt and guilt that plagued me would subside. I told myself I was lucky to be alive, that what I was doing wasn't so bad. Which goes to show you how one's perception is altered, how far off course one can navigate when she's doing the two-step with the Devil. I realize now that when God is forsaken, Satan steps in and dances. He was surely dancing with me!

After my set, no fewer than three guys had paid to see me in the VIP. Sergei was suddenly a believer, and I was growing calluses on my knees. But I was back and I was safe, I thought . . .

Three weeks later, I was still camped out in the dressing room, not even attempting to disguise the fact that I was abusing opiates. I'd stopped working out altogether, and my once rock-hard body was getting soft. Sleeping on an old sofa, subsisting on coffee and cigarettes, my life was spinning out of control.

One night, just as I was finishing up my set, who should sail into the Pony and order a Michelob with lemon? None other than Lyle! When I joined him at the bar, I learned he was newly divorced and raw. Seeing that I'd returned, he chalked it up to fate, said I was his angel come to rescue him. Funny thing is, I was thinking the same thing of him: at last, someone to take care of me! I'd become accustomed to Zane keeping me somewhat normal. Left to my own devices, I'd forget to eat and would spend my free time watching Jerry Springer and his cast of malcontents, fooling myself into thinking my life, compared to the lives of those nut cakes, wasn't half so bad.

Lyle and I took up where we'd left off, but this time it was guilt-free because there were no wife and kid to skulk from. I ended up right back where I'd first started in Daytona: shacked up in Lyle's love-nest duplex! If it weren't for the fact that Lyle needed to keep up appearances for the sake of his boy, I'd have moved into his house in town. As it turns out, I preferred this arrangement; I had my own place but none of the responsibilities of maintenance and upkeep.

Compared to the lowlife I'd been associating with, Lyle was a prince. He had one vice: me. And now that he was no longer married, that didn't stack up to a hill of beans. Lyle could see right away that I was in bad shape, and he was truly worried about my wellbeing. He'd plead with me to get off the pills and tear out articles from the newspapers about people who'd died from overdoses, trying to scare me into sobriety. But as only an addict knows, there was no way I could get clean on my own.

One morning, I was seated at the tiny dinette table in Lyle's duplex, coffee cup in hand, when my eyes fell on another news clipping he'd left for me. Before I could wad it up, an ad for a local methadone clinic screamed at me. It was early—early for me anyway—and my mind was less befuddled than it would be as the day progressed. Perhaps that's why I studied the advertisement. I knew I was a walking time bomb. My liver had to be shot, my kidneys already were, and I could feel my heart thudding through my chest. Maybe this was the answer, I thought, to substitute another substance for my drug of choice and wean myself off the opiates. It was worth a try, I decided. When I called to make an appointment, I was told to come right in. "Praise God," I rejoiced. "Maybe I'll finally get this monkey off my back!"

And that's how I changed my addiction from downers to uppers.

Opioids made my miserable life dreamy and pleasurable, all the while keeping that nasty old reality, to say nothing of a guilty conscience, at bay. But methadone was a different high altogether, a ride on the wild side where life passed in a blur and actions occurred with such speed that they were instantly relegated to the past and seemed of little consequence. Best of all, it pumped up my serotonin levels like the opiates had never done. Methadone is comprised of the same chemical stimulant found in Adderall, a common prescription for the treatment of ADHD. I was the Attention Deficit Queen! After only one "treatment," my addiction for downers was cured and I was worshipping at another pagan altar. The clinic was a godsend. I'd show up daily, get my dose of liquid methadone, and be on my merry way. The idea was to gradually decrease the dosage until I was totally drug-free. Given my high tolerance and the severity of my addiction to oxycodone, I was administered the highest dose, 150 milligrams.

When the docs started decreasing my dosage, I simply compensated by purchasing 40 milligrams of meth on the streets. It was easy to find, and money was never a problem. Before long, I was strung out on methadone and way worse off than I'd been on opiates.

Methadone has some nasty side effects. Whereas before I'd been passive and dopey, I was now juiced and combative. All it took was for someone to look at me funny and I'd be at his throat. There were physical consequences as well. My head itched something fierce, and I'd dig at it until patches of hair came out and my scalp was covered in scabs. I had diarrhea, and my hands shook. Worse yet, I couldn't sleep. Instead, I'd be up all night manifesting obsessive-compulsive behaviors like "cleaning." My cleaning bouts consisted of my ripping objects from drawers and closets and sorting through them, examining each item with the rapt fascination of a hoarder. Sometimes I'd supplant "cleaning" with "art." I became engrossed with glossy magazine ads, would cut them out to create collages that were never completed. After having passed out at four or five in the morning, I'd awaken in the afternoon amid a pile of underwear, clothing tangled on hangers, CDs, DVDs, papers, jewelry, toiletries, and magazine ads. Lyle took to installing locks on drawers and doors, but there weren't enough locks in the world to stop my madness.

One afternoon, after a particularly rough night, he said, "Let's take a little vacation. I think it would be good for you to get away from all of this."

"Sure!" I agreed, thinking I hadn't had any fun in forever. "I'll ask Sergei for some time off."

So we packed our bags. Actually, Lyle packed, as I'd get too derailed to accomplish any task that took much organization. I grabbed Bentley and some dog food, and we headed south for some R&R. Lyle was eager to visit Sebastian, a sleepy, laid-back fishing village just north of Vero Beach. I imagine he thought I'd be safe there, far from the orgy that is Daytona, maybe even get clean. He booked a room at Captain Hiram's, a resort fronting a marina on the Indian River.

Shortly after checking in, we rented a little speedboat, and the afternoon passed in a blur like they all did. Before I knew it, the sun was setting, and Lyle and I were at the Tiki Bar knocking back spiced rum punches and grooving to a band called Panic Disorder, a name that, for some reason, I found hysterical. Hooked on opiates, I'd long since lost my taste for liquor; it simply didn't do anything for me. I never imagined there could be another drug that would replace my affection for Oxy-Contin. But now I discovered something amazing: alcohol mixed with stimulants produced a superlative high. I was flying, but in slow motion, and it was incredibly pleasurable. Best of all, the liquor eventually knocked me out. Eureka!

That night, I slept like a baby. I didn't awaken until ten in the morning and probably wouldn't have woken up then if it hadn't been for Lyle barking into his iPhone.

"I'll be there as quick as I can," he said. "But it's gonna take me a couple hours. Sit tight."

"What's the matter?" I asked, my noggin pounding from a killer hangover.

"It's my mother," Kyle said. "She fell and hit her head. She's in the ICU, and they've got her on a ventilator."

"Oh no! I'm so sorry."

"Yeah." Lyle was stuffing clothing into his travel bag, willy-nilly. "So much for our getaway."

"That's okay." I didn't try to disguise the disappointment in my voice.

Lyle turned to me and said, "Well, hey! There's no reason for you to leave just yet. Stay."

"I should go with you," I said.

"No. That's silly. There's nothing you can do, and we're all paid up through the weekend. Somebody might as well enjoy it." But then he paused, considering. "That is, if you think you'll be okay by yourself?"

It was a question, not a statement, and I knew the reason for his concern. But the thought of idling away a few days here by myself was appealing. Suddenly, I could hardly wait for him to leave.

"Lyle, this place is about as safe as Mayberry," I said. "I've got Bentley to protect me, and everything I need is here at the resort. There's no reason for me to leave the property. What could go wrong?" I leapt out of bed and wrapped my arms around him. "I'll be fine."

Lyle left for Orlando, and I was left with nothing but time on my hands. I got through the morning without incident, took a turn on a jet ski, ate a lunch of dirty oysters at the Sand Bar, and attracted a few admirers. Bentley helped break the ice. Everywhere I went, whether it was the gift shop, the marina, or one of the open bars, people stopped to admire my precious doggie. I made friends quickly.

That night, a group of us gathered at the Sand Bar and we partied. Two guys attempted to latch on to me, but I managed to keep them at arm's length. I felt beholden to Lyle, and I needed another man in my life about as much as a zit on my birthday. But all of my good intentions flew out the window after slurping down a few rum punches mixed with 190 milligrams of methadone.

I don't know how it happened. When the bar closed at 1:00 a.m. the party moved to my room. What I do know is that I was on all fours in the hotel parking lot screaming at the top of my lungs when the cops came to haul me away. As it turns out, I was lucky. One of the resort's owners happened to be the father of a friend of mine. Liz had been my running partner when my dad was falling from grace. Our families had resided in the same upscale waterfront enclave, and Martin and his wife, Beverly, socialized with my parents. Despite the fact that my room was trashed, Martin didn't press charges. The police dragged me off to the hospital where it was determined I was not only inebriated but had enough methadone in me to detonate the heart of a racehorse. I was Baker Acted and admitted to the Center for Emotional Behavior and Health for a mandatory seventy-two-hour detox.

Later, Doctor Dean confessed that he hadn't quite known what to make of me, and he'd seen it all. I was so far gone that I couldn't speak. Beyond the fact that I was overdosing, he determined that my drug abuse had somehow opened a Pandora's box of deeply hidden psychoses: bipolar disorder, perhaps schizophrenia. He didn't rule anything out. But before he could get to the root of the problem, he had to stabilize me.

It wasn't until three days later, when the demons fled, that I could walk and talk again. Even then, my brain was not functioning properly. Doctor Dean tried to reason with me, to impress upon me the severity of my overdose, how close to death I'd been. All I wanted to do was leave, get the heck out of there and get me a smoke! Legally, I had every right to go. But Doc was persuasive and convinced me to stay.

CEBH was a decent place, clean and as homey as such an institution can be. And Dean was cool. Handsome as all get out, he was a dead ringer for Christopher Reeves, and I needed a Superman to fix me! Doc started me on a whole slew of meds: one to counteract the nausea, one for anxiety, one for depression, a mild stimulant to wake me up in the morning, and a narcotic to help me sleep at night. This was the ideal regimen for me; I loved popping pills, and I figured this treatment might actually get the job done. I participated in group, shocking them all with my dissolute tale. After a month of therapy, Lyle picked me up and chauffeured me back to Daytona.

I stayed clean for eighteen hours.

This marked the beginning of a particularly dark period for me, one in which I kept recalibrating my reality. I'd make excuses for my inability to drive without getting into an accident, the fact that my clothes and bed linens were pockmarked with burn holes from cigarettes I'd failed to ash, why I couldn't seem to eat or drink without getting food all over me or spilling something on the floor. Lyle was always nagging me about leaving the house unlocked, the front door open, or the stove burners on. But I held it together enough to perform at the Velvet Pony, and as long as I could do that, I told myself I was okay.

One day, I awoke at about two o'clock in the afternoon only to realize I was out of cigarettes. Lyle was at work, and I decided I had no other alternative but to drive myself to the nearest convenience store to buy a pack. After quickly making up my face and downing three methadone wafers, I pulled out and headed toward the center of town. If you've never been to Daytona, just picture a zoo where all the animals have been let loose, and you'll have a reasonable idea of what it's like. As always, the main drag was clogged with traffic, and I immediately got confused. I was suddenly in the throes of a panic attack when I found myself behind an ambulance at a stoplight. What am I doing? I wondered. I put the car in park and got out. It seemed like the reasonable thing to do at the time. Next thing I knew, an EMT was standing before me.

"Are you okay?" he asked.

I shook my head no. Almost immediately, there was a cacophony of horns honking. People tend to get pretty upset when they're stopped in traffic. The police arrived, dealt with my car, and directed traffic while I was deposited in the ambulance and driven to the Behavioral Services Department at Halifax Health.

Halifax was not CEBH. No one there knew of me or my family, and I was not given preferential treatment. Instead, I was treated like the skanky addict I'd become. I was kept on a regimen of drugs that knocked me out as I detoxed. And it wasn't pretty. But I still was. And at one point, I awoke to find myself naked on my cot and live on camera. Seems I'd given the night staff something to talk about.

When I'd detoxed and was finally coming out the other side of crazy, I was allowed to call home.

"Mom," I pleaded. "Get me out of here. They're keeping me drugged, needles all the time."

Mom contacted her old friend Sam Block, a top-of-the-heap lawyer with a high-end Vero Beach practice. Mother explained my predicament, that Halifax refused to release me, and asked what she should do. Sam wanted to know if I'd been charged with a crime, and Mom told him that I hadn't. He advised her to insist on my release, telling her they had no right to hold me against my will, but not before cautioning her to think about the consequences. He asked her if she was capable of caring for me. Mom didn't know the answer to that question. She only knew she had to get me out of there.

Mom broke me out of that Bellevuesque hell and drove me back to Vero. I stayed with her until I regained my land legs. But as soon as I was able, I returned to Lyle and the Velvet Pony.

It didn't last long. Eventually, Lyle grew tired of picking up the duplex after my madcap all-nighters, of worrying whether I'd burn the place down when I crashed with a cigarette in hand. I doubt I was much fun in the sack anymore, and although he truly wanted to save me from the fiends in possession of my soul, he realized he was making no progress in that regard. I didn't allow myself to delve into the reason behind Lyle's decision, to admit that I'd become a monster. I told myself I wasn't in love with him, that there was an endless supply of men eager to do my bidding.

Bill was one of those men.

A mild-mannered, nondescript sort of fellow, Bill was a retired engineer with lots of time on his hands. He hung out at the Pony, but he never requested time in the VIP. He seemed content to look and not touch, which was about as perfect as it gets in my book. To this day, I'm not sure what floated Bill's boat. Maybe he was what he seemed, a wimpy mama's boy who'd never had a serious relationship. But I'd been around the block often enough to know that was probably not the case. Perhaps he whacked off in my sneakers. Who knows? I needed a place to crash and Bill's high-rise condo fit the bill. His place was nice, though dated, and it afforded a grand view of the Atlantic. I never enjoyed that view, for it always brought me back to Patrick. I'd see him in my mind's eye, peering out from behind bars in the state prison. On the positive side, I had my own bedroom, and I locked my door at night. Bill seemed content with that. I stayed with him for a few months, and in all that time we never had an argument. If I went on one of my "cleaning" or "art" binges, he'd just pick the place up and put things back to rights. That all ended the night a few of us dancers got it in our heads to party at my favorite haunt, Rain.

I'd been talking up the nightclub ever since I'd returned to the Pony, telling the girls how great it was. On this particular evening, a few of the dancers decided to give it a shot. Once there, I ordered my usual, a bottle of Cristal. Unlike old times, however, I found I really dug the champagne on top of my methadone buzz. I guess I got a little sloppy, tipped over a glass, and the expensive bubbly sloshed all over the table. The waiters came rushing to sop up the mess. I wasn't too concerned; I figured they'd dealt with worse. Then the girls and I hit the dance floor, putting on a bit of a show free of charge, so to speak, and the crowd loved it. It must have been about three o'clock in the morning when I called Bill, telling him to come fetch me, as I was in no condition to drive. I was miffed to find that Bill was a bit testy. Apparently, he didn't appreciate being called upon to taxi at such an hour, especially when he hadn't been invited to the shindig. Naturally, I gave it right back to him.

"Oh, come on," I said. "What else have you got to do?"

"Sleep," he mumbled before hanging up the phone. Twenty minutes later, he was there with bells on.

Once in the car, I started in on him. I was so wired I felt like I was coming out of my skin, and I was suddenly, violently angry.

"You're such a pansy," I sneered. "No wonder you never had a girl-friend."

Even stoned, I had this gift; I knew just what buttons to push, those that would inflict the most pain. All the while he was driving, I kept on in this fashion. Bill simply held his tongue while I heaped abuse upon him. When we pulled into his assigned parking slot, I headed for the entrance.

"I can't have you here any longer," Bill said, his voice low and controlled. "Collect your things and get out."

His words stopped me in my tracks. Still, it took a moment for my fuzzy brain to process. When I realized he was serious, I lunged at him, beating him about the head with my Versace bag. He just stood there taking it. When it finally dawned on me that I was not going to engage him, I stopped my attack. We took the elevator, facing off as far apart from one another as that miserable cubicle would allow. Once in Bill's condo, I haphazardly gathered up some of my things, all the while hurling insults at him. I was out of my head, but the anger raging within me kept me pumped and focused. In short order, I departed with Bentley in tow. If I hadn't been so strung out on meth and champagne, I might have had the good sense to sleep it off in the lobby and try to make up with Bill in the morning. Instead, I stumbled out onto the street and started walking.

I must have been a vision, dressed in my sequined cocktail gown, perched on five-inch heels, toting a bag in one hand, a dog on a leash in the other. Even at this hour there was traffic, and I got my share of honks and wolf whistles. It wasn't long before my fury subsided, and I was left feeling shaky and disoriented. I couldn't recall how I'd come to be out there walking Bentley. As my head cleared, it dawned on me: I'd reached a new low.

I was on the streets.

CHAPTER FIFTEEN

The Time Warp

EVENTUALLY, A TRUCK DRIVER STOPPED. HE LEVERED OPEN THE DOOR TO HIS CAB, SAID, "HEY YA, SWEETHEART! NEED A LIFT?"

I must have said yes because before I knew it, Bentley and I were jigging down the highway, safely ensconced inside that trucker's cab. He said he was en route to Jacksonville.

"That okay with you?" he asked.

I said, "fine."

That was the second time I was rescued by a truck driver. I confess to a certain fondness for the guys who pilot those big rigs. The three I've encountered had hearts of gold. Normally, I'd have been up all night, would have driven the guy nuts with my mindless chatter. But I'd consumed a bottle of Cristal on top of my meth, and I was asleep and snoring long before he'd turned onto I-95.

I awoke with a throbbing head and a crick in my neck. The sight of Bentley lying curled beside me was a bit of good news. We were zooming down the freeway, my rescuer at the wheel.

"You must a been tired," Al said when he noticed me stir. "Slept right through a thunderstorm."

"Um," I replied, not up for small talk. "Got any water?"

He pointed to a small cooler at my feet.

"In there," he said. "By the way, my name's Al. Al Hubbard. Stopped at St. Augustine to let the dog out for a minute. He had to go."

"Oh." I opened the cooler, withdrew a bottle of water.

"You got a dog bowl for him? He's probably thirsty, too."

"Uh . . ."

"Didn't think so. We'll pick one up. Where you headed?"

"Nowhere. I don't know."

"Lotta people going in that same direction. Would think a pretty girl like you might have more alternatives."

"None of your business, Al." As kind as he was, this guy was starting to get on my nerves, and the fact that a search of my handbag yielded only two methadone wafers didn't improve my disposition. I was well on my way to a meltdown.

"Don't mean to pry, so forgive me for asking. You got any clothes to wear other than that getup you're in?"

"I'll have you know this dress cost over $800," I snapped.

"I don't care if it cost eight million. It ain't appropriate for where we're going."

"Can we stop someplace for coffee?" I asked, ignoring his insult.

"Not dressed like that we can't. People will think I abducted you or maybe that you're cuckoo, which probably isn't far from the truth."

"Point taken," I said. "You'll probably have to front me some cash so I can buy jeans and a tee." I rummaged through the contents of my bag. Days like these . . . Well, this day was probably like none I'd ever experienced. What I mean to say is, when confronted with the havoc wreaked by my addiction, I often vowed to get clean and turn my life around. Here I was in a semi with Al Hubbard, who could have been a murderous psychopath but instead was about to kill me with his good intentions. I had packed with all the efficiency of a two year old; I had no money, no pills, one sneaker (naturally), a spangly top, a lacy push-up bra, a red wig, three pairs of designer sunglasses, my makeup (Thank God!), two mismatched socks, a light bulb (???), some CDs, my iPod (no charger), no phone, no wallet, no identification, no credit cards. I swallowed two methadone wafers and immediately felt better. It wouldn't last, though, and I would quickly need a fix or I'd start detoxing—vomiting, shaking, the whole nine yards. I doubted even Al would stick around for that party.

Now you would think that this was the perfect opportunity for me to kick the habit, and you'd be absolutely correct. But did I? No! I wasn't ready. By this time, I'd attended enough AA and NA meetings to subscribe to the mantra "You have to hit bottom." And I had a ways to go. Besides, God had His plan. Not that He'd ever want me in this situation. But as I was, I guess He had more to show me before I surrendered and He dragged my shaggy behind out of the gutter.

The truck stop was a revelation. Like all of us, I'd frequented plenty, had darted in for a quick pee and was back on the road in less than five minutes. But now I found myself in truck stop heaven. It was like a miniature city. Anything a person desired could be found there: restaurants offering a variety of cuisine, barber shops, baths with showers, and mini department stores. We even found a dog bowl for Bentley, as well as a pair of flip-flops, some shorts, and a tee for me. The flips and tee were much too large for my small frame, but they would do. Better still, I scored some pills in the women's restroom.

After our shopping foray, Al and I left Bentley in the rig and went for dinner.

"You pick," he said. I decided on an ersatz steak house, and that seemed to please Al. The methadone wafers I'd consumed were now but a memory, and I was starting to get strung out. The fact that I'd had a quarter of my daily dosage contributed to my unusual appetite.

"I'm starving," I announced as we seated ourselves in a booth by the window. The view of the highway left something to be desired, but I've always been a sucker for a window seat. The waitress came by, and Al ordered a beer.

"Don't suppose you have Cristal," I asked, and I wasn't joking.

"Ha, ha," the waitress said humorlessly. "We got Heineken, Miller, Budweiser—"

"I know, I know," I said, putting my palms in the air to stop her. "Any wine?"

"We got white zinfandel, sauvignon blanc, chardonnay, cab—"

"I'll have a bottle of the chard." Al raised his eyebrows but didn't comment. When the waitress turned away, I glanced at Al. "Thanks for the clothes," I said rather smarmily. I was such a bitch. The guy had done everything he could for me, and I was still living in an alternate universe, one in which I ruled. Clearly, I hadn't hit bottom. But I was heading there really fast.

"So what do you do, Al?" I asked, thinking to make polite conversation. "When you're not trucking?"

Rather than answer my question, Al posed one of his own.

"What do *you* do, Meghan?" he asked. "When you're not turning tricks?"

Al's query caught me up short. I was semi-sober, saner than I'd been in a very long time, and his question resonated in my vacuous cranium. What do I do? What did I used to do? What am I? And there was such a longing in my heart. I wanted to find that girl who used to want . . . something. But I wasn't ready. Almost, but not quite. So I gave him an inane answer. I didn't realize it then, but this was to be my first baby step on the road to my recovery. God was starting to wake me up. And in a small part of my muzzy mind, I knew this was true. Because I was beginning to want Him to.

We had a decent meal in that truck stop. I polished off a bottle of wine, which subdued my methadone craving. Al downed three beers and remained the perfect gentleman. Afterward, we retired to the semi, and Al's first order of business was to see that Bentley had his own steak dinner and fresh water in his new bowl. There was no sexual tension between the trucker and me, which I took as a blessing and as an affirmation.

Everything would have been perfect if not for the fact that I was starting to get the shakes; I needed my drug.

"I've got to go," I said, opening the door and preparing to drop out of the cab.

"Take the dog," Al mumbled. Then he turned on his side and was asleep in an instant.

I snatched Bentley up in my arms and bounded out of the cab. Bentley, good doggie, immediately did his business in a patch of grass. My first order of business was to duck into the ladies' room and make up my face. There wasn't much I could do about my clothing, but I twisted and tied the tee hem, transforming it into a halter, and yanked the shorts down to showcase my tiny waist. After making those minor adjustments, Bentley and I headed for the bright lights of the truck stop in search of amphetamines, my new lover. The steak house seemed as good a bet as any. I lashed Bentley to a post outside and sauntered into the bar. I didn't have two nickels to rub together, but that had never stopped me before, and it sure as shooting wasn't going to stop me now.

I paused before selecting a seat and checked out the customers, all of whom were doing the same to me. This was critical. I needed to find my mark, and quickly or things were going to get ugly. Most of the patrons were of Al's ilk, not a bad thing but not what I required, given my present circumstances. At the end of the bar, however, sat a likely candidate, a lanky fellow with a reasonably handsome face. He glanced my way, flashing me a rakish come-on grin not to be ignored. Sizing up the rest of the patrons, I figured this chap was my best bet and moseyed on over, which was all I could manage in flip-flops. (In heels I would have made quite an entrance, but a girl works with what she has at her disposal.)

"Anybody sitting here?" I favored him with a coquettish smile. Right on cue, he patted the empty barstool.

"It's reserved for an angel," he said. "Must say I'm delighted you finally appeared."

Not bad, I thought as I climbed up next to him. I could get it on with this trucker. The bartender came by, gave me the once-over, obviously having pegged me for the broad who'd ordered a bottle of chardonnay not more than two hours ago. Like all good bartenders, he kept his mouth shut.

"What'll it be?" he asked.

I pretended to consider, waiting for my new boyfriend to pipe up, which he finally did. "Whatever the little lady wants, it's on me," he exclaimed.

"What're you drinking?" I asked, batting my lashes, real flirty.

"Jack, neat."

"Too strong for me. I'll just have a glass of chardonnay." The bartender raised his eyebrows and then turned to pour my drink. I sat there pretending to be shy, knitting my fingers together, when all the while I was dying for some speed.

"So, where are you headed?" macho man asked.

"Jeez! Everybody keeps asking me that," I complained. I caught myself and switched gears. No man cottons to a whining, nagging female.

"I don't know. I'm coming off a bad relationship." I shook my head and did my helpless act. "I . . . I'm just . . . betwixt and between. How about you?"

"You'll never believe this . . . I'm in the same boat! Just broke up with my girlfriend . . ."

"Well, aren't we a pair of lonely hearts?" I said, raising my glass. We clinked glasses, and I thought this was all going text-book perfect.

"Don't tell me you drive one of those big old monster Peterbilts?" I asked.

"Yes, ma'am, I do."

"Ooo, don't call me ma'am. Makes me feel so old."

He laughed. "What are you?" He leaned in conspiratorially and whispered, "Eighteen?"

I cuffed him playfully, put a finger to my lips. "Shhh! Don't you know I left without my driver's license? And for your information, Mr. Smarty Pants, I'm twenty-five."

He whistled softly. "You look like a kid."

"Good genes. And speaking of jeans, I wish I had me a pair. You must think I'm a hick, dressed in this god-awful getup."

"No!"

"I was so mad when I left, I couldn't see straight. Didn't pack too well!"

DANCING WITH THE DEVIL • 113

"Shit happens."

"I'll say." I extended a hand. "I'm Daisy, Daisy Collins."

He folded my itty hand in his paw. "Darryl Armstrong at your service, ma'am. Oops, I mean, Daisy."

Well, Daisy and Darryl got along splendidly. We got tipsy and, after collecting Bentley, went back to Darryl's truck.. Darryl turned out to be a pretty good kisser. One thing led to another until poor Daisy was struck with a blinding headache.

"My head is killing me!" I moaned. "I'm not used to drinking wine!"

"I'm sorry, baby. You want some aspirin?"

"You wouldn't have any painkillers, would you? I think I've got a migraine."

"I might have a prescription in the glove box, from when I broke my wrist last fall."

"Oh! That'd be great."

Darryl rifled through the contents of the glove compartment, and all the while I was practically salivating. Finally, his search was rewarded, and he withdrew a plastic pill bottle. "Ox-y-con-tin," he said, reading the label phonetically.

"Perfect!" I grabbed the bottle and tossed down three pills.

"Careful! That's strong stuff. I took one and it knocked me out."

"I have a high tolerance," I said, giddy with relief. The poison kicked in almost immediately. I was grateful to Darryl, and I let him know it. When I was done with him, he was a happy mother trucker. As I let Bentley and myself out of the cab, I palmed the pill bottle. Darryl would never miss it. And if he did, so what?

I stumbled along until I found Al Hubbard's rig, and I hoisted myself up, Bentley in my arms.

"You were gone a long time," Al grumbled, half asleep.

"Got the curse, had to rinse my underwear," I told him. "I'll need a couple bucks in the morning to buy some Tampax."

Men generally cease and desist at any mention of menses. They simply do not want to go there. I'd learned long ago that on occasion menstruation proves useful.

"Um . . ."

See what I mean?

The uppers and the downers worked in tandem, and I slept. In the morning, Al shook me awake.

"Want some breakfast?" he asked.

No, I didn't. I felt awful and only wanted to return to my dream. But I knew I was at a crossroads, so I pulled myself together and forced my brain to work.

"I'm not hungry. You go," I said.

"Okay, but we're pulling out at eight sharp," Al peeled a few bills from his wallet and handed them to me. "Get whatever you need between now and then."

I had twenty-seven oxys, which would make do for the time being, but what I really wanted was to be riding that methadone rollercoaster. I had to make a decision. I could stay with Al and . . . I don't know what. Go into rehab? Or I could find Darryl, ride shotgun with him, go wherever that led. I could hitch a ride back to the Pony and resume my old unsatisfactory life or forge a new path. I took some pills, washed them down with bottled water, and made up my mind. I was going to stay right here, I decided. I liked the truck stop; it had everything I needed. I could work this gig for a while.

I chucked both truckers with no qualms whatsoever. When it was time for Al and Darryl to hit the road, they did so solo. I wonder what they thought. Did they worry about me? I hope they read my story some day and realize how grateful I am for what they did for me. I was getting low. But those guys let me know there is hope for the species, that there are human beings out there who are basically good. There are men on the planet who aspire to more than using and abusing for their own gain. Somewhere along the way, I'd forgotten that.

That first day at the truck stop was a learning experience. I hung out in the ladies' room, striking up conversations with girls who I thought might have what it was I needed. It wasn't too long before I scored. She was a bottle-blonde with two inches of brown roots showing, pretty but pasty-faced and wasted. I can spot them a mile away.

"Hey," I said as I looked in the mirror while applying lip gloss. I made a show of casing the joint even though I knew we were alone. She nodded, washing her hands in the sink, not meeting my eyes. I opened my bag, tossed in the lip gloss, making sure to reveal the greenbacks wadded up inside.

"I'm a little strung out," I whispered. "You got anything I could buy off you?"

The girl's mouth tightened, and a look of fear passed over her face. I could see she was ready to run, so I snatched a wad of paper towels from the dispenser and handed them to her. Momentarily deterred, she took them.

"Look, I need uppers. I don't care what," I said.

The girl tossed the paper towels in the wastebasket and pivoted, heading toward the entrance. But then she hesitated, turned to me, and said, "How do I know you're not a cop?"

I laughed. And I guess my reaction was sincere enough to allay her suspicions, for she appeared to consider my request.

"Come on! I'm in a bad way," I wheedled. "Help a girl out, won't you?"

I thrust Darryl's bottle of painkillers in her face. "I'll pay you and you can have these. They don't do it for me anymore."

Her eyes latched on the oxycodone, and I knew I'd hit payola.

"My boyfriend can help you," she said, reaching for the pills.

"I'd like to meet him," I said, dropping the vial into my purse.

"Okay," she said, her face hardening. "Come on then."

I followed her out of the air-conditioned restroom into the sweltering heat of a Florida summer's day. The humidity enveloped me like a steaming sauna towel. Most days I didn't pay attention to such things, too anesthetized to care, but on that afternoon I was overloaded with sensory data. It was coming at me fast and furious, and all I wanted was to escape to my drug-induced haze. It was too prickly and uncomfortable in the sober world.

So I met her pimp. He gave me the once-over, sizing me up, and I could tell in an instant I was his new girl. I was both relieved and happy. I knew it wouldn't end well, that I was putting off the inevitable. But I chose to skate across the thin ice of my methadone-induced high rather than plumb the depths below. There was a reckoning coming, but I put it off for this sweet oblivion. Damien was his name, and I grooved on that. I'd finally come face to face with the Devil, and he wasn't that bad looking.

"Well, come on in," he said. "And welcome." And we danced.

CHAPTER SIXTEEN

Dancing with the Devil

BRITTANY WAS NINETEEN AND A SWEET KID. It didn't take her long to realize that I'd replaced her in Damien's affections. I think she was actually a bit relieved about that. My being there took the onus off of her. Brittany and I gladly hooked for him, turning over our earnings in exchange for nirvana. I didn't work that scam for long, maybe a day or two. Time had become a crafty bastard. Sometimes it would speed up; other times it would lag. Day, night—who knew the difference? All I wanted was to stay high, and that's exactly what I did. Until I awoke one morning to find that Damien and Brittany had cut out, leaving me to fend for myself.

As luck would have it, Al was passing through on his return trip. He spied me loitering outside the ladies' room and was immediately in my face.

"Girl, I wondered what became of you," he said. And the disappointment in his eyes was hard to miss. Despite my leathery alligator skin, it stung.

"Hey, Al," I said, trying to keep the desperation out of my voice. "How's it goin'?"

I knew I looked a wreck, that I'd fallen even lower than when he'd last seen me. But our exchange was interrupted when a stocky middle-aged security guard swaggered over. He was doing his job, preventing me, the scumbag that I'd become, from contaminating decent folk.

"You got to get outta here," he said, placing a meaty paw on his holstered revolver. "Get going, or I'll have you forcibly removed."

"That won't be necessary, officer," Al intervened. "The lady's with me."

The "lady" wasn't lost on me, and I silently blessed Al.

"Come on, honey," he said. "Let's go dress for dinner."

With that, he grabbed my arm and led me, stumbling, to his rig. Once safely ensconced in the cab, Al let me have it.

"What the hell do you think you're doing?" he demanded. "Do you have a death wish or what?"

I can usually talk my way out of any predicament, fabricate a plausible excuse for even the most bizarre circumstances my drug finds me in. But not this time. "I . . . uh . . ."

Al took pity on me.

"You need help," he said. "I'm taking you to the hospital."

"No! Call my mom," I pleaded.

"Hello, Mrs. Rose?" Al held my cell phone to his ear.

"Yes?"

"Sorry to bother you, ma'am." Al glanced at me, concern written across his face. "Your daughter's not well."

"What do you mean? Has she been in another accident?"

"No. I don't know what's the matter with her. I think she took something. She's not acting right."

"Where is she?"

Four hours later, my brother was there to take me off Al's hands. Once again, he came to my rescue. Michael bundled me into his car and drove me the three hours back to Vero Beach and the Indian River Medical Center. Upon our arrival, Mom relieved him. (The two of them had tacitly agreed to share the burden that I'd become.) I don't remember much of that time, as I was in and out of my head. But I do recall lying in a hospital bed, Mom pressing a glass of water to my lips, urging me to drink. I got a bit combative and brushed her hand away.

"Lea' me 'lone," I mumbled.

Several hours passed before blood work revealed the methadone in my system, and I was duly Baker Acted. Shortly afterward, two uniformed cops arrived to escort me to the Center for Emotional Behavior and Health. I posed about as big a threat as a mosquito, but they had to comply with regulations. They muscled me into a wheelchair, and in the process, one of my flip-flops fell off. Mom retrieved it and attempted to fit it back on my foot. But I resisted and started to struggle. I wanted that thing back on my foot about as much as I wanted the curse! The cops and Mom were baffled; they couldn't understand why I was putting up such a fuss. Mom finally succeeded in wrestling the sandal back on me, and I was whisked down the hallway and out into the night. The cops hustled me into the back seat of their cruiser, and we made the short trip directly across the street to the CEBH campus.

I couldn't wait to be rid of that flip-flop and, while being transported, managed to kick it under the seat. The darn thing had been searing the bottom of my foot!

We pulled up under the CEBH portico, and one badge got out of the car, opened the back passenger door, and dragged me out. Having won the small victory of ridding myself of the flip-flop, we'd nearly made it to the entrance when the other cop realized I was missing a shoe and made a quick survey of the back seat. He snatched up the sandal and, just as I crossed over the threshold and into the waiting arms of the admissions administrator, tossed it in after me. "Don't forget your sandal," he cried as the door whooshed shut behind me.

If you're wondering what the big deal about that shoe was, keep in mind that old Beelzebub periodically grabbed hold of my foot. He surely had done so again, was clutching that flip-flop, attempting to drag me down with him to the inferno. In some small part of my deranged mind, I knew with absolute certainty that this was the case. What I experienced in the ensuing days only proves that fact.

After being administered medications to ease the effects of the detox and put into isolation, I was unconscious for forty-eight hours. When I awakened, I was told I'd slept for the duration, that I didn't get up to go to the bathroom once in all that time. But I wasn't sleeping. I was dead and in hell. I could hear the lost souls shrieking, and I added my voice to theirs. I was in agony, my flesh burning. It was very real and very scary. I believed I'd been damned to an eternity of hellfire.

I was soon to discover my experience was not unique. In the months following that episode, I spoke to Dr. Dean about where I'd gone. He explained to me that other patients had described similar experiences while detoxing, assured me there was a perfectly logical, scientific explanation for this phenomenon, one that did not involve the spiritual realm. I didn't buy his argument. I knew the Devil had taken me, just as he'd snatched those others. Satan had claimed me. My blood pressure had been so high it was a miracle my heart hadn't exploded.

When I came out the other side into the land of the living, I was a model patient. I deep-sixed my smart-alecky attitude, was candid with my shrinks, and participated in group. Dr. Dean had me on so many meds the transition from hooked to clean proved fairly painless. Of course, I would have killed for a cigarette.

Still, giving up my drug was like losing a lover. I felt empty inside, like a cyborg, just going through the motions. Drugs had been my life for so many years I couldn't imagine what could possibly replace them in my affections. After having detoxed for seventy-two hours, I was given the choice of leaving or continuing on with treatment until I was deemed fit. Dr. Dean urged me to stay and work the program.

"Otherwise, you're not going to make it," he said. This time I believed him. I opted to stay.

I was a very sick girl. It was determined that my drug addiction was the manifestation of a deep-seated psychosis attributable to abandonment issues and the abuse I'd suffered at the hands of bad boyfriends. This diagnosis resonated with me, and I surely seemed to be recovering under Doc's care.

Mom visited regularly, bringing clothing, magazines, and candy. We would discuss what I'd do when I was released and decided that I'd enroll in Indian River State College. When not in class, I could answer phones at her office, earn a little money to get back on my feet.

CHAPTER SEVENTEEN

The Boogie-woogie

BEFORE BEING RELEASED FROM **CEBH**, I'D BEEN PRESCRIBED A WHOLE
SLEW OF PRICEY MEDICATIONS.

There was Seroquel, an antipsychotic; Wellbutrin, an antidepressant; Tegretol to combat my bipolar disorder; Paxil, an anti-obsessive (no more "cleaning" or "art"); Klonopin to prevent my panic attacks; a mood stabilizer; and Neurontin, a mood stabilizer to control my mood swings and make everything copacetic. One script cost $700, another five, and Mom was having a conniption. Money was tight as it was; she didn't know how she was going to afford my monthly scripts. And I'd begun smoking again, which really drove her up the wall.

We bickered a lot. I was sober, so I felt guilty, while she stressed over the financial burden involved with my upkeep: schooling, psychiatric treatment, cigarettes, and meds on top of the mortgage and all the household bills.

It's not easy returning home to live with a parent, but I buckled down and tried to re-enter society. There were no local NA meetings, so I went to AA, where I got hit on constantly. And I attended classes, picking up a few credits in interior design. But there was still this big emptiness inside me. I didn't feel like I fit in anywhere.

Mom suggested I join a soccer league, and for the first time in a long time, I got excited over the prospect. That's what I was missing, I told myself. I needed to get back into athletics, compete in team sports!

So I signed up to play with a men's soccer league. Really. And for a time, that was my salvation. Of course, Mom had to buy me soccer gear, cleats, shin guards, and the uniform, but she didn't complain. She was delighted that I was willing to give it a try.

I'll never forget the first time I hit the field at Hobart Park. I'd French braided my hair and wore no makeup. Still, the guys laughed me off. And no wonder. I didn't present as your typical female jock; I was a bit of a lightweight, and some of the players were formidable. The team was a mixed bag, comprised mainly of Brazilians and Mexicans, most of whom had competed on professional teams in their native countries, as well as a few middle-aged white fellows, who did a fairly good job of keeping up.

Needless to say, I was terrified. It had been years since I'd played, and even though I'd been running the beach and practicing my footwork, I knew I was going to get killed. Then that fearless thing kicked in right on cue. I ran out onto the field and immediately get clobbered. My new teammates were giving me the business and continued to do so all night long. Who could blame them? Barbie dolls make easy targets! But it wasn't long before they discovered I could take anything they sent my way, and the fact that I was as lithe and fast as a gazelle didn't hurt any either. When, despite my aches and bruises, I showed up for the next game, they began taking me seriously. And it wasn't long before I was accepted and was just one of the guys.

The Mexicans were a trip—such drama queens! They'd fall to the ground writhing if I touched them.

"Ju keeked me," they'd snivel, hoping for a foul to be called against me. "Ooo, my laag."

I had no patience for their theatrics. "Get up!" I'd snarl. And they would.

The Brazilians were gorgeous. Naturally, I developed a huge crush. Wanderson was his name. Lovely boy, lovely name: wandering son . . . so evocative. The fact that he spoke only Portuguese was a bit problematic. I'd taken two years of Spanish at St. Ed's, which helped somewhat in that regard. And although the language barrier proved a challenge, there was no denying the attraction between us.

It was soccer that kept me on an even keel for many months. I played Wednesday evenings and Saturday mornings. Mom would drop me off and come back and pick me up, or I'd catch a ride home with one of my teammates. Some nights, the guys would want to hang out after a scrimmage. We'd all reassemble at the local pool hall, where we played darts and billiards, and competed some more.

About that time, I began to feel pretty cocky, thinking I'd completely beaten my addiction. I was young and beautiful, and I'd missed so much of my twenties, I felt I owed it to myself to make up for lost time. Going out with the guys had presented no problems. God knows I was looked after by my teammates and well protected. It was a natural progression to think I could handle the bar scene. I started frequenting the local watering holes on weekends. Soon I was reconnecting with old classmates who'd come to town to visit their parents or returned from tours of Iraq or Afghanistan. We'd hug and catch up, and I could always tell the ones who were using.

One night at the Riverside Café, when I happened to be looking particularly foxy, I caught the eye of a smartly dressed dude. He was not much taller than I, unremarkable but for the fact that he was Asian. We all know the good Lord rewards persistence, and although he was not my type, this guy had that going for him. All night long he kept coming on to me, and all night long I rebuffed him, laughing him off.

At one point, he pressed his card into my hand, saying, "Call me. I want to take you to the Bahamas on my private jet."

Suddenly, he had my attention. I couldn't remember the last time I'd been on vacation, and I realized I needed one badly. On closer inspection, I decided he wasn't all that bad looking. Short but cute in a he's-got-a-lot-of-money way. I'd fallen for Patrick, I thought. Surely I could do the same with this chap. I switched gears and started oozing charm. What a harlot I was! But I don't regret a minute of it, for what next transpired is the stuff of dreams.

The next morning while getting ready to accompany Mom to work, I told her of my encounter. "I met this guy at Riverside Café last night . . ."

"And?" Mom rinsed out the coffee pot, seemingly none too interested.

I dropped the bombshell, anticipating her reaction. "He wants to fly me to the Bahamas on his private jet."

"You've got to be kidding!" Mom whirled to confront me.

"I think this guy is for real," I faced off before her. "He drives a Maserati."

"That means nothing!" Mom furrowed her brow. "Besides, you don't even know him. You can't just fly away with him. Who knows what kind of person he is?"

"We're going to find out. He'll be here at seven to pick me up and take me to dinner." I widened my eyes, making light of her concerns. "You can interrogate him then."

Josh showed up right on time, pulling into our drive behind the wheel of his sleek luxury car. He was beautifully dressed, cream-colored silk blazer over hip jeans, and I decided right away I could learn to love this diminutive Asian. Polite and deferential to Mom, he managed to win her over within the first five minutes.

"So, you're from Port St. Lucie?" Mom waved toward a chair, indicating that Josh should sit.

"No, I'm from Indiana." Josh lowered himself into the chair, and I perched on the ottoman next to him. "At least, that's where I was raised. I'm originally from Korea."

"He was adopted when he was only 2-years old," I interjected. "Isn't that amazing?"

"And what brings you to Florida?" Mom seated herself across from us, pointedly ignoring my remarks.

"I was persuaded to headquarter my company in South Florida."

"Your family still lives in Indiana?"

"Jeez, Mom!" I exclaimed. "What is this? The third degree?"

"It's okay," Josh said, waving a hand dismissively. "I get back to see them every now and then."

"What is your company?"

"Actually, I'm in transition right now." Josh leaned forward, placing his palms on his knees. "I design and manufacture computer software. I sold my company last year and am embarking on a new endeavor." He paused for effect.

"Oh?" Mom took the bait.

"I'm partnering with Digital Dominion!"

"Ah!" Mom nodded and smiled. "Of course I've heard of them. Animation."

"Yes. It's very exciting."

"Well!" Mom rose to her feet, and Josh and I followed suit. "It was very nice to meet you, Josh. You two have fun tonight. Drive safe."

"Not to worry, Mrs. Rose." Josh took my hand in his. "Meghan's in good hands."

"I can see that."

"He's really hot to fly to the Bahamas," I said, palming a diet soda from the fridge. "Apparently, he likes to gamble."

"Hmm . . ." Mom looked up from the *Vero Beach Press Journal* and frowned at me.

"He wants to go next week."

"That's impossible, Meghan." Mom put the newspaper aside and gave me her full attention. "You don't even have a passport. Besides, I'm pretty sure the fact that you're still on probation prevents you from leaving the country."

"I'll be off probation in a little over a year," I said. "Officer Clark loves me. He'll let me go."

Mom sipped her coffee and considered. "I suppose he would," she finally agreed. "But it takes three, sometimes four weeks to get a passport."

I held my cell phone high over my head and did a happy dance in the middle of Mom's bathroom. "Josh's flying in from Port St. Lucie on his private jet. We're going to fly to Miami and get my passport."

Mom peered at her reflection in her X7 magnification mirror.

"Good grief," she muttered as she applied her mascara. "That man can't wait to get you out of the country."

"Either that," I said, "or he really wants to hit the tables."

And so, I set off on my most excellent adventure. Mom drove me across town to Sun Aviation and the private runway where Josh's Gulfstream awaited. I bolted out of the car and retrieved my luggage from the trunk, eager to be on my way. The copilot relieved me of my bags and waved me toward the stair ramp. I found Josh seated in one of the plush lounge chairs, grooving to music from a headset. I rushed toward him and wrapped my arms around his neck. With a lazy motion of his hand, he motioned me toward the bar, at the same time raising his glass.

The jet's interior was luxurious and beautifully appointed. There were six passenger chairs, upholstered in a buttery-soft kidskin, that both swiveled and reclined. And everywhere, polished brass details gleamed like gold. The lavish bathroom featured granite countertops, brass fittings, and gilded fixtures. As we soared over the Atlantic, Josh and I toasted one another, clinking crystal champagne flutes. I was clean but still yearning for something that would complete me, something to expunge that desolate, empty feeling that plagued me. I hoped Josh's millions might do that.

We were met at the Nassau International Airport by two hulking giants, either of whom could have played body double to Mr. T.

"My bodyguards," Josh explained as one relieved him of his bulging leather valise while the other saw to our luggage. Thunderstruck, I realized Josh was carrying so much cash he felt the need for his own personal security! A stretch limo whisked us all to the tropical paradise Atlantis. Nothing but the best for Mr. Josh! As we stood in line to check in, a colossus of a man entered the reception area. Heads turned to gawk at this Goliath with a doll-like blonde on his arm.

"Who is it?" I whispered to Josh.

"That's Kobe Bryant," he said, gape-jawed like the rest of us. "And it looks as though he prefers your type!"

We were shown to an enormous penthouse suite in the Cove, the private section reserved for celebrities and millionaires. It was decorated in an island theme with Tommy Bahama-style furnishings. The covered balconies boasted chaise lounges where one could loll and admire the sweeping ocean views. There was a full kitchen and a fully stocked bar, and the separate dining room boasted a massive chandelier. But what really struck me was the fact that there were two sumptuous master bedrooms. Perhaps, I thought fleetingly, Josh intended for us to occupy separate sleeping quarters. When he directed one of the bodyguards to deposit our luggage in the smaller of the two, I knew I was on the hook for paybacks.

I could hardly wait to check out the island, enjoy some fun in the sun at the waterpark or frolic with the porpoises at Dolphin Cay, but Josh was itching to place his first bet.

It was his party, so we hit the tables.

Las Vegas has nothing over Atlantis's Temple of the Sun Casino. With its faux Mayan ruins and magnificent Lalique sunburst chandelier rendered in fiery hues, it could easily hold its own with the Venetian or Caesar's Palace. There was a momentary lull when we entered the casino. All eyes fastened on the incongruous foursome: the compact Asian with a Jessica Simpson look-alike on his arm and his entourage of titans. We were escorted to the casino's private rooms, where the heavy hitters placed bets in $20,000 increments. Josh savored the limelight. He made a show of removing wads of cash from his valise, handing them to his bodyguards so that they might go and purchase chips.

"Can I play the slots?" I asked.

"Sure, baby." Josh strutted to a bank of slot machines, planted himself before one, and proceeded to feed it $100-dollar bills. He motioned for me, and I pulled the lever. In the next instant, the chrome-plated machine erupted in a cacophony of computer-generated bells and whistles, lighting up like New York Harbor on the fourth of July. I shrieked, "Josh! We hit the jackpot!"

Jumping up and down, I threw myself at him. Attendants came rushing out of the woodwork to assist, and a crowd of spectators gathered round as the machine spewed out a seemingly endless cache of coins. In the first five minutes of our initial gambling soiree, I'd managed to score over a grand. And so it went. I was on a roll.

After that rush, and having entrusted the bodyguards with the loot, Josh and I moseyed on over to the blackjack table. He pushed forward a stack of chips, and I hung on him, offering up words of encouragement. Josh gambled for a few hours, proceeded to lose and then win it all back. I stood by my man. He was ahead by about $40,000 when my interest waned. Not only was my stomach grumbling, I was dying to explore the island.

"Baby, let's grab a bite," I wheedled. "We can come back later."

"Sure thing." He motioned for his bodyguards to cash in his chips. Josh was feeling flush; he'd scratched that gambling itch and gotten a bit of relief apparently. Making our way from the casino, we immediately came upon the swank Japanese restaurant Nobu.

"How about this?" Josh asked, pausing in front of the enticing menu prominently displayed just outside the eatery's entrance. I hesitated. I love Japanese cuisine, and the trendy restaurant, with its crisp black-and-white color scheme, was tempting. But its proximity to the casino worried me. I could see a pattern forming here, and I wanted none of it. I needed a break from the ear-splitting, ding-dinging slot machines and the ribald gambling frenzy. I took Josh's arm and steered him outside, where the shadows were lengthening and the air was redolent with the scent of gardenia. We strolled past the opulent Crystal Court Shops, and Josh suddenly became animated.

"Let me buy you something," he said. "You're my good luck charm.

You should be rewarded."

"Sure," I agreed.

"What would you like, sweetheart? A dress? A handbag?"

I wanted both.

"Oh, look at that adorable tunic." I pointed to a brightly colored frock, and Josh nodded his approval. In a little over half an hour, Josh laid down over $3,000 with nary a blink of an eye, and I walked out of the shops with my nifty shopping bags filled with expensive booty: a Burberry bag, a Juicy Couture bikini, and an Armani tunic. This is what I'd been waiting for, I thought. Surely it was a sign: I was being rewarded for my sobriety!

CHAPTER EIGHTEEN

The Soft-shoe

ONCE IN THE PRIVACY OF OUR SUITE, JOSH SUDDENLY BECAME
AMOROUS. I was finding him cuter by the minute and didn't mind making him happy. Forty-five minutes later, having left the Egyptian cotton sheets in disarray, I went to the adjoining bath to shower. As I waited for the water to warm, I paused at the window to take in the spectacular view. The sun was slipping into the ocean, creating a fantastical display. Bruised clouds bled across the horizon as the Atlantic turned from blue to silver. In a matter of minutes, the fiery colors faded like cooling embers, painting the sky rosy shades of lavender and pink.

After dressing for dinner, Josh and I discussed the various venues available to us. We finally decided on Dune, touted for its haute cuisine, French-Asian fusion spiked with Bahamian influences. The restaurant didn't disappoint. The ultra-modern décor was minimalistic, a look I don't normally find appealing, but Dune did it right. With its neutral color palette of black, white, and shades of brown and gray and a variety of textures in fabrics and wall surfaces, the place exuded an aura both sexy and *au courant*. We weren't big eaters, but that didn't stop Josh from ordering a variety of delectable dishes. When we finally pushed away from the feast—Josh $200 the poorer—we hit the tables.

Believe it or not, I found those hours killing time in the casino far more onerous than the time I spent performing in the bed for Josh. I could take care of him in fifteen minutes if I so desired. But trapped in the casino, I was stuck for what seemed an eternity. As he continued to lose at blackjack, Josh finally realized how bored I'd become.

"Here, sweetie," he said, thrusting a pile of chips in my direction. "I'm out of luck. Why don't you take a spin?"

I'd been watching Josh with half an eye while sizing up the room. I'd hoped to get another glimpse of Kobe. Instead, it was Vanilla Ice I spied as he concentrated on the roulette wheel. But my people-watching session was interrupted by Josh's question, and I gave him my full attention. "Sure," I said, eager for a diversion.

I don't know whether the dealer was playing me or if it was just sheer beginner's luck. In any case, I started winning. "Blackjack," the dealer would announce hand after hand. Josh was beside himself, hooting and hollering, and a small crowd of onlookers gathered round, adding to the excitement. Finally, when I was $20,000 ahead, I decided I'd had enough. The wagering and suspense, the thrill of winning—they exacted a price; I was left feeling weak and wobbly.

"You can't quit now," Josh said. But I needed fresh air and longed to escape the unnatural pulsing-neon atmosphere.

We returned to our suite of rooms and Josh made a beeline for the bar and poured himself a Dewar's on ice.

"What can I get you?" he asked, taking a generous swig from his glass.

I had collapsed on one of the sofas and was digging into a beautiful presentation of hand-dipped chocolate-covered strawberries left by the night maid.

"Um . . . Cristal?" I mumbled, savoring the sweet confection.

"Sure thing, baby," Josh said, pouring me a glass of bubbly. As he crossed to me, stemmed glass in hand, his eyes fastened on the balcony around the corner from ours. "Jesus!" Josh exclaimed. "Would you look at that?"

My eyes followed his, alighting on a pair of enormous sneakers neatly aligned there. Then it registered: our suite was directly across from one of the Laker's rooms! Perhaps the shoes had been put there to air-dry, I thought. In any case, there they were, classic white-and-gold Nike Zooms.

"I'm going in!" Josh deposited my drink on the cocktail table and made for the sliding glass door.

"What do you mean?" I asked.

"I want those shoes!" Josh didn't give me a backward glance.

"You can't!" I cried, jumping to my feet.

"The hell I can't. What a trophy!" Josh bounded through the opening. "Can you imagine the mileage I'll get out of this story?"

I followed him out the door. "It's stealing," I said.

Before I knew it, Josh was hurtling over our balcony onto the adjoining one. My own little Jackie Chan was performing daredevil stunts in his pursuit of ill-gotten gains.

"Oh my God!" I wailed as he hoisted himself up and over the adjoining balcony. This guy was seriously unhinged. "What are you doing?"

"Here," he cried, as he tossed one shoe after the other in my direction.

"Are you crazy?" I asked. "Surely they'll figure out who stole them!"

"They'll think the maid took them." Josh dropped back into our terrace. "Trust me, they won't rat her out."

"But . . ."

"We're talking shoes, darling." Josh bent to retrieve his plunder. "Whoever this guy is, he's a mega-millionaire. The loss of a pair of shoes will barely penetrate his consciousness."

"Jeez," I muttered to myself, as I followed him back inside. "What is it with me and shoes, huh?"

Our vacation rhythm became established: Josh and I would meet up for dinner, after which I'd spend a couple of hours with him in the casino before heading back to our suite or going dancing or catching an act at the nightclub Aura. The more Josh lost at the gaming tables, the more I won. In the beginning, my lucky streak didn't seem to bother Josh. Everywhere we went, he threw money around like it was confetti. It was obvious he got his kicks having a looker on his arm. I was an expensive bauble, much the same as the ostentatious gold chain he'd fastened around his neck the minute we'd touched down on Bahamian soil. Like Patrick, he suffered from a Napoleon complex, and he reveled in all the attention, the false adulation heaped upon him at every turn.

Inevitably, I began to see another side to Josh; he seemed to lack morals, an observation one might find ironic given my recent profession. And not only was he an alcoholic, he was a compulsive gambler. I was willing to overlook these character flaws so long as he treated me well. And those first days in the Bahamas, he did. But slowly, a pattern emerged. Josh, having burnt the midnight oil gambling, preferred to sleep until mid-afternoon. I, on the other hand, arose mid-morning and headed for the gym. Serendipitously, my workout partners happened to be a few of Kobe's teammates.

Andrew Bynum and Ronny Turiaf teased me, half-pint that I was. And Lamar Odem taunted, "Oh, mama! Don't hurt yourself with that big ol' weight." But when they got a load of my bench-pressing and running the treadmill at full tilt, they invited me to party with them come nightfall. I declined their invitations, thinking Josh would not appreciate my ditching him for the Lakers.

I felt guilty over the pilfered shoes, but I don't think those mighty athletes suspected I'd been any part of that business.

By the time Josh and I flew back to Vero and reality, a veritable chasm had opened up between us. He was sullen and introspective, seemingly jealous of my winnings, whereas I was miffed at his standoffish attitude and ready to be rid of him. On the flip side, three $1,000 bills were tucked into my Burberry, and I was sporting a pair of half-carat diamond earrings.

"Call me," I said, brushing my lips against Josh's. Then I turned and trotted toward my mother's car. But Josh was concentrating on his cell phone and merely nodded. He never did call, and I didn't regret that one little bit.

CHAPTER NINETEEN

The Bossanova

I JUMPED BACK INTO MY OLD LIFE WITH RENEWED VIGOR, DESPERATELY TRYING TO STAY CLEAN. Wanderson and I picked up where we'd left off, and it wasn't long before we were getting serious. But even though I yearned for one, I was not ready for a committed relationship. I was not fully recovered by any means, and I was taking a variety of powerful psychotropic drugs to keep me on an even keel. After all, I'd been diagnosed as bipolar, depressive, obsessive-compulsive, prone to panic attacks, and *schizophrenic*!

One night after a game, the team decided to adjourn to Cunningham's Pool Hall. But before joining them there, I'd insisted Wanderson take me home so I could shower and change clothes. Mom was at choir practice, so we had the place to ourselves. I showed Wanderson to the living room before retreating to my suite. After blowing my hair dry and applying eyeliner and lip gloss, I donned tight-fitting jeans and a tee. When I emerged, Wanderson's eyes bugged out. "Ju beautiful!" he exclaimed.

I made quite an entrance at the pool hall. My teammates had never seen me dressed in street clothes with my hair down and paint on. Timmy, who'd always made a great show of ignoring me, came on to me

"Well, hello, sweet thing," he drawled.

"Timmy," I said. "It's me, Meghan. You know, the girl who's going to leave you in the dust come Saturday!"

The guys all cut up over Tim's faux pas, and I had to backtrack. Tim would never forgive me for making him the butt of a joke, and I had no intention of doing so. He was a bud.

"Come on, tall man," I said. "Show me how it's done."

And with that, I made as if to chug my beer. Tim didn't let me down. He swallowed his pint in a single protracted gulp.

Life was good for a while. Wanderson, upstanding Catholic boy that he was, behaved like a perfect gentleman. I wasn't used to that, but I appreciated the reprieve. The attention he lavished on me was flattering, and the sexual tension between us, delicious. He'd kiss and stroke me until I was ready to shuck off my clothes and have at him. I guess the boys from Brazil save themselves for marriage. At least mine did. Wanderson was the ideal suitor, just what I needed to boost my confidence.

When I'd first moved back in with Mom, she'd kept me on a tight rein. After three DUIs I'd long since lost my license, and my beautiful Mercedes was relegated to the garage. Mom drove me everywhere, which was a drag for both of us. When soccer came back into my life and it appeared that I was sticking to the program, she started granting me more freedom until eventually I began coming and going as I pleased. I was twenty-five, for heaven's sake! I'd go out in the early evening, ostensibly to an AA meeting, when in fact I was hitting the local pubs. Then I stopped taking my meds—first one, then another.

"Wellbutrin gives me the shakes," I explained to Mom. "Klonopin makes me feel disconnected." She argued against it, but in the end, she was relieved. She simply couldn't afford to keep paying for my costly medications. One thing led to another, and I started doping again. I'd pop a couple of Xanax during the day to mellow things out, but I was still able to function, to play soccer and keep up the deception that I was clean.

Raymond Dean specialized in both childhood psych and addiction, and I was considerably older than his other patients. Ostensibly, he'd taken my case because he, more than anyone, knew my history, having worked with me on and off since the time of my first DUI. But there was more to it than that. He and I had a special connection—nothing sexual, just a genuine affection for one another. I respected him. But when he started crowing that I was his recovered-addict poster child, I knew better. I continued to see him for monthly counseling sessions, informing him that, despite the fact that he prescribed them, I wasn't taking my meds with any sort of regularity.

I was able to pull the wool over Mom's eyes for a while; she didn't realize I'd begun self-medicating again. I was still attending AA meetings, where we dug at our scabs, trying to fathom how it was we'd come to be wounded in the first place. But, as Mick sings, I wasn't getting any satisfaction.

We were in the car, and Mom was at it again. "You know, Meghan," she said, "I don't buy the fact that you're depressed or bi-polar."

Silently, I agreed. "You have ADHD, and you got side-tracked by drugs," Mom said. Suddenly, she had my full attention. This made sense to me; I'd secretly suspected the same thing. When my life was careening out of control, the opioids slowed everything down to a tolerable level. "Why don't you ask Dr. Dean to treat your ADHD?"

At my next appointment, I broached the topic, asked Dean if he could prescribe something for my attention deficit. But Doc was having none of it.

"Meghan!" he exclaimed. "Do you know what you're asking? I've been Executive Director here for nearly twenty-five years. And you want me to prescribe *Adderall?*"

"I've read it's an effective treatment," I countered."

"Yeah, when taken as prescribed. You know, Meg," he said, "you're always going on about Devils and demons . . ."

I nodded.

"Well, kiddo, Adderall happens to be my personal Devil. It's a central nervous system stimulant, the exact same one that's found in methadone. And that's why I seldom prescribe it. It's just asking for trouble."

"I won't abuse it," I said. "I just want to get my life back, Doc. Please. Can't we give it a try?"

Dean cupped his chin in his hand and stared at me balefully. "Okay," he finally said. "But we're going to drug test you on your next visit. This stuff is highly addictive and, Meghan, you don't want to go there again."

I agreed with him.

But then my world began falling apart, and so did I.

CHAPTER TWENTY

The Conga

READ LOWE WAS THE FIRST OF MY MANY FRIENDS WHO ENDED UP A CA-SUALTY OF FLORIDA'S RAMPANT DRUG EPIDEMIC. Read and I went as far back as nursery school. Our families were close, and our friendship continued on throughout the years. In his late teens, Read started abusing drugs, and it was during his short stint at college that he segued from merely using to selling. Read was but a lowly "gopher" in the drug trade. Nonetheless, he was eventually sentenced to prison. On the morning of May 8, 2002, Read's lifeless body was discovered hanging from the Barber Street Bridge. There were no witnesses, and no one knows if Read took his own life to avoid prison or if he was murdered by his suppliers.

David Root was the first childhood pal I lost to alcohol abuse. It was 2005, and he'd been celebrating Independence Day with a few buddies at a local watering hole. The pub was located a mere quarter mile from where he was living, and although he'd had too much to drink, David must have figured he could make that short distance home safely. Instead, he lost control of his vehicle. It flipped and he was killed instantly.

But it wasn't until 2009 when the death knell announcing the passing of my friends and loved ones became a constant ringing in my brainpan. Over the course of four months, I lost my father; Gus, who'd been like a brother to me; my best girlfriend, Olivia; and my precious Nana.

From an early age, Gus had been my brother's soul mate, and I tagged after the two of them like the annoying little tomboy I was, secretly in love with my brother's best bud. In his late teens, Gus became addicted to dextromethorphan, a cough suppressant found in many over-the-counter cough and cold medications. Gus was dancing with the Devil—"robo-tripping"—when he and his girlfriend shot and killed their roommate, stole his debit card and Nintendo games, and set fire to his apartment. Gus and the girl were sentenced to life in prison. In December of that same year, Gus looped a twisted length of sheet around his neck and took the only way out of prison that was available to him.

Dad passed away at the ripe old age of fifty-nine, having literally drunk himself to death—no small feat. When I was informed of Dad's passing, I sequestered myself in my bathroom and downed four Adderall, effectively deadening my grief. I was incoherent at Dad's funeral, but that didn't stop me from making a scene. The fact that I hadn't been given an active role in the ceremony didn't penetrate my anesthetized brain until the service was nearly over and my brother was delivering the eulogy. Het up as I was, I became violently angry. I bolted up out of my pew in righteous indignation, fully prepared to vent my ire. Dad's sister-in-law managed to subdue me when heads turned at my loud complaining over the unfairness of it all. But I wasn't appeased; I knew I'd been slighted. Afterward at the wake, I gave Mom and Michael the cold shoulder while devouring an entire tray of pastries. The Xanax I'd swallowed brought me floating down. Anger forgotten, I was suddenly mellow and ravenous.

Olivia Garrison was a waif-like creature and one of my closest girlfriends. The two of us had a lot in common: we'd both attended St. Edwards, and our parents traveled in the same circles. Like me, Olivia worked as a waitress and drifted from one bad boyfriend to another. Unlike me, Olivia suffered from endometriosis. All the girls in my clique bemoaned our monthly "curse." But Olivia's suffering was epic, and as she grew older, her symptoms only worsened. Still, she'd somehow avoided falling into that pain medication trap. But that all changed when her doctor prescribed Roxicet, a highly addictive form of oxycodone. Olivia was twenty-seven when she died. She'd been trying to get clean, and her toxicology report attested to that fact. But her boyfriend had ingested a handful of Xanax just before the two of them climbed into his truck. They were twelve miles outside of Vero Beach when he lost control of the vehicle. Both of them were ejected through the windshield. He died instantly, and Olivia never regained consciousness.

After Olivia's funeral, her brothers and a few of our former classmates assembled for an informal wake. When I looked around at those familiar faces, it was disturbing to see how many of them were on that same destructive course that Olivia and our other fallen friends had followed. I had to admit that I was one of them. Before the gathering broke up, we all vowed to honor Olivia by getting clean and making successes of our lives.

It didn't take long for my resolve to waver.

CHAPTER TWENTY-ONE

Mambo

JUST BEFORE MY DAD DIED, WANDERSON WAS SIGNED TO A PRO TEAM IN BOSTON. The two of us had hatched a plan for me to join him there once he'd settled in. But I couldn't get my act together. I was using regularly again, and I'd lost interest in everything; all I cared about was getting and staying high. I stopped playing soccer altogether, and it wasn't long before Mom kicked me out. She couldn't put up with my being doped up all the time: policemen at the door day and night, dragging my sorry behind home from who knows where; dealers in my room in the wee hours, where she'd find me exchanging contraband for pills.

I was a big gaping wound. My life was solely comprised of one tragedy after another, with me trying desperately to avoid the pain at all costs.

I shacked up with a series of guys. It became a routine, comforting for its familiarity. Initially, they'd turn a blind eye to my dopiness and tantrums, but they'd soon tire of me and my melodrama. I didn't let it bother me, told myself it wasn't my fault. I was careening through life and cutting a destructive swath, would as soon dissemble as tell the truth, and could tear a man to shreds with my vicious tongue. At one point, when I'd managed to distance anyone who'd ever cared a whit about me, I cleaned up my act somewhat, reducing my Adderall consumption. It was out of necessity; I needed money or a sugar daddy. Miraculously, I landed a job waiting tables at a fish shack in Fort Pierce.

I enjoyed the work at Sharky's. Once again, I immersed myself in that fast-paced hustle-bustle that had always appealed to me. As soon as I managed to save up a little cash, I enrolled in a lifeguard recertification class at the North County Pool. Lifeguarding would be my salvation, I decided. Perhaps, in the process of getting certified, I could save my own life.

Although I'd cut back, I was still using, and the instructor, Brianna, took an instant dislike to me. I realize now she probably suspected that I was high most of the time. In any case, she managed to make my life even more miserable than it already was. She rode my ass, was darn right nasty and insulting, and my battered ego suffered all the more. The one good thing that came out of this situation was that some of my old devil-may-care pluck returned, and with it, my resolve to pass the course with flying colors despite Brianna's best efforts to prevent me from doing so.

My first trial was coming up. Besides having to complete 300 yards of freestyle and breaststroke, I was to dive into the deep end of the pool, retrieve a ten-pound brick, swim to the other end, and hoist it onto the deck. This task was to be accomplished in three minutes.

I started training, running the beach again, and I reduced my daily Adderall intake to six 30-milligram tablets a day. Still, on the morning of the trial when Brianna blew the whistle, signaling that I was to begin, my heart was beating wildly. I dove into the pool with the speed of a torpedo. In the next instant, I hit the bottom and palmed the weight. I raced to the end of the pool and practically threw the weight on the deck. Brianna offered no congratulations, but I knew I'd aced it. I just didn't know by how much. Later, when I asked her my time, she allowed that I'd done it in two and a half minutes, nearly tying the record for Indian River County! How would it have gone had I not been speeding on Adderall? Perhaps not so well. But I sorely needed a success to cling to, and this accomplishment provided a shred of self-validation that buoyed me.

I kept in contact with Mom, occasionally hitching a ride with her to and from the pool or my apartment. She encouraged me in my endeavor to lifeguard again, but she was wary. She knew I was still using. Sometimes she'd take pity on me, ask me over for dinner, occasions when she'd ply me with orange juice, all the while keeping me at arm's length. Mom didn't invite me to move in with her, and I didn't ask.

Once again, I was living quasi-independently. Translation: I was sharing digs with my newest boyfriend, Charlie Fortune. I'd known Charlie from when we were both seniors at John Carroll High School. There had always been chemistry between us, yet we'd never dated. When I reconnected with him, it seemed that fate had thrown us together, and it wasn't long before we were a couple. Charlie truly loved me, and I cared deeply for him. But my drug was my one true lover. Like Lyle, Charlie did everything in his power to help me get clean. I'd pretend to go along with the plan, but secretly use, still not ready to go cold turkey. So our ride, Charlie's and mine, was a bumpy one.

I'd completed the certification course and, despite Brianna's pushback, was hired on as a lifeguard at Pepper Park Beach in Fort Pierce. Granted, it was on a part-time basis, three days a week from six in the morning to six at night.

Mornings, I'd get to my post and be treated to a magnificent sunrise. Soon, I got to know the regulars, the surf fishers and guys with metal detectors hoping to unearth a Spanish coin washed in from one of the shipwrecked galleons out on the reefs. Occasionally, I'd rouse a drunk passed out on the dune and send him on his way. Once, I stumbled upon a beached bottlenose dolphin. I made frantic phone calls, and in no time the coastline was crowded with members of the SeaWorld Rescue Team supplemented by a gaggle of well-intentioned locals. Despite a concerted effort, our rescue attempt ended badly, and I cried myself to sleep that night, thinking the world a cruel and unforgiving planet. But for the most part, it was peaceful as I surveyed my realm at 6:00 a.m. I felt as though I was getting my life in order; I was a county employee with a meaningful occupation, and I held down a second job waiting tables. I was beholden to no one, or so I told myself. But I was completely and utterly lost. That big hole in my chest was like a sinkhole threatening to suck me down into the void. "Take no prisoners," the Devil cackled gleefully. Little did I know that the only thing that could ever fill that hole was Jesus, that when I asked Him to come in and do so, He would. But I wasn't ready to surrender. I was still deluding myself, thinking I was my own pilot, master of my destiny.

Three months after my dad died, Nana passed away. Mom's mother had eleven grandkids, and all of them were special in her eyes. But our relationship was especially close. So much so that when she needed a hip replacement and Mom and her siblings were scrambling to find someone to stay with her after the procedure, I volunteered. It was during one of my relatively clean periods, and I was up for the task. I loved my Nana and more than anything wanted to lend a hand in her time of need. Nana and I were, and are, soul sisters traveling this galaxy in God's perfect synchronicity. We both felt the connection. Despite my little problem, Nana accepted my offer, and I will forever be thankful for the opportunity to help her get around, assist her in the shower, and wash her hair as she had done for me when I was a tot.

Nana suffered from chronic obstructive pulmonary disease. She'd had hospice care in her home for over a year, and we all knew her days were numbered. Two weeks before she passed, Mom and I picked her up and took her to her favorite restaurant for lunch. She tossed back two martinis and polished off almost all of her lunch. Afterward, when we were getting her settled back in her little villa, she had an attack.

"Emergency," she gasped. "Get oxygen!"

Mom and I knew how to activate the tanks and set them up, but Nana was in such distress that, in our panic, we fumbled with the machinery. Eventually, we got her the oxygen she needed, and the crisis passed. But I believe it was that episode that clinched it for Nana; she didn't relish a repeat performance.

"Nana called," Mom's voice came to me over my cell. "Hospice wants her to start taking morphine in her nebulizer."

"What? Don't let her do it," I snapped.

"Why? She says it'll help her breathe."

"It'll kill her, Mom. Trust me," I said. "It'll go straight into her bloodstream, and—"

"Meghan, hospice has suggested—"

"I don't give a damn," I interrupted. "I'm telling you . . ."

Everyone else in the family except my Uncle Jeff went along with it. What did they know? I knew drugs, and Jeff did too. Uncle Jeff was bipolar and had been a guinea pig for a lot of psychotropic meds. Anyone who's had that kind of experience is generally very knowledgeable.

"Are you crazy?" he asked my mother when he heard the news. "*Morphine*? Come on!"

"Hospice thinks it's for the best," Mom said. "They ought to know."

I held my cell phone to my ear, digesting Mom's words.

"I can't say why," she said. "But I feel so strongly that I need to be there. I was going to wait until Saturday, but I think I'll take a day off and go tomorrow."

"I'll come, too," I said.

"What about your work?"

"No problem. They'll let me off. I think we should go."

"Can you get someone to drive you to the house by ten?"

"I'll be there."

On the drive to Satellite Beach, I discussed my future plans with Mom.

"I'm going to go into the Coastguard," I announced.

Mom shot me a quizzical look. "Can you do that with your record?" she asked.

"Sure. I'm not a felon."

"But with your history, having been diagnosed—"

"It's crap, Mom, and you know it," I said. "I'm not schizophrenic!"

"I do know it, Meghan." Mom sighed. "What are you taking now? Adderall?"

"Nothing, Mom. I'm clean." I gazed out the window, avoiding her eyes.

"Humph!"

Per Nana's request, we were armed with several newly released paperbacks and a liter of Smirnoff. It was clear Nana's plan was to hunker down and wait for the end, but not without a good read to keep her company and a martini at five. We were definitely not prepared for the scene that awaited us at Nana's villa. Jake, her Cairn Terrier, was staked outside.

"Hey, Jake," I said, patting him on his graying head. "How you doin'?"

He was not doing well. Dogs know what's going down even when we humans remain clueless.

The hospice gal was hanging out in the kitchen, checking messages on her iPhone.

"Hi!" I said. "How's Nana?"

"She fine," the woman said. "She restin'."

Mom and I exchanged troubled looks before making our way to the back of the house.

We found Nana in her bedroom. She was in the hospital bed that hospice had delivered, and she didn't look at all like my pretty Nana, who'd always been so particular about her appearance—clothes, hair, and makeup. The morphine had taken her to another place. In and out of consciousness, she was letting slip her moorings to this earth, relinquishing her connections, and I didn't want her to go.

"Nana!" I cried.

"Mama!" Nana fixated on a spot on the wall. Mom and I raptly followed her gaze. Nana turned to us and, with complete lucidity, said, "Mother's come for me. She's so beautiful."

We nodded, absolute believers. She'd seen her own mother coming to lead her to heaven. In the next instant Nana said, "Maybe we should call a priest."

Mom and I searched each other's face, both of us thinking surely this was precipitous, but terrified of making a misstep.

"I'll call Holy Name," Mom said. "See if we can't get a priest here pronto."

Forty-five minutes later, the Vietnamese priest whom Nana adored, but because of his accent, none of the rest of us could understand, showed up at her doorstep. Things were happening here! We couldn't believe this was actually the end for Nana. But God had his own plan, and we were finally getting with the program. Mom and I witnessed Nana's last rites. It was very teary. Barely able to swallow, Nana received communion; she was loosening her tether to this lifetime, and she was not sad, but rather eager to go. We were sad and couldn't bear the thought of her leaving.

"You don't have to stay," Nana said upon awakening. As always, she was perfectly selfless and solicitous of others. "I'm fine."

"We want to, Nana," I said.

Mom and I stood vigil for a time, but Nana was sleeping and there was little for us to do. Eventually, Mom started cleaning. Cleaning is Mom's little addiction, her obsessive-compulsive disorder. She tackled the kitchen sink base cabinet, a particularly odious job. No one had addressed that cabinet in years. While Mom cleaned, I stayed at Nana's bedside. At one point, the hospice aide came into the room. She gently shook Nana's shoulder, rousing her.

"Barbara," she said, "can you eat something?"

"No," Nana mumbled. "Go to the bathroom."

"Okay, sweetie." The aide hastened to help my Nana up and out of bed, and *glory be*! Nana fairly leapt out of that hospital gurney and dashed to the bathroom unassisted. The aide and I followed along behind, but we were superfluous. Nana had it under control. She did her business and returned to bed, and we followed along like lackeys. Sometimes the dying are imbued with a burst of energy in order to accomplish their final tasks. Nana certainly had been. No one was going to find that she'd wet her pants or worse.

Nana slept then, and Mom and I decided we'd go home and return in the morning.

I got the call at a little after nine. Mom's voice was thick with tears.

"She's gone," Mom said. "Thank God we had the priest come when we did."

"Noooooo!"

What ensued then was a kind of dream. My big Irish family and I went through the motions. Apparently, that's normal. When a loved one passes, there are so many details to attend to, it takes one's mind off the reason for the details. I distanced myself in other ways. But I was there for Nana's funeral, and let me tell you, it was a bang-up celebration of life!

I was high but not nearly so out of it as I'd been at my dad's send-off. Holy Name was packed. Nana, this little lady of little means, had touched so many lives. My brother was the oldest grandchild in attendance, and in typical Michael fashion, he took charge. He arranged for all the grandchildren and the great-grandkids to bring up the gifts—the unconsecrated bread and wine—and there were a lot of grands. We processed down the aisle, Michael's firstborn holding her infant brother in her arms, followed by the rest of the clan, youngest to oldest. I don't think there was a dry eye in the pews.

When the last eulogy had been delivered and everyone was smiling and weepy, my uncle Greg held the little wooden box containing Nana's cremains high over his head as if affording her one last glimpse of her beloved church. My family and I filed out of the sanctuary, and the entire assembly followed. We gathered just outside the sacristy where Nana had spent so many hours in silent adoration. The Vietnamese priest said a few words that no one could understand, before motioning for the immediate family to come forward. Uncle Greg handed him the box containing Nana's ashes, and the priest placed it in a small pit that had been prepared in the memorial garden. He beckoned for each of Nana's children to come forward and instructed them to toss a bit of earth over the ashes. While this was happening, an extraordinary thing occurred. Seemingly out of the ground where my Nana was being interred, an enormous monarch butterfly appeared! All the onlookers, myself included, gasped in amazement as the gorgeous, winged creature dipped and swooped over the many mourners who'd congregated outside for the burial. That butterfly was in no hurry. It paused first over one person, then another, bidding individual farewells. At one point, it hovered near a stained-glass window, as if seeking one more earthly sighting of the church interior. After the initial shock, Mom burst out laughing. Then the rest of us caught on, and soon my aunts and uncles were sharing in the merriment. The butterfly lingered for another minute or so and, as magically as it had appeared, vanished into thin air! We in the family knew Nana had orchestrated a final appearance. As was customary, she'd done it with her usual flair, clothed in finery crafted by the Creator of all Creation.

"She made it!" Aunt Becky said, her voice evincing both awe and delight.

Later at the wake, the tale of the monarch was oft repeated.

"Who released the butterfly?" Nana's friends asked. And that became the big joke of the evening. It's that kind of thing that carries one through such grief. God bless Nana, she'd given us a sign! Still, in the days and weeks that followed, the finality of her death resonated. There were no more butterflies and no more signs. She had truly left us. We were happy for her. As Aunt Becky had proclaimed, she'd surely entered heaven's realm. But we were also bereft and missed her something awful.

Thus began my final degradation.

CHAPTER TWENTY-TWO

Limbo! How Low Can You Go?

AFTER NANA'S PASSING, THE LOOSELY WOVEN FABRIC OF MY EXISTENCE BEGAN UNRAVELING AGAIN. My lifeguard position at Pepper Park was eliminated. Cutbacks! Municipalities everywhere were finding themselves in the red, needing to tighten their belts. I, the last hire, was the first fired. It was a low blow, for I could no longer pretend that I had a career. I was nothing more than a waitress in a fish house. Then the vilest, most despicable man I have ever encountered came into my life.

James Casey and I had attended different high schools and didn't travel in the same circles. During my teens, I'd occasionally see him and his dad, Warren, at school sporting events. So I knew of them. Now, however, Warren seemed to show up wherever I happened to be. Almost overnight, he became a regular at Sharky's. It seemed only natural for us to forge a casual friendship. Before I knew it, Warren was driving me to and from work. I didn't give it much thought. I was dopey and didn't delve too deeply into the why and wherefore of things. I simply figured Warren was cut from the same mold as Bill—the guy who'd finally thrown me out of his condo in Daytona—that he was happy to dote on an attractive young woman with no questions asked. I never suspected Warren had ulterior motives, never wondered why he was so willing to drop whatever he was doing to taxi me around town. I didn't realize then, as this madman insinuated himself into my life, that he was gradually making me dependent on him in incremental little steps. By the time I wised up to Casey's plan, it was nearly too late to reverse the disastrous course he'd set me on. It was after Nana's passing, when I was dejected and vulnerable, that Warren began upping the ante. And there was a method to his madness; he was beginning to separate me from the herd before swooping in for the kill.

Warren was transporting me from my job at Sharky's to my current abode, a ramshackle apartment on South Beach, when I started whining about the fact that Charlie was threatening to put me out. Warren was a taciturn fellow. I considered him dull but useful. But he was cunning.

"Why doncha move into my place?" he said as though he'd only just thought of it. "Just until you get back on your feet."

That sounded good to me. I needed someone to steer my course, for I was lost without a compass.

"I'll think about it," I said while my soggy brain tried to weigh the pros and cons of such an arrangement.

That very night I got into it with Charlie. He'd had enough of the drug-addled mess I'd become, my slovenly ways and violent temper. When he ordered me to leave, I called Warren, said I'd thought it over and was ready to move in with him. That jackal was there picking me up within the hour.

I'd become a vagabond, wandering wherever my habit took me. As I slipped ever lower, abasing myself and allowing myself to be abased, I told myself it was okay. It was okay that I was passed from man to man, that I used them until they had their fill of me. It was okay that in the process I was forever losing things. I'd get angry, pack up in a snit, and leave clothing, cell phones, toiletries, and shoes behind—usually, only one shoe to a pair, though. Little Miss Un Zapato!

Now, at last, I would have a safe haven, someone to look after me, and I would owe him nothing in return! Warren delivered me to a modest little house west of Vero. It was located on a dirt road framed by deep culverts on either side, not the most desirable of addresses. He'd rented it solely on my behalf, but I wouldn't find that out until much later. There was nothing fine about it: cheap metal blinds at the windows, ratty carpeting. But I had my own bedroom with a mattress on the floor and my own bath, and there was a flat-screen TV in the otherwise empty living room. Warren didn't require any servicing, so I figured I'd gotten the best of the bargain.

Warren Casey was an exceedingly strange man. When I was down and out and needing a friend, he was there. Everything in my world at that time was colored in a rosy drug-induced haze; I wasn't seeing clearly. I thought him kindly and avuncular.

At first, all went smoothly. In the evenings, after I'd worked a shift at Sharky's, Warren would order a pizza and we'd watch a movie or I'd go to my room and "clean" or create my collage masterpieces. Warren supplied me with everything I needed: tabloids, cigarettes, food, pills, whatever. He even gave me a laptop. And that kept me entertained, downloading YouTube videos and researching various branches of the service. I'd become fixated with the idea of enlisting in the military. Apparently, a lot of nutcases suffer from the same obsession. I was going to save the world! Never mind the fact that I was the one who needed saving. Warren's generosity was insidious. When I complained that my job was a drag, that I'd taken heat for dropping trays or spilling drinks, Warren would commiserate. "You don't need that place," he'd say. "Quit. Walk away. You're too good for them."

But then I was fired. And that put an end to that conversation.

"You're a good worker, Meghan," the manager said. "Come see me when you get that monkey off your back."

I narrowed my eyes and smiled humorlessly, hardly able to process the fact that I was being canned from such a lowly establishment. But there you have it: I was. This development fit perfectly with Warren's plan to make me completely dependent upon him. That he was suddenly relieved of the responsibility of driving me to and from Fort Pierce was an added perk. With no job and nothing to occupy my waking hours, I spiraled down to the lowest point of my addiction.

My routine was to fly on Adderall when the sun was out and to float down on Xanax when the shadows lengthened. I told myself that Adderall was a legitimate prescription and the only means by which I could function. In reality, I wasn't functioning at all. Time flew by with nothing to distinguish one day from another. Speeding as I was, I completely lost my appetite and seldom ate. But I made up for it by chain-smoking. Warren had thoughtfully provided a metal bucket beside the molded plastic chair on the front porch, which I proceeded to fill with cigarette butts. Xanax in the evenings brought me down, but not enough that I slept through the night. I'd be up until three or four most mornings, manifesting my wacky obsessive-compulsive behaviors. At some point, I'd simply pass out, only to dream bizarre, drug dreams of fantastical places peopled by humanoids arrayed in bubble clothing or some other such nonsense.

Sometimes, when I regained consciousness after crashing, I'd be plagued with indistinct memories of Warren having assaulted me. My skin crawled at the thought of his hands on me, rearranging my drugged body. Perhaps he'd snapped nude photos of me? I never caught him in the act. I was paranoid, I reassured myself; surely I'd only imagined those incidents.

Warren was a man of many talents. For one thing, he was a computer guru. He'd stolen the identities of several poor sods and lived high on the hog off their credit cards. I thought that was despicable, but I didn't waste any time worrying about it. When he hacked into my AOL account, however, I was furious. Somehow he'd managed to change my password, thus ensuring I wouldn't be communicating with friends or potential suitors. When, after repeatedly trying to open my email, I realized what he'd done, I flew into a rage. Warren tried to mollify me, but Adderall fueled my ire. I went for him, clawing him about the face. He retaliated by doubling up his fist and socking me in the eye, literally knocking me off my feet. I scrabbled away from him, found my cell, and dialed 911.

This was to become a ritual: a blowout that ended with my spending a night in the hospital, followed by a three-day drying-out stint in CEBH, where everybody knew my name.

I wasn't the first girl Warren enslaved, Caylee was. I never met her, but over time, I pieced together enough information from the random references Warren let slip to form a mental picture of her. Like me, she was a petite, blonde addict. She lasted a year, living low, under Warren's roof before their big blowout. He beat her, too. But that proved to be Caylee's get-out-of-jail-free card. While Warren languished in the county jail, cooling his jets in the cooler, Caylee laced up her Keds and ran. She fled to South Carolina, moved in with her mother, and got herself clean. Unlike mine, the charges Caylee brought against Warren stuck.

Despite my dopiness, I sensed Warren was rattled by the prospect of his upcoming day in court. When he suggested we take a road trip to South Carolina, the sole purpose of which was to track down Caylee, I figured he was up to no good. I had no idea what he planned to do with her should he be successful in his quest, but there was a pistol rattling around in his glove box.

I fiddled with the radio dial as we traveled north, finding the local rock stations and singing along with Lady Gaga and Adele. The trip was a bust for Warren. He never did locate Caylee. It didn't matter, though. When Warren went up before the judge, he was sentenced to a fine and a year's probation, little more than a slap on the wrist to that Machiavellian creep.

A few months after I'd moved in with him, Warren produced an application for me to sign.

"What is it?" I asked.

"It's a health insurance policy," he explained. "Your meds are getting too expensive. You need insurance to offset the costs."

I didn't need any encouraging, didn't bother to read the document. All that fine print was beyond me. I believed him and readily scrawled my signature. What a guy! He was ensuring I'd always be flush in pills.

Later, I learned that Warren's wife, Katherine, had passed away in 1998. Forward-thinking man that he was, Warren had taken out a life insurance policy on her. When she died, he came into a tidy sum.

Now that I'm sober, I have my doubts about that document being a health insurance policy. I'm willing to bet it was a life insurance policy. At the rate I was going, Warren wouldn't have long to wait before cashing in.

During my year of corruption with Warren, I attempted to make a break on a number of occasions, but I always ended up slinking back to him. After another argument that landed me in the ER followed by a stint in the CEBH, I veered from our set pattern. When I was released, I deliberated. I could phone Mom. She'd take me in, nag me to distraction, and fight to keep me clean. Or I could call Warren and continue my decline. As long as he could control me, he'd supply me with the drugs my body craved.

I called Mom. At 95 pounds, I came to her malnourished and gaunt. My withdrawal had nearly done me in. When we arrived home, I immediately took to my bed.

"I'm sick," I mumbled, and Mom left me alone. My heart was coming out of my chest, my hands and feet swollen up like balloons. I tried to sleep it off, but my pillow was slick with sweat and every muscle in my body ached. It felt as though I had the flu times ten. I stayed in bed for two days, leaving it only to empty my bladder. Mom kept a tumbler of water by my bedside, for I was alarmingly dehydrated. On the third day, I lurched into the kitchen with the unsteady gait of a toddler. Mom immediately placed a tall glass of orange juice before me, her panacea for the world's ills, and I slugged it down. However precariously, I was back in the land of the living.

So long deprived of sensory input, I was as fragile as a blown egg. The world was a jarring and unfamiliar place, and that hole in my heart was demanding to be filled. Mom did her best to fill it. She dragged me to weekend mass at St. Sebastian, and I became the darling of her church friends. They congratulated me on my re-entry into sobriety. But although I wanted it badly, I wanted my pills more.

Weekdays, I accompanied Mom to her shop, whiling away the hours answering the phone and playing on the computer. At noon, Mom would drop me at an AA meeting, and I'd tell my story, actually thinking I might stay clean this time. But I was so raw I felt like an alien on a toxic planet. And I wasn't working the program because I didn't really buy into the 12-steps. Naturally, it didn't take.

Warren had taken to loitering around Mom's shop in hopes of catching me on a cigarette break and luring me with pills. I resisted for a while, but it wasn't long before I gave into temptation and was using. Just a few pills, once again trying to manage my addiction. I could tell Mom suspected, but she put up with my dopiness until my nightly "cleaning" bouts put her over the edge. One evening, she returned home after a rare night out only to find me "cleaning" her closet. I'd dragged out nearly all of her clothing, her handbags, and her shoes and had heaped them all in a tangle on the bed. She lost it, went berserk, screamed that I was driving her insane. I suppose I was.

I called Warren. Within the hour, he picked me up and drove me to my new abode.

In my absence, Warren had abandoned the house west of Vero only to take up residence in a warehouse, a low-slung, cement-block building in an industrial park. He'd reverted to type, living like vermin in a slum. That was to be my new home, a rattrap with no kitchen and no hot water.

I'd fallen to a new low.

I don't remember much of that hellish, dark period; I was between worlds, alternately wired or heavily sedated. Still, the next time Warren laid hands on me, I somehow thought to contact an old acquaintance and pleaded with him to take me in.

The Anaconda

LUCKY TIMES IS WHAT I CALLED HIM. AND THE TWO OF US WENT AS FAR BACK AS THOSE EARLY DAYS WHEN I WAITED TABLES AT MONTE'S. Like Warren, L.T. was twice my age and a predator of sorts. Lucky for me, the man suffered from a savior complex. He was forever taking in strays, and I was the alley cat whose nine lives had just about run out. L.T. agreed to let me stay with him, but not without a stipulation: I had to stay clean. I agreed. At this point, I would have agreed to anything; I didn't have a lot of options.

True to his word, L.T. put me up in his home office, which was hunky-dory except for the fact that there was no door to afford me privacy. I carped mightily over that indignity, but I realize now he was just trying to keep an eye on me, to make sure I wasn't using or stashing pills. Mom ignored my complaints. She thought the arrangement with L.T. was perfect. So long as she didn't have to put up with my "cleaning."

During those first weeks with L.T., I tried to honor our bargain and cut back on my pill consumption. But it wasn't long before Warren got to me, and I was worse off than I'd ever been. As the Bible says, each time I fell, seven more demons entered in, and my behavior became ever more erratic and destructive. Eventually, even L.T. had enough of my insanity and showed me the door.

When flush with scripts, I usually had the presence of mind to stash a few pills away for a rainy day—beneath the lining of a handbag, in the toe of a sock, under my mattress. I had lots of hiding places. Trouble is, when one is high, one tends to forget where one has secreted things. Oftentimes, my "cleaning" bouts were merely a frantic search for my hidden stash. I'd been doing that very thing when Mom sent me packing.

I'd inveigled myself back into her good graces and was staying at her place for the umpteenth time when, after ransacking my bedroom and bath with nothing to show for it, I realized desperate measures were called for. If I didn't score quickly, I'd start to detox. And I couldn't stomach the thought of the cold sweats and vomiting, the excruciating headaches and the shakes. So I went in search of Mom's jewelry. Although I'd forgotten mine, I knew all of her hiding places. In no time, I'd scored. I called a friend, told her I needed to hitch a ride, and sweetened the deal by offering to share pills.

Mom had some nice pieces, gold and diamond baubles that Dad had given her back in the glory days. The lot of it was probably worth $20,000 or more. I only pawned about a third of it, netting me all of $500.

One of Mom's friends called her to say she'd seen me at the Treasure Coast Pawn Shop, told her I didn't look well, that I was pawning jewelry. She'd just happened to be there to retrieve the jewelry her own daughter, a former St. Ed's schoolmate of mine, had stolen. What a world!

I came waltzing home as high as a kite. Mom stopped me at the front door with a face that could smite dragons.

"Where are my things?" she asked.

"I—" My woozy brain refused to produce a plausible explanation. I made as if to enter, but Mom barred the way.

"Where is my jewelry?"

"Uh—"

"I know you pawned some of it, but there's more. Where's the rest of it?"

"I've got it," I said, eager to please. "Sorry. It's right here."

I opened my purse and withdrew a small box containing Mom's treasures. "I only pawned a few things—"

"Which cost me $2,000, Meghan. Two thousand dollars that I don't have!" Mom snatched the box away from me and immediately began sifting through the contents. I honestly didn't understand why she was so upset. What was the big deal? Jeez!

"Get your things," Mom said. "I can't trust you. Go!"

I left. I called L.T., but he said he couldn't have me in his house, that his neighbors had started complaining about my antics—screaming tirades, policemen beating on doors. Some vestigial shred of dignity prevented me from crawling back to Warren. Suddenly, I was faced with the fact that L.T. and Mom had given up on me, and I had no more fallbacks. I'd finally arrived where I'd always known I'd end up: back on the streets.

I had the good sense to get myself to the Newport Club, where AA meetings occurred until midnight. I hung there, catching no less than three meetings, until closing time. When the place was being locked up and it became apparent I had nowhere to go, Jon, one of the regulars, took pity on me and offered me a bed for the night. I was grateful for a place to crash. In the morning over coffee, Jon suggested that I apply for a position at a discount chain hotel on South US Hwy 1. He knew the manager there, said he was constantly in need of housekeeping staff.

I was hired, and the best part of the bargain was that, in lieu of wages, I was offered a room. I moved into the hotel, where I cleaned toilets, changed soiled sheets, and eked by. It didn't take long for Warren to find me, but I was slowly coming around. I took the pills he brought me, but not three or five at a pop. More like two or three a day, just enough so that I could function and perform my assigned tasks without beginning to detox.

At long last, I was forced to take a cold, hard look at the trajectory I was on. It was a dead end, "dead" being the operative word. I was twenty-six. I had no career, no home, no car, no driver's license, and no significant other. Over the past eight years, I'd slipped lower and lower until I'd finally reached my nadir. No one but that madman Casey wanted me. And even he didn't want me; all he wanted was to cash in on the insurance policy he'd taken out on me. I was utterly alone and without hope.

"Dear God," I prayed in desperation, "help me. *Save me!*"

And God answered my prayer. But He didn't shout; He whispered in my ear, "Call your mother."

It took a few days for me to heed His advice.

"Mom," I wailed, "I can't live like this. Please—"

Mom interrupted my litany of complaints. "You need to call Restoration House Ministries."

"What?"

"It's in Fort Pierce. They have a bed, and they'll take you if you're ready."

"Oh, Mom, we tried rehab programs—CORE, the Haven . . . They didn't work."

"You didn't work the program. Goodnight, Meghan."

This conversation was probably repeated a half-dozen times before I realized the only way out of the hell I was living in was to call the number Mom had provided.

The voice that answered my SOS was low and pleasant. "Restoration House, Olivia speaking."

Thoughts of my sweet girlfriend who had so tragically lost her life immediately came to mind. But this was another Olivia—a shrewd, savvy soul who'd seen or heard nearly every depravity known to man. She knew of me, my history and present circumstances, for Mom had paved the way. And she was wary. But what she said was, "Are you on probation?"

"Yes," I said.

"Well, you're going to have to take care of that."

"And how do I do that?" I said, thinking that here lies the roadblock.

"Write a letter to the judge and tell him you need to be released to our care."

I would soon learn that the directors of the Restoration House Ministry prayed over each and every potential candidate, ultimately relying on God to make the final decision. I have no idea how I came to be accepted into the fold. Perhaps I was ready and they were somehow privy to that fact. Perhaps my mother was ready, at her wit's end. In any case, miraculous as it seems, I was whisked into the program.

"Be here on the thirty-first," I was told, which was two days away. Halloween—how appropriate!

I phoned Mom with the news.

"Restoration House wants me there at nine o'clock on Monday," I explained. "Can I stay with you over the weekend, get my things together?"

Reluctantly, she agreed.

"Oh, and we need to write Judge Wilde, ask him to dismiss my probation."

"Good heavens," Mom grumbled. But she wrote a compelling letter explaining how I'd been accepted into a long-term substance abuse treatment program and hand-delivered it to the courthouse. Judge Joe Wilde came through for me, releasing me from all terms of my probation. I'd been freed from the legal system's clutches! But I was not free. I was about to embark upon a journey that would require me to muzzle my willfulness and commit to working a very restrictive program.

I was ready to take this step, to commit to a year or more of in-house treatment. Mom hauled out suitcases and I packed. And I packed . . .

"Meghan, you needn't take every article of clothing you own." Mom clucked in annoyance. "Certainly not all your designer bags and sunglasses. Where you're going isn't the Ritz, you know."

But I was in the packing zone, on an Adderall high, and undeterred. "Meghan, they're not going to like you," Mom said. "They'll think you're a spoiled brat if you flounce through that door with Gucci and Versace in tow. Worse yet, they'll think I have money."

"Oh, Mom! What does that have to do with it?"

"They'll expect me to fork over big bucks that I don't have."

"It's always about the money, Mom!"

"It is when you don't have it, sweetheart."

Ready or not, I dawdled the next morning. Could I really go through with this? I wondered.

"Come on, Meghan. Get a wiggle on. We're going to be late," Mom ragged. She was whirling around like a dervish, fastening luggage snaps, schlepping suitcases to the car. Somehow, without my assistance, she managed to get us on the road by eight thirty.

"I need a cigarette." I stared out the passenger window sullenly.

"Meghan, I'm sure they're not going to let you smoke," Mom said, keeping her eyes on the road.

"Come on!" I coaxed. "I'm about to give up everything. Heck, even a condemned man gets a final smoke."

"Oh, brother!" Mom was irritated, but I didn't care. I was dying for a Marlboro and desperate for anything that might delay this pilgrimage to purgatory.

We stopped at the Walgreen's on Oslo Road. Ironically, it was less than a mile from where this sorry saga had begun all those years ago when I'd nearly died of alcohol poisoning. Mom peeled a ten from her wallet and thrust it toward me.

"Could you buy them?" I asked. "I don't have any ID."

"Good grief!"

Mom tromped out of the store and tossed the pack of cigarettes in my direction.

"I don't have a lighter," I said, palming the goods.

"What? I'm not buying you a lighter, for heaven's sake! You must own twenty of them. Didn't you think to bring one?"

An elderly fellow seated on a bench in front of the pharmacy caught my eye. He nodded to me, and I returned the greeting.

"I know that guy," I said. And before Mom knew what was happening, I was levering open the door and hiking in his direction.

"Hi! You know Bill, don't you?" I said. "Bill" being the semi-secret code word to AA kinship. I was certain I'd seen this fellow at meetings.

"Sure do, sugar," the man drawled. "Why do you ask?"

"Newport Club, right?"

"That's right, sweet." He extended a hand. "Name's Ed. Ed Lansaw."

"Hiya, Ed!" I exclaimed, thinking we seldom put names to faces at AA meetings as we all were supposed to be *anonymous*. "Can I bother you for a light?"

"Sure thing." Ed withdrew a lighter from his pants pocket and held it before me.

"Thanks," I said, inhaling deeply, trying to wrap my head around the circumstances that had led me to this pass.

"You're more than welcome." Ed lit up as well, took a drag, and sighed contentedly.

"I'm celebrating my eighth year," he announced.

"Wow! No kidding. Eight years sober?"

"No kidding. Life is good."

"Yeah? I'm on my way to Restoration House," I blurted. "Probably be there for a year or more."

"That's wonderful!" Ed blew a smoke ring, and we both watched it dissipate before he turned to me.

"Go for it," he said. "You're such an attractive girl. You just need to get your head screwed on right."

I laughed at his choice of words, and I could tell that Ed instantly regretted them. "No disrespect intended, darlin'. All of us, on occasion, take a wrong turn that ends us up in La-La Land. Time you found the right path, I think."

Just then, Mom sidled up and insinuated her presence. "That's really nice of you, Ed. Congratulations on your eight years. Wish us the best, won't you?"

"I do, ma'am. I surely do."

In the car I gushed about having run into Ed. "Can you believe it?" I asked. "It's like a sign or something."

"I'm sure it is a sign." Mom glanced in the rearview mirror before pulling out of the parking lot. She had a mission, and she was eager to see it through.

It was an overcast morning, and the sky commenced to weep a steady drizzle. I concentrated on my jewelry, sorting it, one of my OCD behaviors that I often exhibited when high. Mom drove determinedly to Restoration House, eager to turn me over to someone, anyone, who might better deal with my addiction and the weirdness it begot. When we arrived at the institutional-looking structure, I was engrossed in my sorting.

"Here we are," Mom said, flinging her door open. She went to the trunk and, unmindful of the rain, began muscling out my suitcases and lugging them to the front porch. When she'd deposited my belongings on the stoop, Mom rang the bell. "Come on, Meghan," she urged impatiently while waiting for someone to answer her summons. "It's after nine."

Reluctantly, I stepped from the car and went to join her. Minutes ticked by. Finally, the door opened, and a striking black woman waved us in.

CHAPTER TWENTY-FOUR

Can-Can

FROM THE MOMENT I ENTERED THAT HUMBLE ABODE, MY LIFE BEGAN TO CHANGE. NOT SLOWLY EITHER, BUT WITH LIGHTNING-FAST SPEED. I was embraced. And let me tell you, if you've never been hugged by a passel of well-intentioned black women, you have never been hugged. They really mean it when they put the love moves on you! I immediately melted, instinctively knowing that I'd come to the right place. It was plain to see these women were troopers, enlisted in God's army to save souls, one sorry sinner at a time. I was the sorriest of the lot and ready for them to have at me.

Introductions were made, but the only faces I put to names were those of Miss Frances and Miss Olivia. That is until an elderly black lady stepped forward and whispered in my ear, "I'm Miss Mareya, dear," she said. "And you can have a cigarette if you want to."

Miss Mareya was tiny and fashionably dressed, and I was instantly reminded of my Nana.

"No," I said, digging through my handbag. "I'll just have to give them up in the long run. Here, you take them."

Mareya snatched up my Marlboros in her arthritic fingers and from that moment on was my staunch supporter. Not so the big cheese, Miss Frances, who glared at me suspiciously. Frances had an aura of authority about her, and it was apparent little escaped her penetrating gaze. Who could blame her? I'd entered Restoration House giving off vibes like some arrogant fashionista, this despite the fact that I was shaking in my Jimmy Choo boots. And I mean that literally, for I started detoxing right there on the spot.

"I don't feel so well," I mumbled, suddenly clammy.

"Miss Charlene," Frances said, "show Miss Meghan to the bathroom, then escort her to her room."

A pretty strawberry blonde in her early thirties darted toward me and took my arm.

"You girls stop your gawking and haul Meghan's stuff back to the classrooms," Miss Frances ordered. "Miss Mareya and I will have to sort through the lot of it."

Miss Frances rolled her eyes at the thought of the distasteful task before her. "Make sure there's no contraband," she added theatrically.

"Come on, hon," Charlene said as she steered me toward a corridor on the far side of the reception office. "The bathroom's right down here."

The other girls shuffled forward and began shouldering my bags as Charlene and I rounded the corner. "You gonna be sick?" Charlene pushed open the door to a very dated communal bath that had probably never been appealing. Now, fifty years after its installation, it was dismal at best. I didn't care. It was clean and I'd seen worse.

"Yup," I burped, falling to my knees before the toilet.

"I was sick when I came here, too," Charlene admitted as I retched into the ancient commode. She held my hair away from my face, seemingly unperturbed by my sudden onslaught. "It was nasty. Why do we put ourselves through such misery?" It was a rhetorical question; she didn't expect an answer, which was good because I was in no condition to give one.

"Ugh . . ." I gurgled while at the same time pegging Charlene. She was an airhead and a chatterbox but sweet as fresh-picked Iowa corn. I figured once I recovered we'd be fast friends.

Later, when I was alternately sweating feverishly and quaking with chills, Charlene came to my bedside with a large tumbler of orange juice. The cloying smell of the sweet citrus turned my stomach, but Charlene's gesture reminded me of Mom and I was comforted.

"Thanks, Charlene." I took a tiny sip. "Um, that's good."

"You'll be better soon," Charlene said. But neither of us believed that. In fact, it wasn't long before I went to hell again, heard those tortured voices screaming in agony and felt the excruciating pain of fire consuming my body. Difference is, this time I knew I'd be delivered.

On November fourth, three days after I entered Restoration House, I wobbled unsteadily from my bedroom to the bath. It was early and there was no one about. I showered and washed my hair, helping myself to someone's shampoo and cream rinse, figuring she wouldn't mind, whoever she was. I was just stepping out of the shower when Charlene entered.

"Well, hello," she said with a laugh. "Look at you. You're human!"

"Muh, muh, eeek!" I mimed, doing my best ape impersonation.

Charlene cut up. She got me right away. "Oh, gawd!" she hooted. "You're so full of it! We've been waiting for you." I didn't know what she meant by that, but somehow I found her words reassuring. Suddenly, as I stood there in front of the mirror, trying to countenance the reflection that stared out at me, I realized I wanted to be accepted here, to be part of something . . . something good, to grab hold of my life once again and get back on track. Miraculously, I felt a little warm spot in that hole in my heart. A good vibe was oozing into it, slowly beginning to fill up the achingly empty space.

In the next instant, beautiful Reba glided into the bath. She froze upon catching sight of me, pointedly giving me the once-over. Her eyes lingered on my breasts and tiny waist. I didn't mind. I remembered her from the throng of girls who'd gawked at me when I first entered RH. Statuesque, with softly curling light-brown hair, she was a real looker. Girls like her appreciate a little competition. "Hey there," she drawled, her accent only adding to her charm. "How's the baby girl?"

"She's fine, Reba!" Charlene hovered over me protectively. "She just needs to get cleaned up, that's all."

"Well, I see she's already done that, and with my shampoo and conditioner, no less!" Reba arched a brow and gazed at me balefully.

"Sorry," I shrugged. "I haven't a clue where my things are. Hope you don't mind—"

"Nah! Ah'm just teasing," Reba admitted.

"Stop already!" Charlene draped an arm about my shoulder. "For goodness sake, let the poor thing get her bearings."

Reba grinned at me, and there was only the faintest hint of malice in her smile. I took to her instantly. Like me, she was cocky and full of herself—perhaps not the best traits, but great coping mechanisms for former addicts.

"Hi, y'all!" A skinny black-haired girl with a guileless face bounced into the room. "Hey, Meghan. How you feelin'?" she asked.

"Okay," I said, despite being dehydrated, hollow, and weak as a baby.

"Well, you look good, girl! Way better than I did when my sorry Tennessee Walker's ass started cleanin' up. Ah'm Miss Maridee. Maridee Teeter. And ah'm real pleased to meetcha, sweetie." Maridee extended an arm and I shook her callused hand. She reminded me of Popeye's Olive Oyl, gangly and awkward, but pretty nonetheless.

"Goodness, what time is it?" Miss Charlene asked, a note of panic in her voice. "We don't dare be late for breakfast."

"Chill, Miss Char," Reba said. "We've got five whole minutes before Frances-stein breaks down the doors." Charlene and Maridee chuckled as they ducked into shower stalls.

"So, whatcha in for?" Reba asked.

"Murder," I confessed. "I killed myself. They gave me a year to eighteen months."

"Yeah, me too. It's pretty much the same MO around here. Damn, I'm dying for a cigarette!"

"I just handed off nearly an entire pack to the cute old broad," I said.

"That's Miss Mareya," Reba offered. "She's a character, never sleeps, roams the halls like a phantom . . ."

"I wish she'd roam back in here with my Marlboros. I'd kill all over again for just one ciggy."

I didn't know then that the four of us were to become like sisters, an unspoken pact having been forged between us. Reba, Charlene, Maridee, and I became the Missketeers. And we would learn that there truly was strength in numbers; our bond not only helped us resist the temptation to use again, it also prevented us from releasing the monsters that had taken up lodging inside our comely young bodies. The fact that we were no longer alone in our battles— battles against our addictions, our poor self-images, and our overwhelming feelings of hopelessness— proved to be a blessing that only compounded over time.

I had been at the program exactly one week, and I was quickly adapting to the prescribed regimen of life in RH. On this particular morning, we girls were in the classroom, immersed in our parenting skills class when Miss Frances's shrieks sullied the air. Most of the girls at RH had children they'd been separated from due to jail time and now rehab. I had no babies of my own, but I thought the information being dispensed might someday prove valuable, so I'd been paying attention. But at the sound of this commotion all thoughts of nurturing vanished. I glanced around at the other girls seated before their utilitarian desks and realized that they, too, were focused on the ruckus emanating from the reception area.

Our instructor, Miss Anne, voluptuous, tall, and herself a recovering addict, appeared similarly distracted.

"She hep up ova sumpum. Mmm-mmm," she muttered. "Why she carrying on like that? Any y'all know why her knickers in a snit, you'd best tell me."

My eyes went first to Charlene, then to Maridee. I could see by their expressions they were in the dark. But when I looked toward Reba and saw her face go white, I figured she was behind the current uproar.

"What's up, Reba?" I whispered.

"I may know what she's upset about," Reba admitted.

"Yeah?" Miss Anne's brows knit up on her wide face, and she skewered Reba with a piercing glance. "And what might that be?"

"Uh . . ."

"Girls!" Miss Frances screeched. "Get out here now!"

Stricken, the girls and I rose from our desks and charged toward the door. Miss Anne beat us to it and, with her considerable bulk, barred the way. The girls and I looked to one another, confused. Suddenly, we were at an impasse. Was this a power play? I wondered.

Finally, Miss Anne allowed us to filter out, single-file, through the doorway, but not before she'd given each of us the evil eye. Rumor had it that Anne, having emigrated from the Bahamas, was a former voodoo priestess. Whether or not that was true, she was one formidable broad and not to be crossed.

We all reassembled in front of Miss Frances's desk, shoulders hunched and bug-eyed. Fully incensed, Miss Frances was nearly foaming at the mouth. In her hands was a plastic bottle filled with a yellow liquid.

Everyone is flawed, and the residents and staff of Restoration House were at the top of the heap. Former addicts not only exhibit quirky behaviors, they are often either gullible and easily deceived or overly suspicious and untrusting. Miss Frances would be counted among the latter. Still, when she'd discovered the bottle of ammonia stashed over the acoustic ceiling tiles in the girls' dorm, she'd foolishly taken it at face value. Somehow, a bottle of ammonia had found its way there, of all places. But when she'd begun to clean with it, wiping down her Formica-veneered reception desk and sanitizing the waste receptacles, she'd detected the unmistakable odor of urine.

She flung the offending plastic bottle toward Reba, just as though she were tossing a soiled diaper into the trash. Instinctively, Reba reached for it, palming the bottle effortlessly.

"Miss Reba! What in sweet Jesus's name is this?"

"I . . . I . . ." Beads of perspiration popped out on Reba's face, and she cast her eyes about, loathe to meet Mrs. Frances's glare. I'd never seen the haughty, impassive Reba so discomfited, couldn't imagine what it was she'd done that had caused such a ruckus.

"When was your last pee test?" Miss Frances asked.

"Uh . . . Last Wednesday, I guess." Reba's voice quivered.

Maridee and Charlene shot me quizzical glances and I shrugged. We had no idea what this was about, but it was a deviation from the crushing boredom we normally faced, drug-free and empty, and we found ourselves shamelessly enrapt. The only thing that kept us sane in the RH confines was the daily drama dished up in that sanctuary for recovering addicts. It far superseded that of any soap. *Days of Our Lives* could eat its heart out.

"Uh-huh. And you peed clean, right?"

"Yes, ma'am."

"You always do, don't you?"

Reba merely nodded.

"So why you hide this bottle of piss up in the ceiling tiles right next to your Virginia Slims?"

Charlene recoiled and Maridee gasped audibly, her eyes as big as saucers in her thin face. My shock quickly turned to glee. It was all I could do to keep from laughing. I clamped a hand over my mouth and feigned a look of horror, but my shoulders were shaking from the effort of suppressing my glee. This was simply too rich: the cool and unflappable Reba had committed an offense of such magnitude she was quaking in her boots and stuck like a bug on flypaper. I took a perverse delight in watching her squirm. A memory popped into my head: a middle school science teacher explaining the concept of the survival of the fittest, that when a predator cut an animal from a herd those spared felt only relief. That's how I felt. It was Reba who was in trouble, not me. I silently thanked my lucky stars for that bit of good news.

"And when did you have your last cigarette?"

"I . . ." Reba looked as though she wanted nothing more than for the floor to open up beneath her, a gigantic Florida sinkhole to appear and swallow her up.

"The truth!"

"Last night after church," Reba said. "I sneaked one when you let me run back to retrieve my Bible."

"Been smoking all along, haven't you?"

"No, ma'am, just every once in a while. But heck, we all know Miss Abigail—"

"Miss Abigail has nothing to do with it!" Miss Frances roared, nodding toward the plastic bottle in Reba's hand. "Do you know your urine is all over this desk? And the floor? And God knows where else? It's disgusting!"

"I'm sorry—"

"Sorry!" Miss Frances was fully incensed. Tall, with piercing eyes, Frances is a formidable woman to begin with. One instinctively knows not to push her, for it's obvious she's not the backing-down type and, like me, afraid of nothing. Just now she looked as though she could take on Hannibal Lector and emerge victorious. Suddenly becoming cognizant of the other girls and me, standing there agog, Miss Frances took a deep breath and collected herself. After a moment, she spoke in her naturally commanding voice.

"Miss Anne, you and the girls go to the kitchen and start preparing supper. I'll deal with Miss Reba."

Like a mother hen, Miss Anne clucked as she shooed us out of the office and down the hall. Once in the commons, we girls all started chattering.

"Gawd have mercy, that gal be in big doo-doo!" Maridee exclaimed.

"You can say that again," Charlene agreed. "Wouldn't wanna be in Reba's size eights tonight."

"Will Miss Frances throw her out?" I asked Miss Anne, hoping her answer would be no. Of all the girls, Reba was the most like me. I'd dared to think we might be roommates after graduating the program.

Miss Anne considered for a moment before replying. "I don't believe so, honey. Reba's got nearly eight months under her belt. It'd be too big an investment for us to give up on her. Least that's what I think."

"Well, I should say!" Maridee agreed. "Goodness, we're all sinners. I bet the crucified Lord Himself would cut her a break."

"Maridee, you're a nut," Charlene snorted. We all dissolved in hopeless giggles. It was the pent-up emotion, our not having been singled out like Reba, and the strangeness of our situation—all of which conspired against us until we simply couldn't process anymore. There was nothing for it but laughter and comic relief. Even Miss Anne joined in, seeming to have forgotten her position of authority. When we were all convulsed in chuckles, hooting and hollering to beat the band, Miss Frances strutted in and the room temperature plummeted.

"Charlene, chop up some red pepper, onion, and celery," Miss Anne said, erasing the smile from her face. "Maridee, get out the big pot and put it on to boil. And Meghan . . ." I raised my eyebrows, eager to fulfill my assigned task, but Miss Anne faltered. By now they'd all realized I was a lousy cook, could barely toast bread without burning it.

"You set the table," Miss Anne finally said. I scurried to the china cabinet to do just that, grateful for not having been asked to filet a mangrove snapper or attempt some other cooking skill that I was thoroughly incapable of performing.

Still shaky from having just detoxed and jazzed, given the recent excitement, it's little wonder my hand-eye coordination was a bit out of whack. I palmed a handful of china plates, whirled away from the breakfront, and the next thing I knew, the whole stack was slipping through my fingers. There was an enormous crash as shards of glass flew about the room.

"Shit!" I exclaimed, stunned by my own frailty and the destruction it had wrought. "Shit! Gosh darn it! Shit and double damn!"

Don't you know, time slowed down? This happens every so often, generally when one is only wishing that it would speed up instead or, best case scenario, catapult one to another universe. But that wasn't to be my lot. Not only had I managed to destroy sacrosanct Restoration House property and add my own drama to the already supercharged atmosphere, my cussing completely changed the dynamic.

Reba's transgression was forgotten; Miss Frances and Miss Anne turned and stared gape-jawed at me. And Maridee and Charlene were no help whatsoever, suddenly appearing as inanimate as wax figures in Madame Tussoud's.

"What?" I wailed, taking in their stunned expressions. "I'll pay for them. Jesus! It's not the end of the world." It took a minute for time to speed up again, and when it did I started collecting pulverized bits of china.

"Damn it!" I exclaimed when a fingertip spouted blood. "Charlene, could you please give me a hand? Fetch a Band-Aid, maybe a broom and a dustpan?" Next thing I knew I was eyeballing Miss Frances's practical brown oxfords. Flummoxed, I looked up and took in her stony countenance. What now? I wondered.

"Miss Meghan," Miss Frances said, somehow managing to draw my name out into three syllables. "You have a dirty mouth!"

"Okaaay," I said.

"You must refrain from such coarse language within these walls."

"Yes, ma'am," I agreed, trying to fathom the degree of my transgression. I'd cussed. So what?

"Leave that mess and go to your room. There will be no dinner for you tonight."

Shit, I thought. Thankfully, I refrained from giving voice to that expletive. Instead, I rose to my feet, glanced sheepishly at Charlene and Maridee before turning on my heel and hiking toward my cubicle. Truth be told, I was relieved to have been excused; I was exhausted and I'd had my fill of theatrics for the day. Bad news is, my stomach was growling. But I was able to scuttle into Reba's room unnoticed and shoot the breeze with her for a while.

"How you doing?" I asked her, keeping a watchful eye on the hallway.

"Fine," Reba replied. "What's all the commotion?"

"You'll be happy to know that I've taken the onus off of you and transferred it to myself," I said. "I am the new, bad, potty-mouthed girl, and now Miss Frances has a fresh recruit to torment. You can thank me anytime."

Reba perked up right away, and I figured the two of us would have more adventures soon enough.

I wasn't wrong.

CHAPTER TWENTY-FIVE

Watusi

MY PREDICTION PROVED CORRECT: REBA'S TRANSGRESSIONS SUDDENLY SEEMED INSIGNIFICANT. Miss Frances, Miss Olivia, and Miss Mareya now had another challenge to address: me. I guess things do happen for a reason. I figured the reason I was in the hot seat was to take the heat off of Reba. Maybe if I hadn't cussed a blue streak she would have been dismissed from the program. Instead, she was allowed to stay, but not before all of her privileges were taken away. She was not allowed outside to exercise, which, as it turns out, didn't bother her a whit. Unlike me, Reba was not an exercise freak. She was not allowed off campus except for church, where she was constantly under surveillance. There would be no opportunities for her to slip out and sneak a smoke. And she had to write innumerable papers on Biblical passages. It goes without saying, she had to scrub down Miss Frances's desk, the floors, the waste receptacles, and any other surface that might have come in contact with her bodily fluids. Worst of all, we girls were to distance ourselves from her—a punishment that, in my estimation, seemed overly severe. We were, in effect, to shun her.

As for me, having only just embarked on the drug-free diet, I was dope sick. Everything was a bit off kilter as I tentatively began the process of settling in. I was learning the ropes at Restoration House, becoming familiar with the key players, and it seemed totally unnatural for me to suddenly be shunning one of our own. I didn't take a shine to it, and neither did Charlene or Maridee. In the ensuing days, whenever one of the staff was present, we three studiously avoided Reba. But when the coast was clear, we interacted with her every chance we got, slipping her notes or choice morsels of food in an effort to keep up her spirits and let her know we were in solidarity with her. What we didn't know is that the staff expected us to do just that; our every move was being monitored. They had never intended for us to abandon Reba. Rather, we were expected to support her and help her through her trial. Which is exactly what we did.

I truly believe that the men and women who operate Restoration House, those who instruct the girls and boys and administer their programs, are God's own angels. They are masters at their ministry, transforming shaggy-assed drug addicts into contributing members of society. There is a prescribed pattern that they follow in this endeavor, one that yields a better-than-average success rate. None of us working the program were aware of that; we just thought the staff was overly tough on us. It wouldn't be until much later that we'd come to appreciate their tactics. They knew just how to uncover our weaknesses, how to break us down and force us to face our faults, and then rocket us back up again so that one day we might not only be drug-free, but also the beautiful, productive creatures the Lord intended.

How were we to know that Reba's current travail was merely an opportunity for personal growth? We thought she was being singled out and treated unfairly, which is what prompted our secret interventions. And that only cemented our bond. Although it remained unspoken between us, we were in this together. We'd bicker among ourselves plenty, just as siblings do. In the face of adversity, we'd stick by each other while navigating this strange new landscape of drug-free living.

Looking back, I marvel at the fact that from the minute I entered Restoration House I was able to give up drugs, cigarettes and alcohol. I could feel it immediately, a seductive vibe, and I was suddenly eager to get on with the program and reclaim my life. I must admit, there was something pleasurable about surrendering, giving it all up to God and those remarkable women. So I did just that, and straightway that hole in my heart began to fill up with all kinds of amazing stuff—things like *hope* and *joy* and *gratitude*. Talk about miracles!

It wasn't long before I settled into a routine. At six o'clock in the morning, we shot out of our beds like rockets, immediately setting about to erase any telltale signs that might indicate we'd formerly been sleeping therein. One was to be not only clean, but fastidiously tidy, at RH. It's little wonder that so many of the graduates gravitated toward service in the armed forces, as the regimen and routine of the military proved enticing for all their familiarity. Once our beds were made, we assembled in the communal bath for showers and grooming. Preparation for the day ahead, however, did not include applying makeup. At first I found this perturbing, but in time I grew to appreciate how freeing it was not to have to make myself up into a glamorous, faux starlet. The world was to see me as God made me. But I soon learned this restriction was often ignored. When one was to make a *testimony* before potential donors, nail polish, hair coifs and face paint were not only allowed, they were encouraged. Since RH was funded by grants supplemented by charitable donations, we would often be asked to talk to rich folk and guilt them into giving more money. If the end result might possibly influence the outcome of our potential pitch, we could present as Kim Kardashian. But in those early days, it was not unusual for me to do a double take when I spotted my image reflected in a mirror and wonder who that plain young woman was.

And I packed on the pounds. Forget the freshman fifteen. Overnight, I ballooned from a quavering 110 pounds of Adderall-fed frenzy to 140 pounds of laid-back happiness. The food was so good and so plentiful. Not only did the local grocery chains drop off bags of canned goods and perishable items, all slightly past their sell-by date, but the restaurants in the surrounding area did so as well. There was never a question of going hungry. Food—and I mean wholesome and well-prepared food—was always available. The only problem was deciding what the daily menu would be. There were so many choices.

I'd given up all of my addictions, and I thought, "Why not? Eat!" And so, it appeared, did everyone else except for Miss Mareya, who dined off the premises and was tiny, like my Nana had been, and Maridee, whom we all suspected had a tapeworm running the length of her scrawny body, gobbling up all she consumed. It's no wonder more than a few of us grew to be pleasingly plump.

Miss Anne was a fabulous cook. She excelled at island favorites such as fried plantains and black beans with rice. And her conch fritters, featuring big chunks of conch with little else in between, were the best I've ever tasted.

Charlene did Paula Deen proud. Southern fried chicken, chicken-fried steak, anything one might dip in egg wash, dredge in flour, and immerse in oil—that was her forte. Skinny Maridee was a pastry chef wannabe; her biscuits, key lime pie, and red velvet cake were culinary masterpieces. And Reba was a wizard with eggs. She'd combine all the fresh produce the local supermarkets had dropped off—fragrant Italian parsley, grass-like chives, plump plum tomatoes, and savory green onions—with whatever protein she could scrounge up—a thick slice of ham, maple-cured bacon, the odd morsel of smoked salmon—and the results were unvaryingly spectacular. Reba's ham and cheese omelet with mushrooms was one of my all-time favorites.

Weekdays at RH were spent in the classroom and, for the most part, were brain-numbingly boring. Weeknights oftentimes found us in church or practicing with the youth or adult choirs. Sundays were devoted to worship services and fellowship. The only day of the week we were cut a little slack was Saturday, and we looked forward to that reprieve with as much longing as any school kid.

On Saturdays, we were allowed to sleep until seven and dawdle over our breakfasts. Afterward, Miss Frances might suggest an activity such as bowling or sunbathing on the beach or mall walking. Every suggestion that involved fraternizing with the boys who were housed in a separate wing was met with our approval. It was always fun mixing it up with our male counterparts, for outside of church services, we seldom had the opportunity to do so. Even though most of us had sold our bodies in exchange for drugs, we were woefully naïve when it came to interacting with the opposite sex. Now that we were clean, we all yearned for normal boyfriends. Miss Frances and Miss Anne made it clear that we were not to seek out the boys, and the fact that we were separated from them most of the time should have precluded any such infraction. But girls will be girls and boys will be boys, and inevitably someone was in trouble for having committed that transgression.

Miss Frances had connections throughout the community. One Saturday early on in my recovery, she announced that we'd been invited to try out for a baseball league being formed by a group of firefighters. One of Miss Frances's nephews was a fireman, and he was responsible for relaying this tidbit of information. When she asked if any of us would be interested, my hand shot up as though it had a mind of its own. Would I? You bet! I loved to compete, and it seemed an eternity since I'd had an opportunity to do so. The fact that a bunch of hunky firemen were to be my potential teammates only added to the allure of this prospect. None of the other girls wanted to try out, but they all wanted to go so they could check out the beefcake. All the boys were on board, eager for the challenge.

When we arrived at the ball field, the firefighters were engaged in batting practice. I could see they had some pretty good hitters and that they'd be formidable. But that only served to add fuel to my fire. Baseball had never been my sport, but I'd played enough with Michael and Gus to know how to swing a bat and palm a fly ball. I'd gotten my speed back running the beach. Running the bases would be no problemo.

By the time it was my turn at bat, I was a ball of nerves, yet I could hardly wait to strut my stuff. As I took my place at home plate, there was some snickering from the firemen. But the RH boys cheered me on. Unlike the firefighters, they were respectful. They knew what I was capable of.

The first pitch whizzed by my head with lightning-fast speed. Wow! These guys weren't holding back. This was fast pitch! I swallowed hard, concentrating on the next pitch. Again the ball zinged by me. Strike two! Beads of perspiration popped out on my upper lip and brow. I needed to nail this, but now there were derisive hoots of laughter from the firefighters' ranks. Laugh at me, would they? My temper flared, and you know how that usually works out. I choked up on the bat and narrowed my eyes, focusing on the man on the mound. The pitcher wound up and let loose a special delivery package that rocketed toward me. I tightened my grip on the bat and swung with all of my might. Then, as sometimes happens, time became a variable; things that had sped up suddenly seemed to reverse into slow motion. There was a resounding crack as the ball connected with my bat, and the Restoration House contingent went wild. I started to run, not paying any attention to where the ball was headed, figuring if it had fouled I'd find out soon enough.

"*Run!*" Miss Frances screamed, her imperious voice rising above the rest. And time sped up again.

"*Run, Meghan!*" the girls echoed. "*Run!*" I sprang off the batting mound, my legs pumping like pistons. As it turned out, there was no need. I was nearing third base when the ball sailed over the fence far beyond the grasp of the outfielders. Still, one fellow leapt up off his feet in hopes of intercepting it, but to no avail. A homerun. I'd hit a homerun!

Miss Frances and Miss Anne were hugging one another delightedly, and Maridee and Reba were jumping up and down like schoolgirls.

"Way to go, Meghan," one of the RH boys hollered, and another put two fingers to his lips and whistled loudly. Score one for Restoration House! Needless to say, I was immediately inducted into the team. All the boys made the cut, too, which was a relief. I didn't think it would sit too well if I'd been accepted over one of them.

For the next several months, Saturdays would find me playing ball on the league, and I enjoyed every minute of it. It was a wonderful outlet for my burgeoning energy; not only did I enjoy the camaraderie I shared with the RH boys, I also made some great friendships with the firefighters. The older I get, the more I subscribe to the belief that there are no coincidences in life. The relationships I forged with those firefighters would dramatically impact my future. But I was not to realize that till much later.

Although Saturdays proved to be a welcome diversion from the normal routine, Sundays were nearly as structured and demanding as weekdays, the only concessions to the weekend being that we were allowed to dawdle over a leisurely breakfast. By eleven, we'd donned our demure attire and were ready to be carted off to church in one of the two big vans that serviced RH. The dress I'd been assigned, a donation that had been handed down from one new girl to the next, was nothing short of horrid. As far as I could tell, the fabric was homespun cotton, limp from too many launderings. It was white, featuring a high neckline and puffed sleeves, and when I put it on I felt like Laura Ingles Wilder in *Little House on the Prairie*. It was a far cry from the couture to which I'd formerly been accustomed, but then it was a far cry from my stripper duds, too. I vowed to spend my next phone privilege pleading with Mom to buy me a decent white dress.

The 13th Street Church of God was housed in a cavernous, clapboard structure conveniently located a mere two miles from Restoration House. It was a humble but pleasant edifice, with its worn oak pews and colorful stained-glass windows, through which light radiated in rainbow hues. The enormous altar was nearly as wide as the church itself. And that was a good thing, for it would accommodate an entire flock of congregants. Despite having been raised Catholic, I took to worship right away. Unlike the hushed decorum of mass, with its prescribed ritual and traditional music, Sunday services at the Church of God were raucous, untidy affairs.

The Reverend Willie I. Robinson officiated, assisted by co-pastor James W. Adderly, but all were welcome to preach. And preach they did. On and on they'd orate, with encouragement shouted from anyone in the pews who felt inspired to contribute their own emphatic hallelujahs and amens. The music wasn't staid either. Up-tempo and boisterous, the hymns were always open to improvisation. A chorus could be repeated three times or thirty, and a song might segue into another seamlessly, never having been rehearsed that particular way. And that kept the choir members on their toes!

There were four choirs—the men's and women's ensembles, the youth choir and the adult chorus—and I would eventually sing with three out of the four. All of them performed, at one time or another, during the service. At the benediction, all four groups combined to sing a medley of hymns, creating a huge sound, and leaving the church pews fairly vacant, as most everyone was on the altar singing!

Miss Pinky, the picture of a kindly grandmother, tinkled the piano's keys with a ragtime flair that caused one to wonder if perhaps they'd been transported to the Cotton Club by way of a stray melody. Toby, one of our own RH boys, beat the drums with the ardor of Ringo Starr, and tambourines wielded by individual parishioners added to the mix. Sunday worship was like a big celebration. There was no standing on ceremony. Parishioners were invited to the dais to testify, and their stories were alternately harrowing and inspiring. Afterward, when the snuffling subsided and the Kleenex had been tear-dampened, Robinson would have the collection plate passed a second time. Even amid those humble circumstances, $300–$400 would magically appear and be donated to that person who'd given testimony

I hadn't been allowed to don the white dress and graduate from St. Ed's, but now I proudly wore white every Sunday. The significance was not lost on me: all of us at RH were to be born again, our sins washed away in the Blood of the Lamb. Quite a few of the girls with some sober time under their belts had already accepted Jesus Christ as their personal Savior and were now full-fledged members of the church. Given my competitive streak, it's no wonder I longed for admittance to that select fold. If I somehow managed to accomplish that earlier in my recovery than any other girl had, so much the better.

I realize this sounds strange: the foul-mouthed hussy suddenly transformed, spouting Bible verses, and yearning for Jesus as much as she ever lusted for a Louis Vuitton bag. But in the last few years the Devil had redoubled his offensive, staking a claim on my soul, and I'd begun to think of suicide as my one-way ticket out of that hell. How difficult could it be to overdose, to simply go to sleep and not wake up? I'd wondered.

Unless I did an about-face, and turned the corner into a new existence, there had been nowhere for me to go but deeper into depravity. In the end, I found I was too Catholic to take my own life. I'd spent a furlough in Hades, and didn't relish the thought of taking up permanent residence there. "Please, God, I can't do this anymore," I'd prayed. "Help me."

And God had answered my prayers and those of my mother and the St. Sebastian gang and all those friends and relatives who'd been pulling for me. Somehow I'd been accepted into Restoration House, and almost immediately, that gnawing emptiness within me had begun to fill up so that now I was fair to bursting with an eagerness to get on with whatever God's plan happened to be for this fortunate girl.

So yes, I liked worship. I thrilled to the exuberant praise, the emotional highs and lows that it routinely delivered. When one is stoned, feelings are numbed. There is no pain, but there is no joy either. Suddenly, the switch to my emotions had been turned on, and life seemed to come rushing at me with a dizzying, pulsating vibrancy. Sure, I felt remorse for all the foolish things I'd done, for the hell I'd put my mother through, and for the lost years of my youth that I'd squandered. But I was also giddy with happiness, for I had been given a second chance. Church service was a great release. I clapped my hands, sang with abandon, and swayed with the music. I listened raptly to testimonies, weeping openly when the stories were crushingly sad. And when Robinson prayed, I raised my hands in the air and praised God for my many blessings, for He had surely saved me!

CHAPTER TWENTY-SIX

East Coast Swing

I'D ALWAYS HAD A TALENT FOR WRITING, AND NOW THAT I'D BEEN THRUST INTO THIS MICROCOSM WHERE CONSTANT MELODRAMA WAS BREWING, THE ITCH TO GET IT ALL DOWN ON PAPER WAS IMPOSSIBLE TO IGNORE. I became the intrepid journalist, nosing around attempting to unearth the dirt. When they'd catch sight of me, notebook in hand, the girls would avoid me, even more than they did when I'd suggest we all run the Fort Pierce Bridge before showers at 6:30 a.m. or work out after dinner. But I was determined to chronicle my trek up this road to redemption at Restoration House.

Just as the girls began thinking me a real pain in the ass, Miss Frances and Miss Pinky started taking me seriously. They made no secret of the fact that they admired my drive and energy. It wasn't long before they began putting me in positions of authority, assigning me small tasks, such as escorting new girls to the health department or hospital, or staying up late to keep watch, relieving Miss Anne of that tedious duty. Their confidence in me was a real self-esteem booster. I realized I enjoyed helping others, and one day it dawned on me that a service-related vocation might factor into my future. The idea took shape and began to resonate. At Restoration House Ministries, we were constantly fed the line that "everything happens for a reason." I dared to think the reason for my addiction and all the harrowing experiences I'd survived was to prepare me to serve in the military.

I was a fish in water, so I leaned toward either the Marine Search and Rescue Division or, once again, the Coast Guard. I would have aspired to become a Navy SEAL, but my gender prevented me from doing so. Still, I decided to start training like a SEAL. I thought that if I was in prime physical condition I might be accepted to a branch of service that demanded that of its recruits. I beefed up my workout, pushing myself to run an eight-minute mile, and increased the number of daily push-ups I performed from fifty to two hundred. It wasn't long before Miss Frances started referring to me as Wonder Girl, but the Missketeers preferred to call me Rambo.

After six months in the program, just about the time I was given some responsibility and cut a little slack, Miss Frances asked me what it was I wanted to do with my life.

"I think maybe I should enlist in the military," I said.

"Hmm," she muttered, mulling over this idea. "You're strong, I grant you. But you're not a big girl, and you're way too pretty. You'd be fair game, hit on a lot. You realize that, right?"

"I can take care of myself."

"I know you can, but in the military you can't simply slug your superior. It gets complicated. Besides that, you also run the risk of getting wounded or, worse, not coming home from a tour of duty. You sure you want to risk that?" Frances fixed me with her penetrating gaze.

I considered her question. Was I? Heck no! I wasn't sure of anything. I was just so eager to stop taking and start giving back.

"Yes," I said.

"Okay then. We'll get you down to the recruiter's office."

Miss Frances had granted me my first home visit, and I was thrilled at the prospect. Just to be free and in the world for a time without answering to her or Anne was like getting out of jail. I was not allowed to stay the night, so every minute of the day was precious.

We were in the car. Mom was behind the wheel and pulling away from Restoration House, and I couldn't believe I was being granted this privilege. I was reconnecting with the universe, and it felt wonderful.

"You look amazing," Mom said, stealing a glance in my direction.

"Thanks," I said. I felt amazing.

"I thought we'd stop by the grocery store and pick up whatever you'd like me to cook for dinner," Mom said. "Is that okay?"

"Okey-dokey!"

"But first I thought we'd have lunch somewhere. What's your pleasure?"

"Gee, I don't know. It's such a pretty day . . ."

"How about the Riverside Café?" Mom asked. "We could sit outside. Have a grouper Reuben."

"Perfect!"

"This is super," I said, eyeing the sparkling river, the stoic pelicans perched on pilings. We sat across from one another at a high-top on the deck. The wind sifted through my hair, and I gazed toward the Barber Bridge.

"What is it?" Mom asked, jolting me out of my reverie.

I sighed and turned to look at her. "Read," I said, thinking of my childhood friend, how his life had ended suspended from that very bridge.

Mom placed her hand over mine. "It's hard not to think of him. But hey! Let's focus on positive thoughts today."

"Right!"

"Do you know who's doing a book signing at the Vero Beach Book Store?" Mom asked.

"Who?"

"Marcus Luttrell."

"No!" I exclaimed, as my jaw fell open.

"Oh yeah. And we're going. So eat up!"

The parking lot was filled with cars, and we had to double around twice before finding a vacant space. Mom and I walked to the bookstore, only to encounter a conga line snaking around the bookshelves. The place was chock-full of Luttrell admirers. And I was one of them.

I knew of Marcus. He was a former Navy SEAL who had distinguished himself when, on June 28, 2005, he'd been assigned to a mission to kill or capture Ahmad Shah, a high-ranking Taliban leader responsible for killings in eastern Afghanistan and the Hindu Kush mountains.

While Marcus and his team were embedded, a group of goat herders stumbled upon them.

Eventually, the SEALs decided to let the herders go. That proved a poor decision. Within the hour, the SEALs found themselves engaged in an intense gun battle. (Luttrell believes the herders reported their location to the Taliban.) In the ensuing battle, all of the SEALs except for Marcus were killed. An MH-47 Chinook helicopter was dispatched with a force consisting of SEALs and 160th Special Operations Aviation Regiment "Nightstalkers" to rescue the team, but the helicopter was shot down by an RPG. All sixteen men on the Chinook were killed.

Luttrell was the sole survivor. Badly wounded, he managed to walk and crawl seven miles to evade capture. He was given shelter by an Afghan tribe, who alerted the Americans of his presence, and American forces finally rescued him six days after the gun battle.

Following his physical recovery from Operation Redwing, Marcus returned to Afghanistan and completed one more tour before being medically retired. He then wrote the book *Lone Survivor* to share the amazing story of his own survival and that of his brothers who'd paid the ultimate sacrifice.

"Go get a book and we'll have him sign it," Mom said, pressing a twenty-dollar bill into my hand. I did just that and then rejoined her in the line. When, at last, it was my turn to step up and speak with Luttrell, I was a ball of nerves. But Mom gave me a shove and I marched forward. The next thing you know, I was confessing my history to this guy, explaining that I was a recovering addict and training like a SEAL.

Luttrell was so compassionate he gave me his undivided attention. He told me to keep on keeping on, said that I'd be okay. When he asked how I wanted him to sign his book, I said, "Meghan Rose."

This is what he wrote: "To my friend, Meghan Rose. Never forget that 'The only easy day was yesterday.'" Tears sprang to my eyes as he closed the book and handed it to me. We shook hands. Once again, I knew I was in exactly the right place at the right time. The universe was feeding me, filling up that hole inside me, and giving me hope for the future.

"So you think you want to join the Navy?" Petty Officer Jahol-kowski asked.

"No, sir. I'm a swimmer," I said. "I want to apply for the Marine Search and Rescue Division, and I was told I have to train with the Navy for that."

"You do, do you?" Jaholkowski said, eyeing me critically. "That's a tough business. What makes you think you can make that cut?"

"I'm an athlete, sir. I can bench-press my own weight, run an eight-minute mile, and swim like nobody's business."

"Is that so?"

"Yes, sir!"

"Give me twenty," Jaholkowski said, indicating that I should fall to the floor.

Happily I complied, doing twenty push-ups without breaking a sweat, before proceeding to do five, one-handed. As this was occurring, the other two recruiters left their desks to come watch my little show. When I arose, I couldn't help but notice the admiration in their eyes. I was feeling pretty cocky, like I'd aced it, but then one of the recruiters noticed my body art.

"Uh-oh. What have we got here?" He slid a finger up my cuff.

"I have six, sir," I admitted. "These." I pulled up my sleeves, baring my wrists. Then I hitched up my pant legs so he could see the tattoos on each ankle.

"There's another teeny one on my hip," I said. "And . . ." I drew my hair from the nape of my neck to reveal the numbers etched there. ". . . this one."

Jaholkowski studied the tattoo just below my hairline. "Hmm," he muttered. He turned toward the other recruiters, but they merely shrugged. Gesturing toward the youngest of his cohorts, he said, "Take off your shirt, Phil. Dutifully, the cutie did as he was told, and my eyes fell to the well-defined pecs beneath his black tee. He was darling in that clean-cut, all-American-boy way. I couldn't help but notice the absence of a ring on his finger. I grinned at him, trying to remember how to flirt. Phil handed the shirt to Jaholkowski, who then held it out before me.

"Okay, Meghan," Jaholkowski said. "Put this on."

I slid my arms into the sleeves and buttoned up the standard issue. It was much too large for me, but Jaholkowski wasn't concerned with that. "Pull your hair up," he commanded, and I did. The three recruiters came to stand behind me. Then I could feel a hand tug the fabric just below the shirt collar.

"I think she'll be fine," Jaholkowski finally announced.

"Me too," Phil said. "The collar covers it. And the ones on her wrists and ankles will probably pass muster, too. Her shirt cuffs and trouser legs will conceal them."

I breathed a sigh of relief, for it appeared that I'd surmounted the first hurdle on this path to my goal.

"Meghan, I want you back here next Tuesday at 10:00 a.m. We'll get started on your paperwork," Jaholkowski said.

"Yes, sir!" I replied. "But you might as well know I have a record. I hope that won't be a problem."

"You got any felonies?" Jaholkowski asked.

"No, sir. Three DUIs and a VOP."

"Bring me a printout of your record. We'll see if we can't work through it."

When I showed up the following Tuesday, Jaholkowski was nowhere in evidence.

"Hi," I said to Phil when he rose from his desk to greet me. "I was supposed to meet—"

"Yeah, sorry about that. He had to be in Palm Beach this morning. I'm going to work with you," Phil said. "Come over here and have a seat, and let's take a look at your transcripts."

I could feel my face flush. "I'm sorry, but I wasn't able to pull my record," I said. I didn't want to admit I was a recovering addict, that my life was not my own and I could not come and go as I pleased.

If Phil sensed my unease, he didn't let on.

"No sweat. I think I can pull it up," he said as he began downloading my record. But as he read through the transcripts, Phil's face became increasingly clouded. At one point, he shook his head and looked at me dumbfounded.

"It says here you were charged with disorderly conduct?"

"That would be when I lost it in the Lobster Shanty parking lot."

"Lost it?"

"Bad boyfriend. He put something in my drink and I . . . I started screaming."

"Wow."

"It was the middle of the day, and I just ran outside the restaurant and started wailing to beat the band. The cops came and dragged me away. I was out of my head, didn't know what I was doing. But the charges were dropped. I wasn't prosecuted."

Phil sized me up. I realized then he didn't know what to make of me. He resumed studying my record, all the while jotting down notes. A short while later, he turned to me.

"Assault?" he said. "You were charged with assault?"

I felt my face redden. "That would be the time I threw a chair at Warren."

"And that was because . . . ?"

"Another bad boyfriend," I said, trying to make light of it, but with little success. "I wasn't charged"

"Assault?" he iterated.

"He was … is a really big, bad guy. Abusive, you know? Looking back on it, I don't know how I got myself into those situations." I could hear myself jabbering as my chances of a career in the military waned.

"He socked me in the eye . . . put me on the floor. When I was finally able to get on my feet I picked up a chair and hurled it at him."

"I see," Phil said. But it was obvious that he didn't.

"I had eight bad years," I said. "Took a wrong path, ended up with the wrong people. That's behind me now. I want to serve my country."

"I'm sorry, Meghan," Phil turned away from the computer monitor and gave me his full attention. I could hear the regret in his voice, and it was all I could do to keep from crying while waiting for the axe to fall.

"I don't think I can make this fly."

My eyes brimmed with tears. God was punishing me, I thought, punishing me for all the bad things I'd done. All I wanted was to serve my country, to do something noble and gain the respect of all those whom I'd disappointed. Now my hopes for the future were dashed. Somehow I managed to rise from my chair and flash Phil an insincere smile. "I understand," I said as my heart cracked apart in my chest. "Thanks for trying."

"I'm so sorry, Meghan. Sometimes this happens, and there's just nothing I can do . . ."

"It's okay." I walked toward the door. All I wanted was to be able to weep openly without someone watching and secretly delighting in my misery. Of course, Phil wouldn't have done any such thing. But I'd lived with women for too long now not to be guarded.

"I know that's disappointing, Meghan," Miss Frances said. "It just means God has other plans for you."

"But—"

"No buts. When God closes a door, a window opens. You've just got to be able to see that and go where you're meant to be."

"But all of my training . . . I thought I had a calling."

"Listen to me, Meghan. Except for you, every girl at Restoration

House is here by court order. If they weren't in some treatment program, they'd be in prison. But not you. You're here on God's orders. *You
thought. You wanted.* Are you paying attention, Miss Meghan? What is it
that God wants, huh?"

I started bawling. Such a wimp I'd become, all open and vulnerable
without my mind-numbing drugs. "I don't know. I really don't—"

"He brought you to us, didn't He? Perhaps you should look around
you, see what opportunities are right before your eyes."

I knew what Miss Frances was referring to. Perhaps my calling was
to work right there in Restoration House. But that's not what I wanted.
I needed to break out of those confines, had a burning desire to distinguish myself and to put my life on the line. I yearned to serve. To atone.

But it wasn't meant to be. So I returned to the RH program, where
I licked my wounds and prayed that God would open that other window
soon.

It wasn't long before a peephole slid open.

Somehow, I'd avoided the physical markers drug abuse normally
inflicts. My teeth were straight and white, and my complexion, clear.
And after six months at RH, my hair was long and silky, for Miss Mareya had finally allowed me to cut off the brittle blonde ends. Good-bye,
Jessica Simpson! I was now a brunette. Despite my previous eight hard
years, God had blessed me; I still looked young for my age. It wasn't any
wonder that Miss Pinky got it in her head that I should sing with the
youth choir.

I jumped at the chance, figuring any opportunity to sing was a
golden one. Besides, it would entail leaving the campus, and that was
always an appealing prospect. I didn't think it through, though, never
imagining the youth choir consisted of *youth*—the oldest among them
being nineteen years of age.

When I look back on my audition for the youth choir, I realize how
hilarious it must have been. I arrived full of anticipation, eager to sing
and be accepted into the group.

The first thing the choir director asked me was, "How old you be, Meghan?"

"Twenty-six," I said, thinking nothing of it.

"Sixteen?" he asked.

"No. Twenty-six," I clarified.

The poor man did a double take. Then he eyeballed Miss Pinky. "She old," he hissed in an audible stage whisper. "And she *white!*" Miss Pinky merely hitched her shoulders. It took a moment for the choir director to regain his composure and decide just what to do with me.

"Okay, honey," he finally said, looking discombobulated. "What you be, alto or soprano?"

"Soprano," I said.

"Good. Let's hear you sing a few scales."

Miss Pinky played an arpeggio, and the director nodded to me. "Ah . . ." he sang, inviting me to match his tone. I did as I was instructed, proceeded to climb the scale, and didn't stop until I ended on a bell-like high C.

I'd been caught up in the exercise, but when I could go no higher I was forced to stop. Embarrassed, I ventured a glance at Miss Pinky and was delighted to find her beaming at me. Then my eyes cut to the choir director, who seemed equally enthused. Apparently, I'd comported myself well!

After that there was no mention of my age or the fact that I was lily white. I was inducted into the youth choir, and because I was petite, I was assigned to the first row, front and center. I imagine, since he couldn't very well disguise the fact that I was Caucasian, the director had decided to openly celebrate the choir's newfound diversity.

Speaking of *old* at thirty-seven, Miss Abigail was by far the oldest girl in the program. With over a year's sobriety, she was granted the most privileges. Abigail was privy to more backstories than the rest of us girls, and it was she who gave me the dirt on Frances. It happened one magical night when we were both up late, having been assigned the task of sorting through sacks of clothing donated and dropped off by some charitable organization or another.

"She was an addict," Miss Abigail said, dark eyes gleaming in her porcelain doll's face. Abigail had fine features and was blessed with a peaches-and-cream complexion, but the total effect was marred by the fact that her teeth were ruined from having done methadone. She was getting them fixed, though, through the health department and would one day, no doubt, be truly beautiful.

"Her drug of choice was crack cocaine," she confided as she withdrew a gargantuan brassiere from a trash bag. "But apparently she wasn't too particular." Abigail waggled the bra before me, rolling her eyes, and I giggled. "You know how some people get."

"Oh, yeah," I said, thinking that toward the final death throes of my addiction, I'd gotten that way myself, none too particular.

"And of course she hooked. Right out on Avenue D."

"No!" I gasped. I knew of Avenue D. It wasn't a place one would want to be after the sun went down, a seedy thoroughfare notorious for its drug dealers, hookers, and violent gangs. Somehow, I couldn't imagine Miss Frances, with her regal bearing and ramrod-straight posture, doing the dirty. There was nothing soft or yielding about her, nothing sexy. Heck, she didn't even listen to secular music.

"Don't let that snooty attitude of hers fool you," Abigail said. "She wasn't any better than the likes of us. Worse, maybe."

"I can't believe it," I breathed.

"It's the God's honest truth. You know Miss Mareya and Miss Frances are sisters, doncha?"

"Yeah. And there's Miss Pinky, too. Mr. Mills, who directs the boys program, is their brother. And Miss Olivia's the youngest."

"That's right. Well, for years Mareya, Pinky, and Olivia did everything they could to get Frances to come clean; they enrolled her in one rehab program after another. But none of them worked. Finally, they got her to agree to go into Teen Challenge, even though she weren't no teenager. And, by George, it took! That was almost nineteen years ago, and ever since Frances graduated the program, the sisters have been hell bent on their ministry to rehabilitate addicts and bring them to Jesus." Abigail had withdrawn a silk scarf from the bag of clothing. Now she tied it loosely around her neck.

"Just our luck!" she exclaimed as she hitched one end of the scarf over her head, stuck her tongue out, and feigned the hanged man.

We both dissolved in giggles. It's not that we weren't grateful. We knew we were lucky, that we'd been saved from a life on the streets. But sometimes the sisters could get on a person's nerves, never mind the fact that they had our best interests at heart.

"Mareya's a hoot," Abigail continued. "When I first come here, right out of jail, I was dope sick just like you was."

I nodded my head, remembering my first days at Restoration House.

"Miss Mareya was in the office, and I went to her and told her I didn't feel well. I was hoping she'd give me some meds, you know? Something to settle my stomach and stop the shakes. But she says to me, 'Honey, I think you got too much sun.'"

I imagined the exchange and snorted at the absurdity of it. "Too much sun? What was she thinking?"

"God knows," Abigail said, chuckling at the memory. "She's got to be eighty. Sometimes I think she's getting a little senile. Anyway, I said, 'No, Miss Mareya, I haven't been in the sun. I'm dope sick. And look at my hair. I think I need to cut it.' You know how awful your hair gets in jail?" Abigail looked at me quizzically. "I swear the water's full of minerals, and without good products . . ." She shrugged her shoulders. "Ugh!"

"I do," I said. "When I was in jail, I finally stopped washing my hair altogether, which was kind of nasty. But my ends were fried from bleaching and just breaking off like crazy."

"Right," Abigail said. "So I run my fingers through my hair and show Miss Mareya how bad it is, hoping she'll let me cut it. I don't know if you noticed, but they got a thing about cutting your hair around here. It's like taboo. She wasn't having any of it. 'No, dear,' Miss Mareya says to me. 'Let me get you some nice conditioner. And I'll try to find something for that sunburn, too.'"

I burst out laughing. I had become very fond of Miss Mareya, but like all the people at Restoration House, she had her quirks. No sooner had we completed this exchange when who should pop around the corner but the petite lady herself. As always, she was smartly dressed and her expertly tinted curls, lacquered into place.

"Hello, dears," she said as she approached us. "What are you up to?"

"Just sorting clothing, Miss Mareya," Abigail sputtered sheepishly.

"You're such good girls to stay up late and work," Miss Mareya said. "How would you like a treat?"

"Sure!" Abigail exclaimed. We were always up for a chance to do something out of the ordinary, and with Miss Mareya, one never knew what that might entail.

"I can't sleep," Miss Mareya said.

Abigail and I nodded. Everyone knew that Miss Mareya was an insomniac. Her inability to sleep often propelled her to haunt the halls of Restoration House in the dead of night. Although she had her own little house west of town, there was a room in the building assigned to her as well. It was a cozy space, which, except for the shiny new flat-screen TV in the corner, was furnished with consignment shop finds.

"I have a hankering for barbecue," Miss Mareya said. "You gals up for some chicken or ribs?"

Were we? Abigail and I nodded our heads vigorously.

"I'll just tell Miss Anne we're going out." Abigail headed toward the front office.

"So how you doing, Meghan?" Miss Mareya asked, fixing me with her bird-like gaze.

"Just fine, Miss Mareya," I replied. And it suddenly came to me that I *was* doing fine. I didn't crave Adderall, or any drug for that matter, and I wasn't dying for a smoke either. I'd made some friends, and my digs here, though not luxurious, were certainly comfortable. I realized, for the first time in a long time, that I was content.

"I'm happy to hear that, honey," Miss Mareya said. "We're all proud of the way you've fit in. And it's nice that you're helping the girls get in shape, running the Fort Pierce Bridge and all."

I blushed. It'd been a long time since I'd been given a compliment, and I was pleased to know my efforts to work the program had not gone unnoticed. Furthermore, I was determined to maintain my workout regimen, and I intended to keep dragging the girls along with me.

"Miss Anne says it's fine," Abigail said, shooting me a conspiratorial grin as she walked back into the room.

"Let's go then, dears," Miss Mareya said. And with that we set out on our late-night exploit. We climbed into her Toyota Camry and headed north with Miss Mareya at the wheel. "There's a wonderful little barbecue place off of Orange Avenue," she explained. "We'll try that." We took a right on Orange, then turned left. Our destination proved to be little more than a rundown shack with a hog roaster flaking orange rust out front. Still, there was a festive atmosphere about the place. People stood about in clusters or converged at picnic tables, talking and laughing, some with open containers of beer in hand.

We clambered out of the car only to be enveloped in the most heavenly aroma, a heady mixture of cracklin' pork, hickory and spice.

"Come on, girls," Miss Mareya encouraged, and Abigail and I eagerly followed her lead. "Go inside, Meghan, and tell them we want some barbecue."

I glanced first at the building and then at Abigail, my face full of apprehension. We two were the only whites present, and despite lacking the caution gene, I had no desire to leave the relative safety in numbers out here on the street and venture into that forbidding structure. Abigail grimaced but she didn't volunteer to take my place. There was nothing I could do but march forward, draw the door open, and enter in. In the next instant, I was immersed in a tidal wave of music and immediately transported to another era. Loud, it washed over me. I could feel the vibration from the souls of my feet to the pit of my stomach. Good stuff, not rap or hip-hop, but that great old R&B from the sixties and seventies that my Mom sometimes listened to, Soul Train and the like. Having been deprived of all but Christian and gospel music during my Restoration House sojourn, I thrilled to the close harmonies and seductive beat.

All of this transpired in less than ten seconds, about the time it took for my eyes to adjust to the dimly lit interior. When they did, I took in at a glance the bare-bones tavern. There was a crudely constructed bar running the length of the far wall, and a smattering of scarred tables and mismatched chairs occupied the center. No more than twenty "brothers" and "sisters" were patronizing the joint, but as my eyes fell upon them, I realized each and every one could have been dispatched from central casting. I felt a bit like Alice, as though I'd stumbled through the looking glass into an alternate reality. Then again, the last eight years of my life had been one series of bizarre episodes after another, so I just went along with it. Feigning a demeanor of confidence, I strode over to the wizened barkeep.

"Hey," I said, flashing my big white teeth in his direction. "Miss Mareya is outside, and she's here for barbecue."

The man's eyes were rheumy, and it took him a moment to focus on me, but when he did he perked up considerably, making no secret of the fact that he was checking me out.

"Hello, darlin'," he rasped. "You one of Miss Mareya's chicks?" By this time the room had hushed, the entire assembly raptly hanging on our exchange.

I nodded.

"Well, and ain't that just like Miss Mareya?" he cackled, seeming to enjoy this new development. "Poor woman never sleep. Up half the night. And if she's not proselytizing, she's looking for barbecue." He turned and hollered toward the back. "Devon, come out here, son. You got customers." A few seconds elapsed, and then a gorgeous black man emerged from the open doorway. He was well over six feet tall, and his muscled physique spoke of long hours in the gym. His eyes lit up when he saw me.

"Ma'am?" he said, gliding out from behind the bar with the athletic grace of a dancer. "How can I help you?"

"Uh," I said, admiring his beauty. Then I remembered my mission. "We'd like some barbecue to go, please."

"Sure thing." He crossed to the entrance, with me close on his heels. Once outside, he made a beeline for the picnic table at which Miss Mareya and Miss Abigail had seated themselves.

"Hey there, Miss Mareya," Devon said, enveloping the tiny woman in a bear hug. "How you doin'?"

"Devon! You a sight for sore eyes, son!" Miss Mareya exclaimed, obviously pleased by the attention.

"You want your usual?" Devon asked, disentangling himself.

"Sure do," Mareya replied. "Make me up a big box to go."

"Coming right up," Devon said. Before turning away to do her bidding, he glanced in my direction and favored me with a wolfish grin. I knew nothing would ever come of this flirtation, but it was reassuring to know that I could still attract a man without having to take my clothes off.

It was a balmy evening, warm but not too humid, and rather than take our meal back to Restoration House, we decided to stay right there and extend our outing. Devon brought our food and then, at Miss Mareya's persuading, sat down with us. We ploughed through plates of ribs, chicken, slaw and beans, our chins dripping red sauce, while Devon regaled us with stories about his tours of duty in Afghanistan. After Miss Mareya had eaten only a tiny portion of her meal, she declared herself to be full, but Abigail and I didn't push away from the table until our plates were clean.

"Thank you, Devon," Miss Mareya said, withdrawing a wad of cash from her handbag. "I expect I'll see you in church?"

"Yes, ma'am," Devon replied, casting a sidelong glance my way. "That you will."

We piled back in the car, and Miss Mareya said, "Did you enjoy that, girls?" Abigail and I both agreed that we had and thanked her profusely. "Good," she said as she cruised on over to D Street.

"Where we going now, Miss Mareya?" Abigail asked uneasily, for the neighborhood aesthetic had rapidly deteriorated. The buildings lining the street were becoming shoddier and more forbidding with each passing moment.

"We goin' to proclaim the Word," Miss Mareya announced.

"We?" Abigail asked, raising her eyebrows.

"That's right, dear."

And that was my initiation into proselytizing. We stood on a street corner where the flotsam and jetsam of humanity surged around us— gang members, hookers, addicts, and pimps—and read aloud from our Bibles. For the most part ignored, we managed to attract the attention of an occasional heckler, who'd mime and ridicule us before eventually tiring of his enterprise and moving on. In the course of the evening, one teenage girl sidled up to us, and I thought we might have a potential convert. Little more than a child, she was a pretty thing and provocatively dressed. Her dazed expression told me she was flying high. She gravitated toward us with an unmistakable yearning in her eyes. In the next instant, she was hustled away by a dangerous-looking fellow with dirty dreadlocks and a cruel cast to his mouth.

After about two hours of this, Miss Mareya, looking greatly diminished, called it quits. "All right, dears," she said, closing her Bible. "We best be going."

By the time we returned to Restoration House, everyone but Miss Anne had turned in for the night, and she was dozing before the television in the commons. She was slumped in a recliner, multiple chins resting on her ample bosom. Except for the rhythmic buzz of her snoring, the building seemed unnaturally quiet.

"You go on to bed now, girls," Miss Mareya instructed. "I'll lock up. And not a word to anyone about this evening, you hear?"

Abigail and I nodded solemnly. We were dead on our feet and gladly stumbled to our beds, both of us harboring a new appreciation for Miss Mareya.

CHAPTER TWENTY-SEVEN

The Cakewalk

"GIRLS, THERE'S SOMETHING I HAVE TO TELL YOU." Miss Frances strode into the classroom where we sat waiting for our lessons to begin. Her face was unnaturally grave, and we immediately hushed, giving her our full attention.

"Miss Mareya has been diagnosed with cancer," she said.

There was an audible gasp from our ranks before we were rendered silent, stunned by this revelation. In the next moment, I recalled certain details regarding Miss Mareya's recent behavior. Last night, I hadn't thought anything of her poor appetite, the fact that she'd seemed uncommonly fragile and overly exhausted, but now these things took on new meaning. Abigail and I glanced at one another guiltily, each of us thinking perhaps we were somehow to blame.

"Twenty years ago, Miss Mareya battled breast cancer and won," Miss Frances continued. "But now—"

"What kind of cancer is it?" I breathed.

"Colorectal. It's in her bowel, but it's spread to her lungs, and—"

"Well, she's got to have chemo," Reba said. "She can get better."

"Mareya's almost eighty," Frances said. "I'm afraid there's not a lot of fight left in her. Besides, the chemotherapy would probably kill her before the cancer did. Rather than endure the side effects of radical treatments, Miss Mareya has decided to have radiation and to give homeopathic therapies a try. Beyond that, she's chosen to let nature run its course."

The implication of this statement was not lost on us: Miss Mareya was going to die.

A wave of grief washed over me, and my eyes filled with tears. Bolting up from my chair, I charged out of the commons and made a mad dash for the bathroom. I couldn't bear the thought of losing Miss Mareya. In the last ten years, I'd lost so many loved ones. How could I endure the loss of sweet Miss Mareya?

You would think that this new development might have cast a pall over all of us. But life went on, and in the days that followed a light-hearted, one might even say joyous, mood prevailed. It was as though a tacit agreement had been forged among us. We never spoke of Miss Mareya's cancer; if she picked at her food or appeared tired, we didn't remark upon it. Instead, when her energy lagged, we became even more animated in an unconscious effort to imbue her with our own irrepressible youth. I guess it worked because almost overnight Miss Mareya seemed to rally. Of course, she was on a vitamin regimen and eating more sensibly. There were no more midnight barbecue forays, and she swore her weekly radiation and acupuncture sessions left her feeling revived and stronger. But we all knew she was in remission.

When the cancer came back, it would do so with a vengeance.

About the time Miss Mareya was diagnosed, a new girl entered the program. With her myriad tattoos, dyed black hair and silver tongue ring, Sabrina's Goth guise was a bit startling, especially given the fact that the hard look she'd adopted stood in such sharp contrast to her natural attributes. Her waif-like build and delicate complexion were more suited to old lace and frothy tulle than the Nine Inch Nails tee and shredded jeans she'd arrived in. Despite her seeming fragility, we would soon learn that Sabrina was possessed of an evil temper and an iron will.

"That girl be full of the Devil," Miss Mareya was heard to mutter after one of Sabrina's signature tantrums.

In her defense, Sabrina's story was more horrifying than any of the others I'd heard at Restoration House, and that was saying a lot. Poor Sabrina entered this life with two strikes against her: Not only had her mother been a hooker and a lush, she'd continued drinking throughout her pregnancy. Sabrina came into this world mad-crazy angry, suffering from fetal alcohol syndrome. When she was only two years old, Child Welfare Services stepped in and removed Sabrina from her mother's haphazard care. But in those formative years, the damaging effects of the neglect and the outright abuse she'd suffered took their toll.

As a toddler, Sabrina presented as developmentally challenged. She was shuffled from one foster home to another, and no one bothered to ascertain her true mental abilities. It was assumed that she was mildly retarded, when in fact she was quite brilliant. But her intellect hadn't been awakened. Frustrated and starved for attention, she struck back the only way she knew how: by acting out. By the time she was fifteen, Sabrina was abusing pain medication. Like me, she began dancing in her early twenties, although the club she worked at was not on par with the notorious Velvet Pony. Also like me, her addiction eventually brought her down to the point where she could no longer dance. That's when she started turning tricks on the streets. Despite the fact that Sabrina's self-esteem was near nonexistent, she desperately wanted to better herself. When she hit bottom and there was no place else to go but up, she, too, had been accepted into Restoration House.

Not only had Sabrina never known the love of a nurturing parent, teacher, or trustworthy confidante, she'd never owned a pet. I knew what solace an animal can provide to a lonely heart. My own adorable Bentley was currently being cared for by my hero brother and his family. And I sorely missed his doggie affection and comforting cuddles.

But Sabrina had compensated for that lack, capturing small lizards and insects and secreting them away in plastic containers with holes punched in the lids. She had an affinity for roaches, was not repulsed by them in the least, and she was especially fond of chameleons. The first time I was confronted with Sabrina's unusual proclivity for lizards and common household pests, I was appalled.

Having just been admitted to RH, she'd taken to her bed while detoxing. Miss Anne asked me to schlep a cup of chicken broth to the convalescent, and with nothing but time on my hands, I'd halfheartedly agreed.

I knocked on Sabrina's door, careful not to slosh soup from the mug clutched in my left hand. I paused, but when no one answered, let myself in. Like all the dorm rooms, Sabrina's was tiny, cramped, and dominated by the twin bed abutting the back wall. Tucked between the covers, the new girl, seemingly asleep, looked almost angelic. A shock of black hair splayed out over the white pillowcase in sharp contrast to her ashen complexion.

"Hey," I said, pitching my voice low so as not to startle her. "I brought you some soup."

Sabrina's eyelashes fluttered, and then her startling gray-green eyes opened wide to encompass me. A look of fear crossed her face, vanishing as quickly as it had appeared. She pressed her lips together, feigning a toughness that, given her present circumstances, was nearly impossible to convey. Still, I hesitated, knitting my brows in consternation. I'd overheard Miss Mareya and Miss Frances speaking about the new girl, how spiteful and unruly she was. I didn't want to be mixing it up with her at this point. But then Sabrina appeared to assess the situation, and her demeanor changed.

"Don't feel much like eating," she mumbled.

"Yeah, I know how it is," I said. "We were all sick when we first came in here." I approached the bed. "You should try to drink some of this, though," I persisted. "Otherwise, you'll get dehydrated. Trust me. That'll only make you feel worse."

"Ugh." Sabrina's slender body shifted beneath the blanket, and I set the steaming mug down on her bedside table. I leaned toward her, thinking to help her prop up her pillow, and once more a trace of fear flicked across her face.

"Can you sit up?" I asked, backing away.

"I guess," Sabrina muttered unenthusiastically. She scooted up, resting her spine against the pillow in a semi-seated position, and eyed me warily. I picked up the mug and offered it to her. Sabrina sighed resignedly, and a bone-thin arm poked out from beneath the covers. As she made to accept the proffered cup, the top sheet fell away, and in the next instant, a cockroach scuttled out and across the threadbare coverlet. I shrieked involuntarily and cast my eyes about for a makeshift weapon with which to annihilate this repulsive creature. Before I could put my hands on a suitable implement, Sabrina had scooped up the offending creepy-crawly and whisked him back under the covers.

Thunderstruck, it took me a moment to process what had just transpired, and when I did my eyes widened. "You're . . . But it's . . ."

Sabrina eyed me curiously, a small smile tugging at her lips. She appeared to be enjoying my distress.

"It's okay," she said. "He's my pet."

"Yeah, right," I replied, edging toward the door. "Some companion you got there."

"I've got lots of pets," Sabrina continued, drawing the top sheet down to reveal three more roaches scuttling beneath the covers.

My stomach turned. "Greaaat," I said, sidling out the doorway. "Well, I've got to run. You'll have to introduce me another time." I couldn't get out of there fast enough and let the door close behind me with a bang. As I fled down the hallway, I heard a faint sound. It was Sabrina chuckling, and the sound of her laughter rankled. I couldn't help but feel as though she'd somehow gotten the best of me.

I don't know why, but I didn't tell anyone, not even Miss Mareya, about Sabrina's unusual "pets." She was an odd girl, prickly and secretive, but there was a vulnerability about her that brought out my mothering instincts. I had no idea that keeping her little secret would one day stand me in good stead.

I've told you how the sisters—Miss Frances, Miss Mareya, Miss Olivia and Miss Pinky—prayed for guidance, that they didn't accept every applicant and would rather have empty beds than a girl who didn't fit in and caused upheaval. So I couldn't understand how it was that Sabrina, with all of her baggage, was now bunking with us. For one thing, she screamed all night. No sooner would her breathing deepen than her nightmares ensued. And they were epic. She'd gladly recount them for us come morning, but in the dead of night none of us could sleep, and it was driving us all crazy. On top of that, she was argumentative and always interrupting in class, adding her own paltry two cents to whatever topic was being discussed. It didn't matter if she had no knowledge or firsthand experience, she always had an opinion. Even Miss Frances seemed to have met her match. "Breaking that one is like trying to tame a wild stallion," she confided to Olivia. "Maybe we made a mistake letting her in here."

One thing was certain: Sabrina was proving to be more than the sisters had bargained for; she sure as shooting wasn't about to become obedient overnight. Given her upbringing, it came as no surprise that she had no manners, no social graces whatsoever. Her posture was horrid, and she continually slouched in her chair. She chewed with her mouth open and belched loudly, whether it be at the dining table or church, with nary an apology. At first we thought her behavior was funny, but the novelty soon wore off. And in no time we were all on her case, girls and staff alike. That only caused Sabrina to dig in and all the more resist our efforts to make her conform.

The final straw was her refusal to accept Jesus Christ as her personal Savior. It wasn't that Sabrina consciously denied Christ. She participated in Bible studies class and prayed before meals with the rest of us. But when it came to formerly accepting Jesus, she just couldn't seem to do it. The sisters would gather her hair at the top of her head and gently lower her head back and over the baptismal font. Once she was positioned, Reverend Robinson poured water over her forehead, and everything was fine up to that point. But when he uttered the words of baptism, Sabrina would start thrashing and caterwauling to beat the band. You'd think she was being tortured or something, and the flesh of her forehead, where the water made contact, turned bright red as if it were scalding her.

This exercise was repeated three times, and on each successive occasion there were more hysterics, more resistance on Sabrina's part. Afterward, when we gathered in the church hall for our potluck lunch, she confided to us that she couldn't remember a thing, said she truly wanted to be baptized.

The sisters were making no progress in that regard. Finally, they came to the conclusion that demonic powers were at work in Sabrina, and the only way to call a halt to such goings-on was to perform an exorcism.

I was raised Catholic, so ritual, even that of exorcism, did not seem particularly foreign to me. But the sisters practiced a brand of fundamental Christianity. The notion of a Roman Catholic priest, arrayed in vestments, practicing an ancient rite at their behest represented a real departure from their comfort zone, which just goes to show how desperate they'd become. I guess it is safe to say they were at their wits' end. They were willing to try just about anything that might result in Sabrina's salvation and allow peace, uneasy as it might be, to be restored at Restoration House.

One night over dinner, Maridee asked, "Is the priest coming here?"

"No, ditsy, he's not," Reba said. "Miss Frances says that he's got to do it someplace where there aren't so many distractions."

"Nah, that's not it." Charlene grimaced. "Real reason is they want to get her as far away from us as possible. They're afraid that when them demons fly outta Sabrina, they'll slip right into one of us."

"Makes sense to me," I said, thinking we'd only recently been wrested from the dark side ourselves and were, therefore, more vulnerable than most.

In the days leading up to the exorcism, Sabrina was skittish and quick to take offense. Although we wanted to stand behind her and offer our support, the girls and I avoided her as best we could. When that wasn't possible, we were circumspect and watched our tongues. But the night before Sabrina was to be exorcised, Reba let slip a wisecrack at dinner, and, forgive the pun, all hell broke loose.

Sabrina, whose table manners were atrocious, had forked a gob of mashed potatoes into her craw. What she didn't know is that they were just off the stove and scalding hot.

"Ugh!" Sabrina exclaimed, spitting the mouthful back onto her plate. "Burned my tongue!"

"Get used to it," Reba quipped. "Your entire skinny body will be consumed by fire if that exorcism doesn't take."

Sabrina recoiled as though she'd been struck.

"I suppose you think that's funny," she said, glaring at Reba.

"Yeah, I do," Reba replied. "It's a joke. No offense intended."

Like a specter, Sabrina rose from her chair.

"It's not funny, bitch," she hissed, putting her face in Reba's. And at that moment, I truly believed she was possessed.

Miss Anne heard the commotion and loped from the kitchen into the commons. "What's going on?" She was gasping, out of breath from that small exertion. But she was too late; the confrontation had already segued into an all-out battle. Reba had pushed away from the table and risen from her chair in one fluid movement. Then she and Sabrina were at each other's throats.

Reba was bigger than Sabrina, but that didn't count for much. Sabrina was wiry and quick, and she fought dirty. Grabbing hold of Reba's ponytail with her left hand, she yanked it hard while at the same time balling up her right fist and delivering a solid punch to Reba's temple. Reba hit the floor, stunned. Abigail and I rushed to Reba's side. The next thing I knew, Miss Anne was insinuating her large presence into the fray. She wrapped her tree-trunk arms around Sabrina and held on for all she was worth. Afterward, she swore it was like restraining a wildcat. Sabrina writhed and kicked until, eventually, the fight just seemed to go out of her, but not before she'd raised a series of welts and bruises on

Miss Anne's shins.

Miss Anne hustled Sabrina away, depositing her in her room to cool off, and we attended to Reba, offering her a package of frozen peas from the fridge to ice down the knot that was quickly rising on her temple. We didn't know if we should simply clear the table and call it a night or sit back down and resume our dinner. But we were always hungry and the food was so plentiful and delicious, we opted for the latter. By the time Miss Anne returned, we were once again seated at the table, enjoying our meal as though nothing out of the ordinary had occurred.

"How's your head, Reba?" Miss Anne pushed away the bag of frozen peas to better assess the injury.

"It's okay," Reba replied sheepishly. "I can't believe I let her get to me. I must be losing it."

"Nah, you're not losing it," Maridee said. "She's lightning quick. It's the Devil, pure and simple. You didn't stand a chance, hon."

Reba appeared somewhat mollified by this observation. "Maybe so," she agreed.

"That girl has a short fuse," Charlene said.

"You can say that again." Abigail shook her head, disconsolately. "I surely hope that exorcism works."

"It better," Miss Anne muttered. "Or she'll find herself back on the streets. Cain't put up with her crap much longer."

I raised my eyebrows, and we Missketeers exchanged knowing looks, nodding to one another in silent agreement.

The day of the exorcism dawned overcast and blustery, much the same as that Halloween morning when I first entered Restoration House. Sabrina, pale and uncharacteristically withdrawn, picked at her breakfast, offering up not a word. Afterward, Miss Frances and Miss Anne hustled her into the van and accompanied her to the rectory where the rite was to be performed. Mr. Miller took over our classes, heroically attempting to maintain a semblance of normalcy, but we girls were fidgety and unable to concentrate. Eventually, he dismissed us with the admonition to, "Go to your rooms and read your Bibles until lunchtime."

We were just clearing away the midday meal when Miss Frances and Miss Anne arrived with a stricken-looking Sabrina in tow. Our eyes went to Frances, seeking some sort of explanation, but she merely shook her head, refusing to comment, and trotted off to her office. Miss Anne, her face grim, was no help either. Instead, she put an arm around Sabrina and steered her to her bedroom.

"What the heck do you make of that?" Charlene whispered.

"God only knows," Abigail said.

"I can't stand it!" Reba exclaimed. "Somebody's got to tell us what went down."

"Maybe we don't want to know," I cautioned. But as soon as the words were out, I knew they were false.

It wasn't until later in the evening that, after much pestering, Miss Anne finally filled us in on the particulars. The girls and I were seated around the television set, but none of us had been able to concentrate on the mindless reality show that was airing, and we'd turned the sound down, opting instead for quiet conversation among ourselves. Naturally, the topic revolved around the exorcism. There'd been no sign of Sabrina since her return. Her bedroom door remained closed, and there hadn't been a peep out of her. At suppertime, Miss Anne had delivered a dinner tray to Sabrina's room, so we assumed that she was resting, recovering from the aftereffects of the rite.

"What happened? I wonder," Maridee asked. "Did it take or not?"

"It musta took," Charlene said. "Otherwise, I don't think the sisters would keep her on."

"Yeah," I agreed. "I like her, you know? Admire her spunk. But she's such a drama queen." Just then Miss Anne lumbered into the room and wearily plopped down on the sofa.

"Tell us, Miss Anne, won't you?" Maridee coaxed. "It's torture not knowing."

"Yes, please tell," Charlene cajoled.

Miss Anne just sat there, her face impassive. Finally she spoke.

"I shouldn't. We not supposed to talk about it," she said. "Before I do, you gotta promise not to rat me out to the sisters."

"We won't tell nobody. Isn't that right, girls?" Abigail said, and we all nodded our heads in agreement.

"Okay then," Anne said, settling back into the sofa as she began her narrative. "When I first met Monsignor Newsome, I didn't set much store in him. He's a little fellow, bald as an eagle and really old. But I had him all wrong. That guy knows his stuff. First thing he does is talk to Sabrina, explaining what it is he's gonna do and that she is to try to stay calm no matter what happens."

"Riiight!" Maridee snorted.

Miss Anne gave Maridee the evil eye for having interrupted before continuing. "Then he explains how he's gonna strap her in her chair—"

"He restrained her?" I said. "That seems kind of radical."

"Uh-huh." Miss Anne nodded. "And a good thing, too. He goes to a closet and brings out what looks like wide leather belts, and he straps her feet to the legs of the chair and fastens her wrists to the arms."

Charlene gasped, and we all scooted in closer to Miss Anne, not wanting to miss a word.

"Once she's bound to that chair real good, he starts in reading from some Bible or something. At first everything was fine, and I'm thinkin' this is gonna be a cakewalk. Sabrina just sat there looking a little scared. But when he got to the passage where he says, 'I cast you out, unclean spirit, along with every satanic power,' she started jerking and thrashing something fierce. Miss Frances and I had to hold her down for fear she'd hurt herself. But that priest was a cool operator. He just ignored her and kept on reading, saying, 'Be gone and stay from this creature.' All the while Sabrina was bucking and shaking like she havin' a seizure."

"Lord, have mercy!" Maridee exclaimed.

"Um-hmm," Anne said. "And when he traced the sign of the cross on her forehead, saying, 'Be gone then, Satan, in the name of the Father, the Son, and the Holy Spirit,' Sabrina's face got all squinched up so's that you could hardly recognize her, and she started in growling and snapping like some wild animal. I swear she foamed at the mouth. Her spit was flyin' through the air just like raindrops."

"Sweet Jesus!" I muttered. "She really was possessed."

"Look like it," Anne agreed. "Twice Monsignor traced that cross on her forehead, and you'd a thought Sabrina's poor head gonna snap off a her scrawny neck. He does it a third time and, believe it or not, a faint red cross appears on Sabrina's brow. Then it was like somebody turned a switch, for the next instant she shuts up her snarling and goes limp as a ragdoll. It was somethin', all right. The priest says a few more prayers, and that's the end of it."

"What?" Reba said. "That's it?"

"Mm-hmm. We waited about ten minutes or so, and gradually Sabrina revives. 'I'm thirsty,' she says, and Miss Frances fetches her a glass of water. Then the Monsignor undoes her restraints and starts talking to her in a real soothing voice. He tells her it's over and asks if she remembers anything that happened."

"Did she?" Charlene asked.

"She says not, and I believe her."

"Probably just as well," Abigail said.

"I reckon so," Miss Anne agreed. "But if that's the case, you girls know more than she does. You just keep your traps shut and not a word to her about it. No teasing or snide remarks to Sabrina, you understand me? Any girl that does will be on permanent restriction."

"We won't say anything, Miss Anne," I said.

"Our lips are sealed," Charlene promised, and the other girls nodded in agreement. The next morning Sabrina emerged from her bedroom and made her way to the communal bath. We all pretended that nothing unusual had occurred, going out of our way to act normal and not to rile her. But Sabrina seemed not to notice; she kept to herself, not saying a word as she showered and tended to her hair.

"It's like she's empty now that the Devil has left her," Reba whispered to me on the way to breakfast.

"I know. It's weird," I replied. "Wonder how long this'll last?"

Little did I know we would soon learn the answer to that question.

Later in the classroom, Sabrina seemed consumed by malaise. When Miss Suzanne, our Bible study teacher, asked if any of us could recite a scripture passage that referenced an animal, Sabrina merely slumped lower in her chair, a glazed look in her eyes. But Abigail's hand shot up, for she knew her Bible backward and forward.

"Yes, Miss Abigail?" Miss Suzanne nodded for her to proceed.

"Be self-controlled and alert," Abigail recited. "Your enemy the Devil prowls around like a lion looking for someone to devour. 1 Peter 5:8."

No sooner had Abigail recited the verse than she realized her blunder. Clumsily, she tried to compensate for it.

"Get it?" she stuttered. "Prowls like a lion?" But it was too late; the word *Devil* seemed to echo throughout the room.

Horrified, I cut my eyes to Sabrina. She'd perked up considerably and was now sitting rigidly in her chair. It struck me that she looked a bit like Edward Scissorhands—pale, hollow-eyed, and gaunt—but she was also animated to the point I feared she might blow a gasket.

Anticipating an impending kerfuffle, Reba jumped in without any prompting.

"Four things on earth are small but exceedingly wise," she recited. "The ants are a people not strong, yet they provide their food in summer." Reba couldn't seem to get the words out fast enough, for they tumbled out one on top of the other.

"The badgers are a people not mighty, yet they make their home in rocks. The locusts have no king, yet they march in rank. The lizard you can pick up in your hands, yet it finds its home in the palaces of kings." Reba took a deep breath and then finished with one word. "Proverbs."

I glanced at Sabrina. Once again she was slouched at her desk, seemingly uninterested in the goings on about her. Reba had diffused the situation and saved the day! I favored my girlfriend with a thumbs-up.

Miss Suzanne had no idea what had just transpired, that disaster had been averted. Bless her heart. She was well intentioned and eager to do the Lord's work ministering to us miscreants, but she was a dingbat.

"Oh, that I had wings like a dove," she waxed, her voice tremulous. "I would fly away and be at rest. Yea, I would wander afar. I would lodge in the wilderness. I would haste to find me a shelter from the raging wind and the tempest." Miss Suzanne smiled sweetly and stared into space, seemingly transported by this passage.

"I sure as heck would like to fly outta here," Reba muttered under her breath. I rolled my eyes in her direction before cutting them to Maridee and then to Charlene. We grinned at one another. The Missketeers had prevailed. Peace would once again reign at Restoration House.

But our victory was short-lived, for in the next instant Sabrina leapt from her chair and began to speak. All eyes locked on her as she proceeded to recite in a singsong voice, "Ran into the Devil, babe, he loaned me twenty bills. I spent the night in Utah in a cave up in the hills. Set out runnin' but I take my time. A friend of the Devil is a friend of mine. A friend of the Devil is a friend of mine."

We all stared at Sabrina in shock. Even Miss Suzanne was at a loss for words.

Sabrina smiled smugly. "The Grateful Dead," she said before collapsing back into her chair.

Don't you know that old Devil had jumped out of Sabrina's skin, only to climb right back in again? There was to be no peace at Restoration House any time soon, for there was a demon in our midst.

Sabrina's histrionics continued to drive us to distraction. She was forever interrupting in class, always jockeying to be the center of attention, and she'd deliberately try to rile us every chance she got. Miss Mareya admitted that the sisters had misgivings.

"That girl be full of the Devil, pure and simple," she confided one evening when I found myself in her RH quarters. It was after midnight, and Miss Mareya had asked me to sit with her. Naturally, I'd agreed. I loved her. Somehow, I felt as though Nana had taken up residence in her tiny, black body. She was as good and pure as my Nana, and I adored her. I knew she was not long for this world, but I pushed that knowledge back into some dusty corner of my brain. She was here now, and that's all that mattered. I would spend as much time with her as humanly possible before she, too, left me.

"I know, Miss Mareya," I said. "She's hateful."

"Will you be her friend, Meghan?"

"What?" I gazed at my mentor incredulously. "You've got to be kidding!"

"No. I mean it," Mareya said. "That girl never had no friend. No mama. No daddy. No one who cared a rat's ass about her. Forgive my French."

I was agog. Miss Mareya's using colorful language was so out of character. The world was tilting on its axis. "So you're saying—"

"I'm saying she needs someone in her corner. Someone strong. A role model. That would be you, Meghan."

"But, Miss Mareya," I said, "I can't stand her. She's horrid."

"She's one of God's own children, Meghan. Remember, you were some kind of horrid once, too. So were all the girls. So were Frances and Pinky."

"But not you, Miss Mareya. You were never bad."

"Well—"

"You weren't."

"Everyone on God's green earth is a sinner, Meghan. I am no exception."

I searched Miss Mareya's face. She'd lost a good deal of weight and appeared frail. But she was beautiful nonetheless; the goodness just radiated out of her.

"So just what is it you want me to do?" I asked sulkily.

We girls kept our toiletries in wire shower baskets, which we schlepped to and from the bath in the mornings and before bed. Sabrina would leave hers right in front of a shower stall, and any unsuspecting girl who emerged would inevitably crash into it. We'd been harping on her to be more responsible. She claimed innocence, but we all knew she did it on purpose.

One morning, I was the hapless victim of Sabrina's little game. "Yeow!" I yelled when my big toe smashed into her shower tote. The sudden pain was so excruciating, so unexpected, that I lost my balance and slipped on the damp floor. My feet flew out from under me, and down I crashed. Charlene dropped her hairbrush and rushed to my side.

"You okay, Meghan?" she asked, helping me to my feet.

"No, I'm not!" I snarled. "Where's Sabrina? I'm gonna kill her!"

"Here I am," Sabrina said, suddenly appearing before me. "You got something you want to say to me?" Her belligerent attitude only added fuel to my fire, and I was ready to throw myself at her. But then I recalled Miss Mareya's words, how she wanted me to befriend this ornery creature, and I backed down.

"Yes, as a matter of fact, I do," I said. "You have a nasty habit of leaving your shower basket precisely where someone will trip over it. How about being a little more considerate, Sabrina? I'm not the only girl who's stumbled over your tote. What do you say, huh?" I looked to Reba for reinforcement. Good girl that she is, Reba chimed right in.

"Yeah, we're getting tired of your crap, Sabrina," Reba said. "Don't get me wrong. We like you. It's just that—"

"It's just that you're making us nutsy," Maridee interrupted. "We'd ask you to join the Missketeers—"

"But we think you're too wacko," Charlene said, finishing Maridee's sentence. "Could you please just bring it down a notch or two?"

And there it was. Without giving it any forethought, we'd ganged up on her. Stunned, Sabrina momentarily seemed at a loss for words, which is saying something. But she quickly recovered.

"Yeah . . . sure. I didn't mean no harm."

None of us believed a word of this, but we were willing to give the kid another chance. Which is how I came to be Sabrina's champion.

I took that Devil girl under my wing, and Sabrina latched on to me like a deer tick. At first, I found her constant presence burdensome. She was like a baby wanting the affection of her mother, which was rather pathetic for I wasn't much in the nurturing department. But I did my best. I prayed for patience when she pestered me with questions, and I tried to be a good role model.

Despite the fact that the military was no longer a career option, I was still training like a Navy SEAL. Exercise was an outlet for me. It raised my serotonin levels, giving me a natural high, and left me with a feeling of accomplishment. I was in prime physical condition. I figured the Lord would provide an opportunity to make use of my strength and stamina, so I kept up my grueling regimen.

Sabrina embraced my exercise program, even attempting to match me stride for stride when running the Fort Pierce Bridge. In fact, it got so that Sabrina challenged *me*, hollering, "You can do it, Meghan," as she trotted alongside me. "Don't give up," she admonished when my perseverance lagged. And when I worked out in the basement, she regaled me with the words Marcus Luttrell had written in my copy of his book, the same phrase I'd painted over my pull-up bar to inspire me: "The easy day was yesterday."

Daily exercise soon had a transforming effect on Sabrina. Not only did her disposition improve, so did her posture. She wasn't nearly as cantankerous as she'd once been, and she no longer slouched in her chair at meals or in class. Little escaped Miss Frances, and it wasn't long before she noticed these changes in Sabrina. There were times when I caught her eyeing me speculatively.

I had conflicting emotions about Sabrina. I was happy to befriend her. The poor kid hadn't caught one break in her miserable life. But I also felt strapped with her, like I'd inherited a needy little sister, and

I had to guard against my resentment. She was such a child, so un-schooled and ignorant. But she possessed a keen mind, and it wasn't long before I decided I'd best do what I could to help educate her.

All the girls and guys at RH, if they hadn't graduated from high school, were enrolled in a GED program, and Sabrina was no excep-tion. Exhibiting a natural ability for math, she zipped right through algebra and geometry, but struggled with literature, geography, and history. I began working with her after dinner, helping her complete her assignments. Almost immediately, I realized her problems stemmed from poor reading skills.

"I have to take her to the library." I sat across from Miss Frances, pleading my case. "We need to get her hooked on the classics."

"We? I reckon the Bible's good enough," Miss Frances said. "Let her read that, why doncha? Kill two birds."

"Miss Frances," I wheedled, "Sabrina's really smart; she just hasn't been exposed to anything that'll fire up her imagination and get her thinking . . ."

"The Bible isn't thought-provoking?"

"Not for Sabrina, it isn't. I was thinking more on the lines of Twain, Melville, and maybe Dickens to start. Myth, you know—good versus evil."

"And you don't think that's in the Bible?" Frances skewed me with a withering glare.

"Miss Frances, please . . ."

Eventually, Miss Frances acquiesced, allowing Sabrina and me to be dropped off at the library one afternoon a week. My enthusiasm for fiction soon rubbed off on Sabrina. In no time, she was breezing through a novel a week, her appetite for literature seemingly growing with each book she consumed. Even more astonishing was the fact that, as she absorbed those masterpieces, Sabrina seemed to become more human, more compassionate, and less prickly. I guess the Devil had loosened his hold on her, just as he had done on me. It made sense; we'd both given up all our vices—cigarettes, alcohol, drugs, even cussing. I suppose we'd have been classified as "good girls." (Can you imagine?) There just wasn't much weakness left in us for that old Satan to exploit, and it appeared as though he'd moved on to greener pastures.

It didn't happen right away, but over time I became truly fond of Sabrina. And she idolized me, following me around like a puppy. She was fiercely loyal, sticking up for me on the few occasions I was challenged by one of the girls or a staff member. I grew to find Sabrina's dogged shadowing of me endearing. I was so much stronger than she, more than able to defend myself. Little did I know, Sabrina's constant surveillance would one day prove a blessing in disguise.

Not long after the exorcism, another new girl entered the program. Dulcie displayed all the usual issues associated with addiction: physical weakness, big empty spaces in her brain and heart, and poor self-esteem, to name a few. We'd all dealt with those problems, and would continue to do so as our recovery progressed, so we overlooked Dulcie's shortcomings and did our best to make her feel welcome. But Dulcie would have none of it. She didn't trust anyone and refused to let any of us girls tend to her when she detoxed and got the shakes.

Even Charlene couldn't charm her way into Dulcie's good graces. Worse yet, Dulcie took an instant disliking to me and didn't even try to disguise the fact that she found me repugnant. I don't know what it was about me that set her off. Perhaps it was because I'd become Miss Mareya's favorite. Or maybe she thought I got preferential treatment, which I did from time to time. But I wasn't the only favorite in the house: Miss Frances favored Charlene, and we all knew it.

Ever since I'd befriended Sabrina, harmony had reigned at Restoration House. That all changed upon Dulcie's arrival. We'd thought Sabrina's former antics disruptive, but Dulcie took discord to a new level. That girl was as eager to strike as a snake in a jar. And it wouldn't be long before I would feel the sting of her venom.

CHAPTER TWENTY-EIGHT

The Chicken Dance

RESTORATION HOUSE PROVIDED A WEALTH OF MATERIAL FOR ME TO JOURNAL. Despite the structured routine, no two days were ever alike, and someone was always getting into trouble or rocking the boat. Add to that the fact that the staff had their own colorful histories, their idiosyncrasies and quirks, and you can understand why I was constantly striving to commit the scuttlebutt to paper. I had to go about this business furtively, for the sisters and the girls were on to me; they had no desire to have their warts and wrinkles exposed for all to see. But that didn't deter me.

One would never think Miss Pinky, in her billowing muumuus, a former gang member, her weapon of choice: a baseball bat. "You don't want to cross Miss Pinky," Abigail had confided to me. "In her day, she bashed more than one head. If you think Frances is tough, you outta see Pinky when she's got her dander up."

And I was shocked to learn that mild-mannered Mr. Miller had been busted for dealing crack cocaine, in and out of jail for many years. During one of those stints he'd begun working the 12-steps, eventually reclaiming both his sobriety and sanity. After fifteen years sober, he is the gentlest, godliest man I know. Just goes to show, you never can tell what skeletons a person has in their closet.

Speaking of skeletons, Restoration House was rife with spirits. Of all the ghostly visitors, and there were many, Bishop Le Fleur was the most frequent. The Bishop had passed away back in the forties, gunned down and robbed in what, at the time, had been considered a random act of violence. In fact, it'd been a well-planned heist. Uncle to Miss Frances and her sisters, Le Fleur had been a strong influence in their young lives, and his untimely death had weighed heavily upon them. At the time of his passing, the Bishop had undertaken an ambitious fundraising campaign for the purpose of building a new church. Lacking the Bishop's determination to see this project through to its completion, the fundraising committee quickly lost impetus until the congregation's hopes for a new facility faded altogether. It was this unfinished business that led to Le Fleur's nocturnal appearances, and I was to witness this strange phenomenon firsthand.

It had become my custom to sit up late with Miss Mareya. Apparently, she enjoyed my company, and I certainly did hers. The result of this activity was that I was always tired, never having gotten enough sleep. But it was a small price to pay, for those times spent in the presence of Miss Mareya were well worth the discomfort. On this particular evening, we were ensconced in her cozy room, engrossed in a made-for-TV movie. At a commercial break, Mareya asked if I would retrieve a book she'd left on the front desk. I didn't hesitate but promptly scurried down the hall to the reception area. There was no one about at that hour, the familiar space awash in shadows, gloomy and foreboding. I'd just palmed the volume when the adjoining door to Mr. Miller's office slammed shut with a resounding bang. Startled, I nearly jumped out of my skin, but in the next instant my curiosity got the best of me, and I padded toward Miller's office door. Cautiously, I turned the handle, opened the door a crack, and peered inside. Mr. Miller had long since left for home, and, except for a sickly looking potted plant in the corner, there was no evidence of life. Perplexed, I retraced my steps and was soon seated in a comfy chair opposite my mentor. When I recounted the incident to Miss Mareya, she laughed and shook her head.

"Girl, that be my uncle, the ghost of Bishop Le Fleur. No need to worry; he's harmless. Just wants his money is all. Gets agitated when he can't find it."

"But why would he come here?" I asked, puzzled.

Miss Mareya muted the television and closed her eyes, seeming to collect her thoughts. In the next moment, she began relating the history of Restoration House.

"This hasn't always been a rehab facility, Meghan." Miss Mareya waved an arm about the room. "It was built as an annex to the old hospital, which was torn down years ago. It served as a men's ward, but sometimes boys were brought here as well."

"How do you know this?" I asked.

"Oh, I know. I was here once . . . when it was newly built, state-of-the-art, and in its heyday," Miss Mareya replied. A wistful look crossed her face and she paused, lost in another era.

"You're kidding!" I leaned forward in my chair.

"No. Over the years we've seen the boys." Miss Mareya returned to the present and focused on me.

My eyes got round as I digested this startling information. It made sense. I thought of the front reception area with its adjoining offices, the tiny dorm rooms—formerly patients' quarters—the enormous kitchen and pantry, the cavernous communal bath.

Suddenly, a thought occurred to me. "And the basement?" I asked, dreading her answer. The basement was where the treadmill and exercise equipment were located, the space where I worked out daily. I'd always thought it possessed a sinister atmosphere. But it was a cellar, I'd told myself, underground and therefore creepy.

"A temporary morgue," Miss Mareya stated matter-of-factly. "It's where they kept the dead bodies." I shivered as the hair on the nape of my neck rose. "It's where Le Fleur was taken when he collapsed and couldn't be resuscitated," Mareya added. "Seems he'd just collected a sizeable donation when he was shot and left for dead. He must have been semi-conscious when they brought him here, although I doubt he knew what hit him. I can't think of any other reason for him to keep coming back, looking to find the money he raised to build the new church."

"Do you have photographs?" I asked.

Miss Mareya pointed in the direction of a pine chest. "Bottom drawer," she said, "in a manila envelope." I darted to the bureau, drew open the lower drawer, and rifled through the contents. In less than a minute, I'd unearthed the object of my search. Envelope in hand, I returned to Miss Mareya and deposited the package on her lap. As I stood over her, I couldn't help but notice cancer's markers, how infirm she'd become. But a small smile played about her lips and her eyes gleamed with anticipation while her gnarled fingers worked the envelope's metal clasp. Once opened, she withdrew a handful of grainy, black-and-white photographs and some yellowed newspaper clippings. Mareya sifted through the lot until she came to a particular snapshot.

"Here you go." She handed me a photograph bearing the image of a small white boy, not more than ten years old. I studied the photo, taking in the child's emaciated frame. "We call him Jeremy. Don't rightly know what his real name was. But see . . ." Miss Mareya made a circular motion with her index finger. "Turn it over," she said. I complied, only to find the letters J and F and the numbers 9 and 48 written in script.

"J.F.," I murmured, turning the photo face up, scrutinizing the image. "His initials, huh?"

"I imagine so. And the date the photograph was taken."

"September 1948."

"You're a quick study, Meghan," Miss Mareya teased. "We see him every so often. Usually, outside the kitchen."

"He's hungry," I said, for the child appeared malnourished.

"Probably died of consumption, poor thing." Miss Mareya clucked sympathetically. "TB or some such."

"And take a look at this." She thrust a newspaper page toward me. Dated August 19, 1950, it was brittle with age. I held it gingerly as I read the article aloud.

"Grover Jenkins suffered heat stroke today while practicing football at Gifford High School. He was transported to Fort Pierce Hospital where he later died, never having regained consciousness." I cut my eyes to Miss Mareya, but she merely nodded sagely, indicating that I should continue. "The Tigers' football coach, Dan Green, stated that he'd cautioned the boys to keep hydrated. 'I even went so far as to provide water and ice,' Green said. 'But with temps reaching the mid-nineties, and Jenkins weighing in at 197 pounds, it was a recipe for disaster.' Jenkin's mother, Milly Watson, stated, 'It's too hot for those boys to be out there running in uniform during the heat of the day. Something needs to be done to prevent more young men from dying.' School principal, Robert Washington, offered his condolences to the Jenkins family. 'Our hearts go out to Grover's kin,' he said. 'He was a good kid, and a great athlete, and he'll be sorely missed on and off the playing field.'"

I returned the clipping to Miss Mareya. "So?" I said, shrugging my shoulders.

"He was my boyfriend," Mareya said. "Grover was still alive when they brought him here, but just barely. My mother let me come see him, say my final good-bye. I'll never forget it." A single tear wended its way down Miss Mareya's weathered cheek, and she dashed it away with a knuckle.

"Oh," I said in a small voice. "I'm so sorry."

"It's all ancient history, Meghan," Mareya said. "But Grover shows up here from time to time, and I have to admit it's a bit of a comfort to me. I think he comes around because he likes seeing me."

I took her small hand in mine and gently squeezed it. "I suppose you're right, Miss Mareya," I said. "Who wouldn't want to spend time with you?"

Staying up late as I did, I soon became accustomed to creaking floorboards and the occasional glimpse of an ethereal figure lurking in a corner or wafting down a hallway before vanishing altogether. It got so I didn't even flinch when a door slammed of its own accord. I once saw Jeremy lingering outside the kitchen. I swear he smiled at me before fading away. And I distinctly witnessed Grover Jenkins tossing a football toward me, but I figured that was because I was between him and Miss

Mareya, and he was probably showing off for her. I didn't speak of the ghosts to the other girls, figuring they'd find out for themselves if they were supposed to. But Miss Abigail was privy to the information, and she and I exchanged stories of sightings, giggling over Le Fleur's dogged persistence, commiserating over Jeremy's eternal hunger, and in awe of Grover's constant affection. It was more material for my diary, my future book, and I wrote it all down, painstakingly recording the stories for posterity.

One evening after dinner, I went to my room to retrieve my journal only to realize it had gone missing. Frantically, I searched my minuscule cubicle, but it was nowhere to be found. I couldn't believe it! I'd poured my heart out in that diary, detailed my recovery and recorded the girls' stories along with anecdotes about the Restoration House staff.

I stormed into the commons and found Abigail seated at the table, sifting through another bag of secondhand clothing donated by some well-intentioned soul.

"Miss Abigail," I cried, "somebody stole my journal!"

"What do you mean?" Abigail turned her baby-doll face toward me.

I loved Abigail, but was she dense? I wondered. Could I possibly make it plainer?

"My journal is gone!" I screeched.

"Are you sure you didn't misplace it?"

"It's gone! I can't find it anywhere."

Just then the back door banged shut, and Charlene sauntered in. "Y'all, look at what I found," she drawled, bearing my journal in hand.

"Where did you get that?" I snapped, crossing the distance between us.

"I was taking out the trash, and I found it in the garbage. Don't know how it got there, hon."

I snatched the diary away from her and examined it closely. The cover was soiled, and I could see that some pages had been ripped out.

My heart was pounding, and I was shaking with fury. At the same time I felt violated, and tears sprang to my eyes. Who would do such a cruel thing? I wondered.

"I know who did it." Sabrina's voice startled me, and I whirled around to confront her. She'd crept up behind me and was leaning indolently against the doorjamb. I should have known she'd be tailing me, for my newly acquired acolyte was never far from my side. "It was Dulcie," she announced. "I seen her coming outta Meghan's room right after lunch. Didn't think anything of it at the time."

"Was she carrying anything?" I asked.

"Couldn't tell. Saw her from behind. She was walking away from me."

"That's certainly not proof she stole the journal, now is it?" Miss Abigail asked.

"Nah, but it probably was her," Charlene said. "She's had it in for Meghan from the get-go."

"Somebody needs to do something," I said. "She can't just get away with stealing my property!"

"I'll talk to Miss Frances about it," Abigail said. "For now, I don't want any of you to say or do a thing about this. Understand?"

"But I—"

"We'll handle it, Meghan." Miss Abigail cut me off before I could complete my sentence. "Let it go."

I was furious; the unfairness of it rankled. I wanted to lash out at Dulcie, to make her pay for her crime. But I was hamstrung. I turned on my heel and stomped out of there in a rage. I hadn't gone but a few steps when I felt a tug on my arm. Sabrina had grabbed hold of me and was clinging to my elbow.

"We'll get her, Meghan," she breathed. "Don't you worry, sister." Angrily, I shook Sabrina off, but she was undeterred and proceeded to lockstep with me down the hall. Exasperated, I stopped marching and squared off in front of her.

"Sabrina, we can't do anything. You heard Miss Abigail," I said. "If we do, we'll only get kicked out of here. And even getting back at Dulcie isn't worth that."

"You just listen to me, Meghan," Sabrina said. "You're smart. I'll give you that. But there are some things I know that even you don't."

"Oh, yeah?"

"Yeah," Sabrina said. "And revenge happens to be one of them."

Sabrina's words struck a chord, and my heart rate slowed as I searched her face. Sabrina winked at me, as though sealing a bargain. A small smile crept across my own mug as I recollected the English proverb, "Revenge is a dish best served cold." I exhaled slowly, and my spirits lifted. I linked arms with Sabrina, and we put our heads together as we sashayed to my room. There were plans to hatch.

CHAPTER TWENTY-NINE

Glam Rock

"WHERE'S MY CHOIR ROBE?" I pawed through the crammed contents of my itty closet. "I ironed it just yesterday. Now I can't find it anywhere!"

"Look, silly!" Sabrina crossed the narrow room and came to stand beside me. She palmed a hanger and presented it to me with a flourish. "It woulda bit you if it were any closer."

"Hi, y'all. I'm so excited I can hardly stand it," Charlene said, popping her head through the doorway. She made a beeline for my bed, and plunked down on it.

"How you holding up, Meghan?" she asked, her white dress billowing around her compact frame.

Sabrina held my robe out before me, and I shrugged my arms into the ginormous sleeves. "She's a bundle of nerves, that's how she is, Miss Char. And you would be, too," Sabrina chided.

"I am not, Sabrina," I said as my fingers struggled to fasten the snap closures. But I was dissembling; a cold stone of terror sat heavily in the pit of my stomach.

"Hey, there!" Reba called out merrily as she and Maridee, both dressed in their Sunday finest, crowded into the small space.

"You look beautiful," I exclaimed, taking in their carefully arranged tresses, the slicks of lip gloss and mascara enhancing their features. We'd all taken pains with our appearances that morning, for today's services were to be extra special: after Robinson's sermon, the renowned Avenue

D Boys' Choir was slated to perform in concert with our own youth choir, and the entire ceremony was being professionally videotaped.

"Thank you, Miss Meghan," Maridee said. "I do feel particularly fetching today." She batted her enhanced eyelashes provocatively, posing like a cover girl. A shriek rent the air and we all froze. Then a series of curses ensued, and Reba took off running toward the commotion. The rest of us charged after her, Sabrina and I bringing up the rear. Reba halted abruptly at the doorway to Dulcie's room, and we all bunched up in a heap behind her. There was no question that Dulcie was the cause of this current uproar, for the new girl was throwing a hissy fit. I was in back and couldn't see the reason for her hysterics, so I jockeyed for a better position. But before I could make any headway, Sabrina forcibly pried me away. I whirled to face her, my mouth open, ready to protest. But my complaint died in my throat when I saw the smug smile of satisfaction Sabrina wore.

"I told you I'd take care of it." Her gray-green eyes glinted mischievously, and I knew in that instant she was behind these shenanigans. Then Dulcie exploded out of the doorway. Stamping her feet and waving her arms, she looked as though she were performing glam rock at a rave dance party. On closer inspection, I understood the reason for Dulcie's strange behavior: her clothing was alive with vermin. She was howling with disgust while plucking six-legged beasties from her jeans and tee and flicking them onto the floor.

"Ooo, gross!" Charlene cried, backing away from a monstrous roach scuttling across the floorboards toward her. "Somebody fetch the insect spray."

"I'll get it," Sabrina offered. She grinned at me conspiratorially before dashing down the hallway. Fearless, Reba wasted no time and began stomping the offending creatures with the soles of her shoes. I followed her lead, but we were fighting a losing battle. Most of the repugnant insects managed to skitter away, secreting themselves behind baseboards and underneath the hall runner. Maridee and Charlene were no help at all, their horrified squeals only adding to the mayhem.

Soon Sabrina returned with Miss Anne and Miss Abigail in tow. Miss Abigail set about fumigating Dulcie's room and the adjoining hallway with Raid Ant and Roach Spray while Miss Anne dealt with Dulcie.

"Shush now," she commanded, peeling off Dulcie's clothing. At Miss Anne's no-nonsense tone, Dulcie finally stopped her caterwauling and allowed herself to be administered to. "Charlene and Maridee, shut up and go get me a plastic bag for these rags," Miss Anne commanded, wadding up Dulcie's clothing in a bundle. "I ain't never seen such a infestation," she muttered under her breath. "Where they all come from, I wonder?"

When the ruckus finally died down and Miss Anne and Miss Abigail had deposited Dulcie in a steaming shower stall, Sabrina and I returned to my room. "What the heck did you do?" I asked Sabrina, my voice quivering with the effort of suppressing my laughter.

"I just put some of my pets in her closet," Sabrina said.

"Is that all?" I gave Sabrina a hard look.

"Weeelll . . ."

"What else?"

"I put a few of them in her bed."

"Good Lord!"

"And in her dresser."

Unable to contain myself any longer, I burst out laughing. As soon as she realized I wasn't angry, Sabrina joined in, and the two of us chortled until tears came to our eyes.

"You got her good, all right," I said, plopping onto my bed. "Hopefully, she never finds out."

"She won't," Sabrina said. "It doesn't matter anyway. Don't think she'll be sticking around here for long."

Sabrina's forecast proved spot on. Dulcie excused herself from worship, claiming a migraine, and the service went off without a hitch. In all the excitement I'd forgotten my nerves, and I sang my two solo lines in a clear, high voice that never wavered. Afterward, when the congregation was thronging around the D Boys, offering up their congratulations, I headed for the annex and made myself scarce. I was proud of the fact that the youth choir and I had pulled it off, that our debut billing with Avenue D had been a success, but I was also chagrined to think I'd been partly responsible for Dulcie's comeuppance. I felt undeserving of praise, and I didn't want to make small talk with the sisters or the girls. Sabrina had acted on my behalf, and although part of me took satisfaction in Dulcie's travail, my better self knew she'd been unfairly treated.

The very next day, Dulcie left RH and wasn't heard from again. I've never forgiven myself for her defection, and I only hope that she has somehow managed to keep clean. In my heart of hearts, I know that is not likely.

CHAPTER THIRTY

The Quickstep

"YOU PASSED THE SCIENCE AND ENGLISH SECTIONS, BUT YOU'LL HAVE TO TAKE A REMEDIAL MATH COURSE," MISS BRISETTE SAID WHILE SCRUTINIZING THE PRINTOUT OF MY TEST SCORES. I shot Mom a quizzical glance. She nodded her approval, and I sighed with relief. I'd been nine months in rehab at RH, and Miss Frances had finally agreed that I should enroll in classes. It was a huge concession on her part and a step in the right direction for me. I'd called Mom and asked her to pick me up and take me to the college, not only because I needed her to pay for the classes but because I desperately wanted her opinion regarding which courses I should take.

"Let's see," the counselor said, eyeing her computer monitor. "Gee, you're all over the board here. Looks like you've taken lots of design classes and some psych, huh?"

"Yeah, but I'm thinking I'd like criminal justice or EMT," I piped in. My dreams of enlisting in the Navy Search and Rescue Division had been dashed, but I still desired to serve in some sort of first-responder capacity.

"But she's got a record," Mom said.

"No felonies, though," I added.

"Oh, I see . . ."

My heart plummeted. I just knew this woman was going to dash my hopes, and I didn't think I could stand one more rejection, couldn't imagine myself working toward a degree that would land me behind a desk in some nine-to-five job that would kill me slowly.

"Problem is, both the criminal justice and EMT programs require you to successfully complete the NREMT exam, and I'm afraid the deadline for enrolling for that was yesterday. You'd have to wait another semester before entering either program. Besides, I don't want you to set yourself up for disappointment," Brisette continued. "Miss Rose, I'm going to speak frankly. I'd hate for you to waste your time taking classes in those fields when the likelihood of your getting hired in either capacity are slim to none. Even without a felony on your record, I'm afraid you'd have a difficult time. The competition is fierce, and although admittance to either program is predicated on a personal interview and on a one-to-one basis, still—"

"You could finish your interior design degree," Mom said brightly.

"No! It's not what I want," I cried. I knew I was acting like a spoiled brat, but I couldn't help it. I'd been so good, reformed completely, and I felt it was high time I caught a break.

Mom persisted, saying, "But at least you'd have a degree—"

Sensing my dismay, Brisette interrupted. "There is, however, one rather exciting avenue open to you," she said. Suddenly, I was all ears. "You probably aren't aware of it, but IRSC has recently established a homeland security program."

"Homeland security?" I knit my brows. "You mean like FEMA?"

"Yes. FEMA is actually a component. It's a vast, new field that, after 9/11, has become extremely important both to our national defense and as an emergency management organization. President Massey is a forward thinker and eager to distinguish IRSC as a cutting-edge resource in this new area. In fact, the groundbreaking ceremony for the new building is just next week."

"And it's okay that she doesn't have a valid driver's license?" Mom asked.

"As far as I know, the admission policy is wide open. This is the first time we've offered courses. It's a relatively new field. The parameters are evolving."

"What classes are available?" Suddenly eager, I edged closer to the counselor.

"Let's see." The counselor turned back to her computer monitor. "There's Weapons of Mass Destruction on Tuesdays and Thursdays at 9:30 to 10:45, then at 1:30 you could take Disaster Preparedness." I could feel the goose flesh rise on my arms. It was as though a piece of an invisible puzzle were falling into place. There was something that felt so right about this unexpected development. I knew for certain God had answered my prayers.

"You what?" Miss Frances said. "Three classes? How am I supposed to get you back and forth to three classes? You not the only girl I've got to see to, Meghan!" There were times when Miss Frances was maddeningly conflicted, and this happened to be one of them. She'd implicitly told me I could enroll for college courses. Now that I'd done that very thing, she was ruing her decision. I understood her dilemma. She knew I was ready to test my wings in the real world, but she was concerned that when, as would inevitably happen, temptation reared its ugly head, I might be unable to resist.

"But Miss Frances," I wheedled, "I couldn't take any classes without first enrolling in a remedial math, and the only one that was available was at the St. Lucie campus. I didn't think you'd mind."

"Humph!" Miss Frances shook her head, obviously irritated. "We just see about that. Think I drive you from here to kingdom come!"

One of the hardest things about being in RH was not being in control of my own destiny. I was completely reliant on Miss Frances and her staff. I could leave any time I wanted, but there was no open-door policy. If I took it in my head to simply pack up and vacate, I would not be welcomed back.

"My first class is in two weeks." I grinned imploringly. "Thursday, the twenty-fourth."

The phone rang and Miss Frances shooed me away before taking the call. "Somebody going to have to pay for the gas," she muttered, and in that moment I knew I'd won a small victory.

Soon I was attending classes at both the Fort Pierce and St. Lucie campuses. The unaccustomed freedom was heady stuff for me, and I soaked up the college atmosphere like a desert flower does water. Except for obtaining my lifeguard certification, my freshman year at St. Leo had been a bust. And I'd never really appreciated my former classes at IRSC because, of course, I'd been stoned. Miraculously, I'd been given a third chance at obtaining a higher education, and this time I wasn't about to blow it. In fact, I secretly vowed to ace all of my classes. I was a different person from that wild Un Zapato child for whom everything had always come so easily until one day it hadn't. I knew I was going to have to work hard, and that made me all the more determined.

I was the only female in my homeland security classes. Dr. Paul Forage, department head for the newly established program, took an instant liking to me, and it wasn't long before I was spending my lunch hour in his office, the two of us mismatched souls having become fast friends. Forage was a wonk and a bit of a nerd, but powerfully built and thoroughly capable of defending himself and country. As for me . . . I was just getting back on my feet and a little wobbly. It was an unusual pairing, but I have to believe the Lord led me to Forage. Unlike most men, he didn't see me as a sexual being. Or if he did, he sure didn't let on.

Forage had earned his PhD in Chinese history and language with an emphasis on the Song dynasty. But he was more than a scholar; he had a lifelong fascination with the military, eventually serving as an officer in the Canadian Reserve Forces. It was his vast knowledge of history and war that led him to develop an emergency management program while teaching at Florida Atlantic University. In 2006, he was recruited by IRSC to develop a similar program.

Forage regarded me as a valuable asset to mold and make use of. He was like a father to me, treating me with dignity and respect. It was only a matter of time before I found myself spilling my guts to him, recounting all of my mishaps and misadventures, even going so far as to confide that my current residence was a rehab facility. To his credit, Forage took it all in stride, never making me feel foolish or inadequate. Instead, he somehow made me feel exceptional, as though my travails had all been background, preparing me for the ultimate test.

"We need women in this field, Meghan." Forage rummaged through his briefcase, searching for the paper sack containing his lunch. "With the new facility under construction, I feel it is important to fast-track you, get you on staff as quickly as possible."

I'd just bitten into the ham-and-cheese sandwich that Miss Anne had prepared for me and had all I could do to keep from spewing a mouthful all over Forage's desk. Staff? Had I heard him correctly?

"You'll eventually want to get your PhD," Forage continued, prying the lid from a small plastic container. "Once you complete the program, I'll bring you on board as an adjunct. But you needn't worry about any of that. I'll help you in every way I can."

Me, a PhD? Was the man crazy? I wondered. I studied his face for an answer to that question, but none was forthcoming. Forage merely picked at his chicken salad. Despite his sturdy build, he had the look of an ascetic about him. One would never suspect that he was possessed of *special* skills.

"But that'll take years," I said, struggling to keep the whine from my voice.

"We can't wait that long, Meghan." Dr. Forage peeled away the shell of a hard-boiled egg, and I watched, fascinated, by the delicacy with which he dispensed with that task. He was such a dichotomy, I thought: a peace-loving warrior.

In the short time I'd known him, I'd come to trust Forage. He'd completed his BA degree in Chinese studies at the University of Toronto, where the subject of ethics had been drilled into his eager young mind. It went without saying that his sense of justice was deeply ingrained. I had complete confidence in him, realizing full well that he'd never lead me on or fill me with false hope. Is it any wonder that his words were music to my ears? I'd wanted to join the Navy, but that hadn't happened. Then I'd hoped to obtain a degree in criminal justice or as an EMT, and that hadn't worked out either. Now I found myself on the cutting edge of a new field of study, homeland security, positioned with the number-one guy, who was going to head up the number-one state-of-the-art facility. Was it coincidence? I didn't think so.

Just that morning, I'd been at a service honoring CeeCee Ross-Lyles, Miss Frances's niece. CeeCee had been a flight attendant on United Airlines Flight 93, and before that a detective on the Fort Pierce Police Squad. Fifteen years after her death, a life-sized statue of CeeCee was unveiled in the Veteran's Park overlooking the Indian River, and I attended the dedication. It was a very moving ceremony. All of us had lost something in the 9/11 attacks—loved ones, a sense of security. It's no wonder I was raw with emotion when Forage spoke of the need for women in the field, that his words struck a chord. There were people in the world that hated us simply because of our Western ways, the fact that American women were openly sexual. How ironic, I thought, that life had brought me to this juncture. Was my calling to defend the moral decline of our culture? No! I knew right from wrong. But I was also cognizant of the fact that there are shades of gray overlying everything. In the end, it was about freedom, a woman's right—everyone's right—to choose their destiny, so long as what they pursue is legal and not harmful to others.

"Okay," I said. "What do you propose?"

I was nearing the completion of my first year of study in the field of homeland security when I graduated the Restoration House Program. Miss Frances and her sisters threw a little going-away party for me. They even bought a sheet cake from Publix proclaiming "Congratulations, Meghan." And all the girls had made cards for me. Miss Frances said a few words, and I got teary-eyed. I knew I'd reached a milestone in my life, yet the finality of this departure was both anticlimactic and exhilarating. I was a different girl from the one who'd entered those doors a year and a half ago. And I couldn't believe I would be walking out of there with no restrictions whatsoever.

When the party was winding down, Miss Frances came to me and put her arms around me. "You don't have to go," she said. "We'll always have a bed for you here, Miss Meghan."

And then I did break down. "Thank you," I said through my tears. "But it's time I try to fly on my own."

"I suppose you're right," Miss Frances said. "You've made us proud, Meghan. I want you to know that."

"I owe it all to you, Miss Frances. Who knows? Maybe I'll take you up on your offer sometime."

"I'd like that."

I'd hoped to share an apartment with Reba or Charlene, but they'd returned to their respective hometowns. I thought about asking L.T. if I could stay with him, but I didn't want to tempt fate with so many potential "triggers." I was in the world clean for the first time in almost eight years and determined to stay sober. I returned home to Mom,

Life was good. My classes were fascinating, and I felt as though I'd finally found my niche. I especially enjoyed the mock disaster drills that Forage masterminded, even going so far as to recruit my straight-laced niece, Caylin, to volunteer as a civilian on one such occasion. It wasn't until the drill was nearly complete that I made the "fatal" error of stepping on a downed faux live wire, causing us both to be "injured" and out of play. The kid surprised me; she was impressively limp and unresponsive as she was carried out in the EMT's arms, playing her part to the hilt.

True to his word, Forage paved the way for me. I completed the two-year homeland security program in a little over a year. But it wasn't until I was midway toward earning my BS degree that my uniform was issued. Proudly, I donned my gear, khakis and black lace-up combat boots, and headed over to Restoration House to strut my stuff.

I passed over that same threshold I'd crossed two years earlier when I was high on drugs, low on self-esteem and about to detox, and who did I find manning the reception desk? None other than Miss Frances! She took one look at me, and her face split in a wide grin.

"Let's go show the girls," she said, rising from her chair. The two of us linked arms and strode the length of the hallway. When we entered the commons, a hush fell over the room and all eyes turned toward us. I searched the fresh faces ringing the enormous dining table, and I was flooded with conflicting emotions. Reba was gone, having graduated the program, as were both Miss Charlene and Miss Maridee. And precious Miss Mareya had passed, her poor body having just given out. Those women had probably been the best friends I'd ever had, I thought, and I would never forget them. These were new girls at the table, and as my eyes fell on first one and then another, I realized they would look to me as a role model, that eventually I would learn each of their stories. Then my eyes lit upon Sabrina. Not slouching but sitting erect, she was playing the part of the perfect guest and beaming at me with undisguised admiration. I returned her infectious smile, thinking how she might imagine my accomplishment as her own. I shook my head at the absurdity of it all.

"Ladies," Miss Frances announced, "I present to you Miss Meghan Rose, homeland security."

Sabrina rose from her chair, clapping her hands and cat whistling. The other girls followed suit, although I'm sure they didn't understand the reason for their show of congratulations. When the applause died down, Miss Frances bowed her head, then looked skyward as though entreating the Creator. I'd become accustomed to such theatrics, so I didn't think much of it. But then Frances fixed her gaze on me, tears welling in her eyes, and I knew something out of the ordinary was about to transpire.

"Meghan," she breathed, "you have come through fire; you have beaten the Devil at his own game."

Goosebumps rose on my arms, for I knew she spoke the truth. I had done that very thing, and somehow I'd lived to chronicle this amazing story.

"Meghan," Miss Frances continued, "I've seen what you've accomplished, and despite all odds, some would say it's crazy luck. I say . . . it's *God*."

My heart filled with gratitude for the Lord's intervention, for the miracle that had landed me in this place when I was at my lowest. I knew everything I had experienced had led me to this juncture in my life, and I felt that final piece of the puzzle completing the picture. Frances had gotten it right. It *was* God. He'd delivered me. My journey wasn't over, but I was safe. I would always be taken care of, just as all of us who surrender and trust in Him will surely be.

CHAPTER THIRTY-ONE

Warrior Dance

THE SKIES HAD OPENED UP, THE RAIN BEATING DOWN WITH THE INTENSITY OF A MONSOON. It had been a long day of practice drills in the field. Forage was a hard taskmaster, and my teammates and I had worked side by side with some of those very firefighters I'd competed with on the ball league not so many months ago. The homeland security students often collaborated with other agencies—EMT, criminal justice, and the like—for in the event of a bona fide disaster we would all be working in tandem. Imagine my delight when I learned that, in cases of natural and man-made disasters, *we,* that is to say, homeland security, were designated first responders. It was our bailiwick to make the initial assessment, secure the area, and set up the command post! This very afternoon, we'd practiced search-and-rescue exercises using the Trauma-Hawk simulator. I was sodden and weary and never so happy to be home.

My new apartment was a bit ramshackle, but homey and spotlessly clean. I dropped down in my consignment shop-find chair and pried off my combat boots. When I reached for the remote on the side table, my eyes fell upon a framed print of Bentley. As always, thoughts of that sweet dog tugged at my heart. Michael and Mary had done a great job of caring for him, but during his tenure with them, he'd developed a penchant for bolting whenever the opportunity presented itself. (I pray he wasn't heading out in search of me.) On one such occasion, he was struck by a car and killed. That dog had stuck by me through all of my drug-crazed years. His loyalty and unconditional love had always been a given. What a blessing our beloved pets are, and how I miss him!

Next to that photo was another framed pic of the girls and me. This one was taken at an election site Miss Frances had delivered us to. We girls had been out of circulation for so long we had no knowledge of local politics. But Miss Frances had been supporting some candidate running for state representative. So there we were, attired in navy-blue tees, holding an oversized campaign sign before us—Reba, Meridee, Charlene, Sabrina, and the rest—all bright-eyed and exuberant.

I massaged my temples and sighed. I'd kept track of Reba and Charlene via their occasional postings on Facebook. Both of them had returned to their hometowns and reunited with their young children. I have no way of knowing for certain, but I believe they've stayed clean. I do know they've avoided prison. And for addicts with prior convictions, that counts as a success.

Sabrina took a circuitous route to sobriety. Upon her release from RH, her old boyfriend picked her up, and it wasn't long before she was dancing again. Her uncle intervened and persuaded her to move back home. Rather than take up residence with her mother, she agreed to stay with him until she could stand on her own two feet. Presently, Sabrina is working for her uncle in the family business. She is married now, with a child and a real pet, a Humane Society mutt. And she's drug-free.

As for Meridee, she's fine. She has stayed in touch with Frances and me, keeping us up to date on her progress at TU, where she's working toward obtaining her degree in education. I have no doubt she'll be a great teacher

Abigail was not so fortunate. Florida's penal system is skewed against the petty offender. In 2013, Abigail was arrested for violation of probation. She was pulled over while driving the RH van with an invalid driver's license. Because she had a prior conviction, she was sentenced to fourteen years in prison!

I closed my eyes and thought back over my days spent at Restoration House and the amazing women I'd encountered. It pained me to think that any of the girls might slide back into addiction. I wished there was something I could do to help ensure that every RH graduate had a fighting chance of maintaining their sobriety. Miss Frances had spoken to me of her desire to establish an aftercare program, one where the recovering addict transitions into society while residing in a monitored and supportive environment. "I'd like to be a part of that," I'd said, for I knew firsthand that's what was lacking in my own recovery. After having lived five or ten years in the drug, it takes more than a year or two of in-house treatment to effect a total cure. What is needed is long-term aftercare. "You'll have to get a degree in counseling," Frances had told me.

Perhaps, I thought, I should do that very thing. My mind was suddenly awhirl with the possibilities. I tossed the remote back onto the end table. I was too hyper to sit and veg, and the thought of staring at a computer screen while researching counseling degree programs wasn't enticing. I opted for my fallback: I changed into my spandex tights and headed for the gym.

I burst through the door leading from the women's locker room, psyched up for my workout, only to be sidetracked by a small throng of gym rats gathered around the community bulletin board.

"What's up?" I hollered in their direction, curious as to why they weren't battling the machines or lifting, as usual.

"We're thinking about signing up for this challenge," Paul said, nodding toward a poster newly affixed to the board. Paul was part owner of Nature's Way Gym, the preferred workout venue for many local fire/rescue and police academy students. Nature's Way didn't project pretense; it was about as far from a day spa as one could imagine. Bare bones, it was a sweatshop with plebian terrazzo floors and unadorned concrete-block walls. There were no TVs or stereo systems, no Pilates classes or stationary bikes, just a plethora of weights, Machiavellian-looking machines, and an underlying odor of sweat and testosterone.

"Signing up for what?" I asked, sidling over to the bulletin board.

"The Navy SEAL Challenge," Paul said. "We're going to compete, train for it." Then he sized me up appraisingly. "You in, Meghan?"

My eyes flew over the poster, my brain processing the information. The Challenge was to take place in Vero Beach on November 30th, three months from today's date. It consisted of swimming, running, climbing ropes and rappelling. The swimming and running would be no problem for me, I thought. But just imagining the upper-body strength required to climb seventy-five feet from the water's surface to the top of the Barber Bridge and rappel back down was daunting. "Sure," I said, thinking I'd better start working my arms PDQ.

"Great," Paul said. "I'll sponsor you. Maybe even spring for some ropes for us to train on."

"That would be super, Paul." Rory's distinctive baritone came to me from across the gym. I whirled about and smiled when I saw him striding toward me, a wide grin spread across his handsome face. "You know she'll probably beat your sorry ass, but let's go for it!"

I trained for the next three months as though my very life depended on it, and it gave me something positive to focus on. Rory proved a terrific coach, encouraging me to swim and run beyond my endurance. He ferreted out obscure government training courses, long since overgrown by Florida flora, and the two of us trespassed, happy to have the US of A providing us with new challenge venues. True to his word, Paul purchased the ropes and had them installed at Nature's Way. My gym friends and I spent countless hours sweating, climbing, slotting our feet into the tiny rungs and heaving our bodies up and up, until we couldn't bear the sight of a rope ladder, let alone climb one.

When the day of the Challenge finally dawned, I was terrified, ready to back out rather than risk making a fool of myself.

"I'm late for the sign-up," I said. "Probably won't be allowed to compete."

"Late?" Mom's voice came to me over my cell, shrill with incredulity. "You've trained so hard, and now you're going to forfeit?" Mom was my conscience. She simply would not let me slide. Instead, she held my feet to the fire.

"I'm sure Paul told me the sign-up was at noon. In fact, it's at 11 a.m. I'll never make it."

"You're just looking for an excuse to back out. You're in the best shape of your life, and there's not ever going to be another opportunity like this. You can do it," Mom said. "Get your butt down there and show them what you've got!"

As usual, Mom was right. I was wimping out, allowing my fears to get the best of me. But her pep talk had its desired effect, and I was suddenly eager to see this thing through.

CHAPTER THIRTY-TWO

The Challenge

"**WILL WE EVER GET THERE?**" I tapped my foot impatiently, fixing my eyes on the unsightly stretch of US Hwy 1 flying by my window—scrub vegetation punctuated by run-down motels, a cemetery, and low-budget car lots.

"We'll make it, babe." Rory was driving like a speedster at the Indianapolis 500, while I fretted in the passenger seat beside him. Good to his word, he covered the distance from Fort Pierce to Riverside Park in a record twenty minutes. We pulled into an unpaved parking lot littered with boat trailers, and our eyes were immediately drawn to the oversized tarp affixed to the top of the Barber Bridge. "Navy SEAL Challenge," it proclaimed.

"Here we go," Rory said as we hiked toward the docks.

As usual in competitions of this nature, the timeline proved fluid. All twenty contestants were supposed to have been signed in and briefed by 11 a.m., the competition commencing at noon. Luckily for me, there'd been some glitches and everything had been pushed back. I joined the group of contestants and ex-Navy SEALs clustered on the dock, and no one breathed a word about my tardiness.

"You'll compete in twos—two ropes, two ladders," a hunky, middle-aged muscleman explained. "For your safety, you'll each be outfitted with a harness attached to a cable controlled by those fellas up on top of the bridge." All of us contenders gazed up at the bridge, and several tiny figures waved down to us as though rehearsed. "No one's gonna free-fall or drown." He eyeballed each of us, and we nodded our heads while digesting this bit of information. "For you first-timers," he continued, "the rope ladder will likely be your undoing. If you drop your arms or lose your footing, you'll probably flip upside down. Should that happen, you'll find it nearly impossible to right yourself and complete the Challenge. You'll be exhausted and you won't have the upper body strength to continue. I've seen it a hundred times. If that happens to any of you, unclip yourself from the harness and slide down the rope. And if, by chance, you do become distressed in the water, those guys," he gestured toward the two Coast Guard cutters bobbing on the surface, "they'll be on you like flies to honey. I want you to remember there's no shame in having tried. Everyone's a winner here."

Then it was time to begin. Each of us had been assigned a number. Paul's was seven, mine eight, which meant that we would be competing in tandem. We watched as the first two contenders were fitted in harnesses and protective helmets. When the bell rang, the two dove into the water and swam the distance to the rope ladders. One guy made it all the way to the top of the bridge and flung himself over the railing, but the other was having difficulty on the ladder. Eventually, as we'd been forewarned, he became inverted. It was torturous watching him hanging upside down while struggling to right himself. After much effort, he somehow managed to do so and continued his ascent. He hadn't gone but a few rungs when he flipped again, and the crowd emitted a collective sigh of dismay. He flailed and flopped on the end of his line like a fish out of water until, at last, he gave up, defeated. Unclipping his harness from the cable, he flew down the rope and plunged into the river.

We all cheered as arms reached out to hoist him onto the dock. There were no losers here! In the meantime, the first contender had disappeared from view as he raced toward the base of the bridge, and there was a momentary lull in the action. I meandered over to the Riverside Café, where I found Rory seated across from Mom on the deck. This vantage point afforded an excellent view of the bridge.

"Want something to drink?" Rory asked.

"A Coke would be great," I said as I took a seat beside him.

"This is much more difficult than I imagined," Mom said. "That ladder? Brutal!"

"The one we practiced on was twenty feet. This is more than three times that, and I have to swim to get to it. I don't know . . ." My voice trailed off. Then a babble arose from the spectators; they gestured at the bridge where a tiny figure could be seen sprinting toward its apex.

"It's him," Rory exclaimed. "He's finished the run. All he has to do now is rappel the rope, swim to the dock, and he's home free."

"Nothing to it," I said, thinking anything but.

By the time Paul and I were poised to dive into the water and begin our Challenge, two more contestants had gotten hung up in the ladders and opted out by unclipping themselves and sliding down the rope. But I couldn't think about that now; I couldn't think about anything but the tasks that lay before me. Then the bell rang and Paul and I sliced into the river. I quickly outdistanced Paul, which allowed me dibs on the nearer ladder. But I'd expended so much energy—swimming all out—that by the time I reached it, my arms were nearly spent.

Somehow I managed to clip myself to the line and begin slotting one foot after the other into the narrow rungs, willing my rebellious arms to pull me upward. I'd made it about a third of the way when I heard a roar from the crowd. I ventured a look below only to see Paul flying down the rope. He'd given up. I couldn't focus on that now because my fingers were beginning to spasm. Then my hand slipped from the ladder, and in the next instant I found myself flung upside down. Over the cacophony from spectators urging me on, I could distinguish my mother's voice.

"Come on, Meghan," she screamed. "You've got it, girl!"

Rory was yelling at me as well. "We don't give up, Meghan!"

I hung there for what seemed an eternity, grateful for the blood flowing back into my useless limbs. But it was rushing to my head as well, and I knew I had to right myself, that I had to finish what I'd started. With a mighty effort, I heaved myself up, my right hand scrabbling wildly in the air until, miraculously, it connected with the ladder. My fingers found purchase on a rung, and I righted myself. I clung to this lifeline as though it were all that connected me to the universe, too exhausted to attempt climbing. Once more, my mother's voice came to me. "Meghan! Up, up!"

"You can do it, Meghan." Rory's voice coaxed me out of my stupor, and I raised a foot and hitched myself up. My arms were on fire, all the muscles in my body screaming for me to stop this madness, to unclip my harness and fly down the rope into the water.

But there was nothing for it; I had to keep going. And somehow I did. I'd nearly made it to the top of the bridge when my arms gave out completely and I let go of the rope. Instantly, my legs flew out from under me until I was hanging parallel to the bridge. In the next moment, I flipped over and found myself suspended upside down once again. There was a huge gasp from the spectators. They knew it was over for me. None of the previous contestants had managed to recover from this predicament twice.

"Meeghaan!" My mother's voice rose above all the others, screaming for me to continue. "Come onnn. Finiiish!"

"You can do it, Meg," Rory yelled.

"We don't give up, Meghan," Paul's familiar voice separated itself from the crowd below. Having managed to swim to the dock, his hopes of completing the Challenge dashed, Paul had joined my camp of supporters and was now urging me on.

I was less than ten feet from the railing, so close to completing this leg of the event, when the guys on the bridge who were controlling my cable added their voices to the din. "Come on!" they hollered. "*You are the woman!*"

I'd done it before, I thought; I could do it again. "Please, Lord," I prayed, "help me!" With a Herculean effort, I heaved my upper body in the most intense sit-up I'd ever attempted, while flinging my arms out and grasping wildly for the rope. God answered my prayer. Once again my fingers made contact, and with all the strength I could muster, I managed to right myself. The spectators roared their approval while the men above me continued their encouragement. *"You got it now! Come on, woman,"* they cried.

There was no way I was going to win this thing, I thought fleetingly. My time was abysmal. But I sure as heck was going to finish, I resolved. Slowly, painfully, I dragged myself up that ladder until I was eyelevel with the handrail. But I was so fatigued I couldn't fling myself over it. Since I was still competing, no one was allowed to offer me assistance. So there I was between two worlds. What else is new? I thought grimly. My upper body hung over the rail bridge-side, but my feet were still tangled in the ladder rungs. An image of Read, my childhood pal whose life had so tragically ended suspended from this bridge, flashed in my brain. "Come on, Read," I muttered. "Let's do this thing." Perhaps it was divine intervention, or maybe one of the empathetic guys controlling my line gave it the tiniest tug. One way or another, I went sailing over that rail and fell in a heap onto the pavement.

I'd thought I was so strong, when in reality I was a weakling. I wanted nothing more than to plug my thumb in my mouth and lie there indefinitely. I'd pushed my body past its endurance, and my brain was addled from the effort.

"Get up! Run!" the former SEALs commanded, and my ridiculously competitive streak surfaced. Unsteadily, I gathered myself, rose to my feet, and began hiking down the bridge. "No! The other way," they cried. I reversed course and let my feet take me in the other direction, and in no time fell into an effortless lope. This was the easy part; I could run forever. It was a relief to let my arms hang at my sides and feel the blood return to my fingers. As I trotted down the bridge, my head began to clear and I thought about the final leg of the competition. Climbing the ladder had been much more difficult than I'd ever imagined. I'd done it, but by the hair of my chinny-chin-chin! The thought of rappelling down the rope was every bit as daunting, especially now that my arms were two useless appendages. I needed to psych myself up and strategize. I would have to twist the rope around my foot to help support my body, I decided. I couldn't rely solely on my upper-body strength to manage it.

By the time I returned to the top of the bridge, I was somewhat reenergized. *"You the woman!"* the SEALs yelled as I approached.

Once my harness had been attached to the cable, I was handed a small red flag on a clip. I hoisted myself over the railing and grabbed the rope. Some of my strength had returned, for I was able to prop myself up while my right foot worked itself around the rope, creating a tight noose that helped support me. Slowly, I inched my way down. As I descended, it proved ever more difficult to maintain the loop around my foot. But I knew I had to keep my wits about me, keep the rope twisted around my foot. It was the only thing preventing me from flying down to the water's surface.

Halfway down, I stopped to clip the flag onto the cable. This was perhaps the most challenging aspect of the competition. My arms were gone, my fingers numb, yet I needed them to accomplish this task. I dug my foot into the noose to keep me from slipping down. Then, with my right hand, I unclipped the flag from my harness. My right foot and left hand were all that held me suspended thirty-five feet above the water's surface. Somehow I managed to release the flag before my fingers refused to work. I struggled to clip the flag to the cable, but it proved impossible.

The crowd roared to life, screaming at me to accomplish this small feat. I was so close to finishing, but I could feel the last vestiges of strength draining from my body. Then, slowly, the pull of gravity caused me to inch downward. "No!" I cried silently. "Sweet Jesus, please help me do this!" Just as my left hand gave out and I began to fall, the clip miraculously connected with the cable. A second more and I'd have missed it, and been disqualified. I zinged down the rope and splashed into the water, never so glad to be in that element rather than suspended above it.

You'd have thought I'd have been home free by then, but that was not the case. My poor hands had taken such a beating that my fingers refused to obey the signals my brain sent them. They fumbled ineffectually at the clip attaching my harness to the cable. Seconds dragged on into minutes as I struggled to free myself. The Riverside Café patrons and the spectators gathered on shore were going wild, all of them screaming for me to finish.

"Almost there, Meg!" Once again my mother's voice screeched above the clamor.

"Dear God," I entreated, "I beg you." And my fingers responded and began working at the clip until at last I was free! Out of my mind with exhaustion, I began to swim, but my form was nothing like it had been when, cockily, I first dove into the river. My arms were of little use now. I couldn't lift them over my head. So I thrashed and kicked my way toward the dock. And I'd nearly made it when pain and exhaustion overcame me. Barely able to tread water, I slowly began to sink. A deafening blast sounded from one of the Coast Guard cutters, telling me my rescuers were on their way.

It must have been the jarring blare of the horn that caused adrenaline to spike through my arteries. That, coupled with the shouts of encouragement from the assembled onlookers, spurred me on. "You've got this," cried my mother.

"We don't quit," yelled Rory and Paul. "Finish!"

Like a plucky toddler, I kicked doggedly toward the dock until I finally reached it. All that remained was for me to climb up on the deck and ring the bell. But I was totally drained. I couldn't do it.

I do not know how long I clung to the edge of the dock, too fatigued to heave myself up, but it seemed an eternity. It was ironic, I thought, to have come this far and to have failed. And if it hadn't been for Rory screaming for me to "use the piling," I might have. But he had cried out, and I'd heeded his cry. I demanded that my right arm rise, grasped the piling, and did a one-handed pull-up. Then, like a pompano pursued by a hungry dolphin, I fairly leapt out of the water only to collapse on the deck.

"*You the woman!*" my SEAL buddies on top of the bridge shouted.

"*Meghan! Meghan!*" Rory and Paul chanted.

"One last favor, Lord," I breathed, dragging my miserable carcass across the deck. "Give me the strength to ring the bell."

And He did.

Why had I done it, the reporter asked? What had been my motivation? The obvious answer was that the Navy SEAL Challenge had provided a way for me to announce my redemption to the universe and come to grips with it myself. More than that, in my sorry past I'd allowed myself to fall so low as to court degradation. Was it any wonder I craved the opposite end of the spectrum: glory? Of course, I wanted to prove myself, to proclaim my victory over evil. I was no longer an easy mark, and my closet boasted a plethora of shoes in pairs. Miss Un Zapato was history; the Devil had forsaken my feet and moved on to easier marks.

It's up to me now, just as it's always been. But I'm finally ready to follow the righteous path, to see where it leads me. I know it won't be easy, that there will be temptations and detours along the way. But this I promise you: I'll never dance with the Devil again.

And I'll let you know how it all works out.

2013 Navy SEAL Bridge Challenge: Having climbed 60 feet, Meghan nears the bridge railing.

Nearly spent, Meghan clings to the dock and struggles to hoist herself up.

Exhausted, Meghan rings the bell to complete The Navy SEAL
Bridge Challenge

The Back Stories

David Root:

In 2001, David Root was celebrating Independence Day with some friends at a bar in St. James City. He'd had too much to drink, but his home was less than a quarter of a mile away. He must have figured he could manage that short distance, for he slid behind the wheel of his automobile and headed out on Stringfellow Road.

David never made it home. Instead, he detonated his own personal fireworks display. David fell asleep at the wheel. He lost control of the car and veered off the road. The car flipped, and that beautiful, talented boy was killed instantly. He was eighteen.

Like so many of Meghan's contemporaries, David's brothers, Douglas and Dustin, started smoking pot in junior high school, never imagining they'd transition to anything more sinister. But, after David's death, Douglas, struggling with grief and depression, began that downward spiral leading to full-blown drug addiction. Over the years, Douglas committed himself to a number of rehab programs. Just as Meghan had done, he would get clean and stay that way for brief periods. But, as so often is the case, he'd gradually find himself slipping back into old, bad patterns with the assistance of old, bad friends. David Sr. and Deborah Root were beside themselves. They'd lost one child to alcohol. How could they bear to lose another to drugs?

In 2010, Douglas had a son, Brody, and the light that had faded from his eyes returned. Douglas still struggled with addiction, but now he was determined, if only for Brody's sake, to get clean.

After David's death, holidays lost all meaning for the Root family. There simply was no joy in them. But with the arrival of baby Brody, Christmas, Easter, and Thanksgiving were happy occasions once more. Perhaps someday the Root family might even celebrate the Fourth of July.

Read Lowe:

In 1983, Tom and Rhonda Lowe purchased a nursery abutting the Indian River Lagoon just north of Vero Beach. Under Tom and Rhonda's management—and given buckets of sweat labor—the business thrived, becoming a local highlight. The Lowes were good friends of mine. I'd known them from the time they'd purchased the nursery. Their son, Read, and my daughter, Meghan, had been pals since they were tykes.

Read was a good-looking boy with a disarming grin that masked a deep-seated dissatisfaction with the world. Just as Douglas, Gus, and many of Meghan's contemporaries had, Read began smoking pot in junior high school, never imagining that would lead to abusing more potent, addictive drugs. In his high school years, Read's drug abuse escalated, and he had several brushes with the authorities for possession. Believing he was struggling with depression, Tom and Rhonda consulted with every psychiatrist, psychologist and drug treatment program in the area, but nothing seemed to work for Read. He, too, had a hole inside of him, and the more he tried to fill it, the larger it became.

In his senior year, Read completed all of his classes at Indian River Community College, the idea being to jump-start his college education and, at the same time, distance himself from unsavory influences. The plan seemed to work; Read excelled at IRC, and his parents dared to think he'd turned a corner. At last, he seemed motivated and headed in the right direction. Read was accepted to the University of Florida and almost immediately fell in with the wrong crowd. After only a few months, he dropped out of school, taking a job waiting tables. It wasn't long before he was arrested for dealing narcotics, and that's when it all began unraveling. The Feds stepped in and made Read an offer: in exchange for no prison time, he would wear a wire and turn state's evidence on the drug lords who'd supplied him. Read refused. He knew if he did what they asked, he would be a dead man.

While free on bond and awaiting his sentencing, Read worked closely with his parole officer and once more seemed to be getting his life back together. When Read and his parents appeared in court to learn his sentence, they were cautiously optimistic, hoping for leniency. But that was not to be the case. Despite the fact that he'd been a "gopher," a lowly grunt in the drug-delivery chain, Read was sentenced to six years in the state penitentiary.

Upon hearing this sentence, Read's response was, "They'll never put me in prison." Four days later, he was discovered hanging from the Barber Bridge. There were no witnesses, and no one knows whether Read took his own life or if he was murdered, although speculation abounds that he was found out by his suppliers and summarily executed.

I can't cross the Barber Bridge without thinking of Read. I imagine his parents and sister, Katie, can't either, just as I'm fairly certain David's mom avoids Stringfellow Road like the plague.

Angus Wallen:

Angus Wallen was movie-star handsome with sparkly blue-green eyes and long lashes that women coveted. Some assumed he was gay but he wasn't. He was just pretty. And a bit of an oddball. As a kid, Meghan tagged along after Michael and Gus, secretly madly in love with her brother's best bud. I'm sure they wanted to be rid of her. But she stuck like Velcro. They had many adventures: they'd ply the Indian River in Mike's Boston Whaler, fish, wakeboard, waterski, in-line skate all over town, climb trees, and play baseball. The three of them were seldom idle. Still, Gus was restless. I realize now that he had a hole in him, just as did Read and Meghan.

In his late teens, Gus began abusing alcohol and his behavior became erratic. As bright as he was, he just couldn't seem to fit in anywhere. When he was seventeen, Gus visited a Navy recruitment office in Melbourne. He'd gotten it into his head that he might serve his country and find his niche. He scored so high on the assessment tests that the recruiters were eager to sign him up. Gus's parents, Cookie and Larry, tried to dissuade him from enlisting. They didn't feel the Navy was the right fit for their sensitive, brooding son. Michael and Meghan were also skeptical of Gus's career choice; he was so introspective and was a gifted writer. But Gus dropped out of high school, earning his GED at a self-study night class so that he could enlist. Once he'd completed boot camp, Gus surprised everyone by getting married. Meghan, Michael and I attended the wedding, a surreal tipsy affair at which Gus appeared far lovelier than the bride. Not surprisingly, the marriage didn't last long.

Gus was stationed at a remote island in Hawaii, where he was frequently in trouble for his drunken escapades. Eventually, he was demoted and restricted to base. It was then that his anorexia manifested. Gus received counseling and treatment on base, but his symptoms persisted, until he was eventually discharged. When Cookie and Larry picked him up at the Melbourne Airport, they hardly recognized their son. He was a skeletal one hundred and seventeen pounds!

The first time I caught sight of Gus after his discharge, I was shocked. He was emaciated, and those beautiful eyes glittered with a crazed light. The door had opened a crack, and Satan had ushered himself in.

Cookie and Larry suspected that there was more than an eating disorder and alcohol abuse contributing to their son's problem. They did everything they could to get to the root of it and fix him—from in- and outpatient rehab, to psychiatric therapy—but nothing seemed to fill that hole inside of him, and Gus's anorexia segued into bulimia.

It was my son who finally discovered Gus's demon. Just as he and I had done so many times for Meghan—picking up the messy pieces of a turbulent life—Michael had volunteered to clean a house Gus had vacated. In the process, he unearthed a cache of empty Robitussin bottles, and the mystery behind Gus's psychosis was solved! Michael reported back to Cookie and Larry, and they immediately began researching dextromethorphan, the cough-suppressant agent in Robitussin, only to learn that, when ingested in large quantities, it produces an LSD-like hallucinogenic high.

For all those years, we'd chalked up Gus's extreme weight loss to amphetamine abuse, but we'd been mistaken. From the time he'd left for boot camp, he'd been abusing cough syrup, swiping bottles off the pharmacy shelves and "robo-tripping."

Early in 2004, Gus was arrested for shoplifting Robitussin and sentenced to jail. But his parents persuaded the judge to send him to court-ordered rehab. When they visited him during his three-month mandatory stint at hard-core rehab and found him sober, it was the first time in five years they'd seen their only son sane and drug-free. Cookie and Larry dared hope their nightmare was over and that Gus could reclaim his future. But that's not how it turned out. Upon his release, Gus became involved with Cara Wynn, a twisted soul with a history of violence. Cara would be his partner in crime.

For a time, we lost track of Gus. Then one day his parents called Michael with the horrific news: Gus was to stand trial for murder!

Gus and Cara had been sharing an apartment in Jacksonville with a young man, Brandon Murphy. One evening, the two watched the 1994 movie *Natural Born Killers*. At its conclusion, they hatched a plan: they would murder Murphy and steal his debit card!

The next night, after consuming a bottle of wine, Cara pointed a gun at Murphy, demanding that he turn over his debit card. Murphy refused. Cara fired wildly, hitting him in the shoulder. Gus wrested the gun from her and shot Murphy in the head.

After dousing the apartment and Murphy's body with lighter fluid, the pair absconded with his debit card, his Nintendo games and other personal items. A witness saw Gus and Cara get into a Nissan Maxima and embrace in the moment before the building exploded in flames.

They made it as far as Biloxi, Mississippi, before being caught. On August 11, 2004, Gus and Cara were sentenced to life in prison.

Gus claimed to have no memory of the incident, and Meghan believed him. People still tell my daughter things she said or did during her drug-crazed years, and Meghan nods and pretends to know what it is they are referring to, when in fact she has no recollection whatsoever. Big blank spaces remain in her brain, and she's sure the same held true for Gus. More's the pity, to be locked away for a crime one has no memory of.

Prison was not a good scene for Gus. He was not a large man and far too pretty. My family and I sent him letters encouraging him to write his novel, but his return missives painted a picture of a dead soul.

If one is determined, it is possible to opt out of almost anything. Gus was determined. On March 2, 2009, Gus looped a twisted length of sheeting around his neck and followed the jailhouse instructions he'd been given to accomplish the deed.

When Meghan heard the news, she was devastated. She'd been in love with Gus since fifth grade. Imagining him in his last moments, so tormented and hopeless, broke her heart.

Meghan, Michael and I do not believe it was Gus who killed Murphy and set his apartment on fire. It was the drug, the Devil in possession of his soul, that did it.

Meghan's God is a forgiving one. She prays that one day, in another happier life, she will see Gus again.

Olivia Garrison (name changed at the request of her parents):
Olivia was an impish creature with a smile that could melt the heart of a hardened ex-con. Meghan and she had been school chums since kindergarten, and it's safe to say Olivia was a constant in my daughter's life.

After high school, Olivia followed much the same path as did Meghan; she worked as a waitress and drifted from one bad boyfriend to another. Unlike Meghan, she suffered monthly bouts of pain due to endometriosis. Year by year, Meghan's sweet girlfriend's suffering escalated so that by the time she was in her early twenties, Olivia could bear the agony no longer. She decided to undergo a hysterectomy, a drastic procedure that would cure her. Olivia's parents supported her in this decision, but her doctor was horrified at the thought of a twenty-four-year-old forgoing the ability to conceive a child. "No!" she'd said. "You're too young to make such a decision. Someday you'll fall in love with a wonderful man and want his baby."

Olivia persisted. "Honestly, I don't care. I'll adopt. My little brother's adopted, and I love him every bit as much as I do my fraternal brother."

In the end, she was dissuaded. Instead, her doc prescribed the powerful pain medication Roxicet, a highly addictive form of oxycodone.

On Valentine's Day, 2009, Olivia and her father met for breakfast at the Countryside Inn, a homey establishment favored by the locals. She was high, head lolling, and could barely keep her eyes open. Her dad knew she was stoned, that she'd been abusing her pain medication. Before they parted ways, Olivia presented her father with a CD she'd compiled. "A Valentine's gift," she'd said. But her dad was so upset with her that he simply tossed it into the glove compartment and forgot about it. A week later, he discovered the CD and popped it into his car stereo, only to find a poignant collection that brought tears to his eyes: "Butterfly Kisses" and a mix of other heart-tugging ballads. But when he heard the lyrics to "Will I Dance with You, Jesus," he was suddenly filled with dread. Somehow he knew that Olivia was going to die!

Olivia's dad pleaded with her to stop taking her pain medication and get clean. She promised him she would.

On the day she died, Olivia was with her boyfriend. She'd run out of Roxicet, and her boyfriend needed to score quickly or he was going to detox. They decided to stop at a friend's house and begged for pain meds of any sort. After much imploring, Olivia's boyfriend was given a fistful of Xanax. He swallowed the lot of them on the spot. Afterward, the two of them climbed into his truck and headed out toward Route 60. They were twelve miles west of town when he lost control of the car. Both of them were ejected through the windshield. The boyfriend died instantly of a broken neck. Olivia never regained consciousness.

Dr. Paul Forage:

Professor Paul Forage suffered from a virulent form of type 2 diabetes. Meghan was just completing her first year of the homeland security program at IRSC when Forage's disease began exacting its toll. He was confined to a wheelchair after his leg was amputated, and his decline was rapid. Forage passed away on September 8, 2015, on his fifty-eighth birthday.

Paul's passion was experiential, humanitarian, peace-building education. In 2000, Paul established the Atlantic Hope Program. Since its inception, over 500 college students have benefited from the experience, one which is designed to teach students from a variety of backgrounds about emergency management and peace-building. The program, and Paul's work, had a seminal impact on students, some of whom have gone on to international careers. As one former participant commented, "Dr. Forage had a tremendous impact on my life. Paul's passion for helping others, and equally important, his willingness to push the limits of traditional training, opened my eyes to so many opportunities and challenged me to pursue excellence in my humanitarian work."

Dr. Paul Forage was a positive influence in so many lives. Meghan will be forever grateful for his mentoring and friendship.

Made in the USA
Columbia, SC
04 September 2019